Barefoot through Mauretania

Odette du Puigaudeau and Marion Sénones

Barefoot through Mauretania

Odette du Puigaudeau

with a new introduction
by
Caroline Stone

Hardinge Simpole

Hardinge Simpole Publishing,
The Roan,
Kilkerran,
KA19 8LS,
Scotland,
U.K.

For a complete list of titles, visit
http://www.hardingesimpole.co.uk

e-mail: admin@hardingesimpole.co.uk

Copyright © Estate of Odette du Puigaudeau 2010
Translated from the French *Pieds Nus à travers la Mauritania* by Geoffrey Sainsbury
First Published in English by George Routledge & Sons in 1937

This edition first published 2010, Copyright © Hardinge Simpole 2010
Introduction © Caroline E. M. Stone 2009
Cover photograph: © Alexander Stone Lunde 2009.

Every effort has been made to trace possible copyright holders and to obtain their permission for the use of any copyright material. The publishers will gladly receive information enabling them to rectify any error or omission for subsequent editions.

ISBN-13 978 1 84382 201 1 Paperback

All rights reserved. No part of this publication may be reproduced, stored in a retrieval system, or transmitted in any form or by any means, electronic, mechanical, photocopying, recording or otherwise, without the prior permission of the publishers.

Contents

List of illustrations and maps — *vii*
Introduction by Caroline Stone — *ix*
Bibliography — *xxii*
Translator's note by Geoffrey Sainsbury — *xxiii*
Author's Preface — *xxv*

Chapter I	On the Slave-traders' Route	1
Chapter II	The Dunes of Fear	33
Chapter III	The Great Tents	49
Chapter IV	At the Emir's Camp	88
Chapter V	The *Salines* of the Dakar	115
Chapter VI	Men and Camels	135
Chapter VII	The Country of Mistrust	170
Chapter VIII	Our Luck Turns	187
Chapter IX	A Haven of Refuge	216

Acknowledgements

I should like to thank the Golden Web Foundation for its financial support during the preparation of this volume, undertaken as part of the Civilizations in Contact Project, Cambridge.

List of illustrations

Odette du Puigaudeau and Marion Sénones	ii
Villa-Cisneros, the Spanish Military Post	25
Nomads on the Beach at Port Étienne	26
Imraguen Fishermen with their Nets	37
Mohammed-Fall	51
Camping in the Scrub	52
Griots Playing in Sidi's Camp	65
Mohammed-Fall in his Tent	69
With the Women in the Emir's Camp.	91
The Emir and his Family	103
Bird dance; on the left the Dancer is imitating the *Marabou*	127
A Native School	133
Menina Dancing	149
Peulh Women	173
At N'Dio, Women Spinning	189
Magic Inscriptions and Ossuary at N'Dio	195
The Sorceress	203
The Eastern Slopes of the Assaba	209
Kiffa, the Military Post	211

Maps

Itinerary	xxiv
Administrative Districts and Military Posts of Mauretania	35
The *Salines* of the Dakar	114

Introduction

Odette du Puigaudeau

Odette du Puigaudeau was born on July 7th, 1894 into a family of impoverished minor aristocrats turned artists. She was an only child and her father, who wanted a son, treated her as one, taking her with him on cycling expeditions round the country, teaching her to shoot and calling her Robert – "Tu seras mon fils." She was raised largely in Brittany, in country houses of spectacular discomfort. There were always problems of money and relations between her parents, and her parents and other relatives, were often tense. Her father seems to have been difficult, quarrelling with his dealer, Durand-Ruel, and with other patrons, which exacerbated the family's financial problems.

Odette was educated at home, which was not unusual at the period. In her case, it was for reasons of economy, but also because her mother felt that school education was unnecessary and, perhaps, vulgar and because her father did not want to be parted from her. At the outbreak of World War I, the family was living at Kervaudu, a small 15th century castle isolated among the salt marshes, and Odette, not allowed to nurse the wounded, as many other young women were doing, was bored, depressed and at a loose end. Without a dowry, she was unlikely to marry and her father, having raised her like a boy, now wanted a submissive Victorian daughter.

In 1920, she finally managed to escape. She went to Paris and found work as a scientific draughtsman, something for which her father's training had admirably suited her. Furious at her defection, he made trouble between her and several of her employers, resulting in her being dismissed. One job involved drawing the vast collection of butterflies, now in the Muséum national d'histoire naturelle, belonging to Mme Fournier, known to her friends as "Twinka". Odette dreamed of getting right away – working on an Antartic expedition or at the Marine Laboratory at Carthage, but none of her plans came to anything.

After five years, she took a break from science and worked for several months for Jeanne Lanvin as a fashion illustrator, another skill which was to stand her in good stead when she came to record the costume, hairstyles and jewellery of Mauritania. She soon decided that she disliked the glitter and falsity of the fashion world and returned to the butterflies.

For a while, Odette was Mme Fournier's "favourite" and about this time she acquired a boat, which she allowed Odette to use as her home for many years. Odette called it Karet, meaning "beloved" in the Breton dialect of the Vannes region.

At this period she frequently returned to Brittany, under considerable pressure from her parents, and in 1928-30 took several trips to the islands, where she made friends with a number of the working women for whom she had the greatest respect. With their men away at sea, they had been forced to take over many traditionally masculine roles. Odette wanted to paint and draw the fish live that she had been illustrating for the Muséum national d'histoire naturelle and it was the island women who helped her to get her the papers she needed to work officially as a deck-hand on the fishing boats.

In the autumn of 1928, she embarked on *L'Abbé de l'Epée*. Her descriptions of life on this and other ships in the tuna fleet are interesting and the articles her experiences generated attracted attention in Paris. Her father died in 1930 and Odette organized an exhibition and sale of his paintings, which was a success and helped her mother financially, and then went back to sea, this time aboard the *Quatre-Frères*.

Odette loved the traditional, hierarchic, picturesque world of the fishermen and sea-weed gatherers and was indignant both at the way they were exploited financially and at how their courageous, independent and "noble" way of life was doomed to vanish by "heartless" modern mechanised industry. This relationship with the Breton seafarers' world was very much the prototype of the one she was to have with the nomads of Mauritania.

In 1932, Odette met Marcelle Borne Kreutzberger, an accomplished artist, then working for the magazine *Eve*. She persuaded her to change her name to Marion Sénones and the two women were to spend the rest of their lives together. The following year, Odette gave up scientific drawing and managed to earn a precarious living writing articles on the Breton islands, famous women and certain social issues. The two women decided that they wanted to do something exciting and adventurous, preferably that would give them interesting material in their respective fields.

Mauritania was little known and sounded original and promising. Furthermore, Odette's seaman's papers entitled them to travel for almost nothing on Breton fishing boats. The coast of Mauritania had some of the richest fishing grounds in the world and hence there would be no shortage of transport. Odette was particularly interested in what she had heard of the Sahara's neolithic past and through museum contacts it was suggested that they should try to get to Arguin, the Adrar and Cap Blanc, and they were asked to make lists of sites and collect samples of material.

Although the Treaty of Paris gave the area to the French in 1814, Mauritania had only been a colony since 1920, the French having been more interested in Senegal and Morocco. At that date, it was bounded by the Spanish Rio de Oro and the Atlantic to the West, the Senegal River to the South, the Sudan to the East and Algeria and Morocco to the North.

As far back as 1854, the French governor of Senegal had begun to envisage the "pacification" of the Moors in order to protect his colony's trade, but things had progressed slowly and against heavy resistance, and in the 1930s there was still a considerable French military presence.

This first journey lasted for nearly a year, from November 1933 to October 1934. Both women showed remarkable courage and tenacity in the face of considerable physical challenges. Odette was rather inclined to dismiss the dangers of her expeditions, although the sobering accounts of the fate of the pilots of Aéropostale, for example, forced to make unscheduled landings in the region and captured suggest that there was more reason to fear than she admits.

Odette and Marion returned with photographs, films, and large quantities of both ethnographic and prehistoric material, which they donated to the Musée d'Ethnographie. They were met with enthusiasm. The press took a good deal of notice to them, they were invited to lecture, commissioned to write articles, awarded prizes and were involved in a major exhibition on the Sahara at the Musée des Colonies. When invited out, they liked to appear dressed as Mauritanians (male, of course) and carrying with them the equipment to prepare mint tea in the approved manner. They became minor celebrities. Odette continued with her career in journalism and among other things wrote a series of articles - *Hommes seuls* – on men's clubs, which she successfully penetrated as Marcel Dupuis, a Belgian journalist.

The taste for disguise was very strong in Odette and her biographer, Monique Vérité, comments perceptively on Odette's rather naïve beliefs about blending in. Of course there were practical reasons for dressing as a sailor on board a Breton fishing boat, but in the desert, Odette not only wanted to dress as a Mauritanian – although a famous photograph shows her on a camel in a light summer dress - but also be treated as a chief, emphatically male, not female, which she felt was her correct position in society. Monique Vérité comments: "She quickly adopted a seigniorial the way of life and, since in the Sahara any kind of physical work is considered unfitting for one of noble birth, she hired people to serve her...."

It was perhaps her prejudice in favour of the aristocracy that would make her refuse to condemn slavery, particularly in her later books, since she perceived it as essential to a way of life that she admired. Similarly, although very acute in her observation of particular incidents, she had a surprising lack of interest in looking beyond the surface to the basic structures and workings of a society based on violence and dominance. Her very positive attitude to Islam was combined with a lack of understanding of its tenets and the fact she judged it by the way she personally was received and treated under very special circumstances.

Her tactic of assuming she would be treated as a chief worked particularly well when she was backed up, somewhere in the distance, by the French military and on the whole her Mauritanian hosts played up to her image of herself, whether through politeness, genuine respect, hope of gain, or fear of the French authorities is hard to ascertain. Odette who, surprisingly, never mastered Arabic, seems to have been able to retain her belief in how she was perceived by the Moors to the end. This did nothing to diminish her powers of observation, or her ability to collect vocabulary in the Hassaniya dialect in order to give the correct names to all the elements in their material culture that she recorded.

In 1936, *Pieds nus à travers la Mauritanie* came out and in the following year *La Grande Foire aux dattes*. At this date, her work is notable for the accurate descriptions of what she saw – the perfect counterpart to her later drawings of the material culture of Mauritania. Although by nature and upbringing she had a romantic bias in favour of their form of society, with its sharp social divisions, she makes it very clear that she understood its disadvantages both for the people oppressed by it and for herself. At this date she was also still convinced of the validity of the French colonial presence and had not yet become so deeply opposed to the impact of progress and modernization on the traditional world, as she did later.

In December 1936, Odette and Marion set off for their second much longer journey, which was to last until February 1938. This time they were on an official mission from the Muséum national d'histoire naturelle and the Ministries of Education and of the Colonies; they even received a small grant.

This journey was to see Odette become not only increasingly anti-colonial, but also against all forms of change and development. She felt that the peoples of the desert had reached an equilibrium that suited them and was prepared to close her eyes to the negative aspects of their system as it affected the unprivileged classes. Aesthetics played a part. She was to collect and record, lovingly, their arts and crafts, which she saw being undermined by the arrival of mass-produced goods from the West. As Monique Vérité points out: "Her anti-colonialism was not born of an objection to conquest, but from the effects of progress, that great destroyer of tradition."

Odette's experiences visiting the salt mines and on the twenty day 700km trek with the salt caravans were to result in one of her most interesting books: *Le Sel du désert* (1940) and her time at Tagant was to lead to perhaps her best and most personal work: *Tagant* (1949). This second journey also gave rise to a series of archaeological reports, written and illustrated with Marion Sénones, in particular on the rock paintings of the South Moroccan Sahara and the Tagant, as well as a number of popular articles.

Odette and Marion were preparing a third expedition to survey the archaeological sites and especially the $3^{rd} - 5^{th}$ millennium B.C.

rock paintings in the Tibesti – Ennedi mountains of the central Sahara, now largely in Chad, when war was declared. They were still hoping to find a way back to North Africa when the German Occupation of Paris and the desert war put an end to their hopes.

Odette, having decided to return to Paris after a brief period in Brittany, flung herself into the war effort, but with typical political naïveté. She founded the S.F.F. (Service féminin français) and had huge ambitions to create a mass movement of women devoted to the service of their country, with no thoughts of social advantage or superiority over those they were engaged in helping. She felt that one of the greatest needs for the French was solidarity: to forget their selfish individual concerns and lose themselves in the greater needs of France.

This in itself might have been admirable, but she wrote articles praising similar Nazi organizations, such as the NSV (National Sozialistische Volkswohlfahrt), for their efficient organization and maintaining there was much to be learned from their methodology. She was apparently unaware of the implications of what she was saying, simply insisting that anything that worked was worth examining and copying. She was not pro-Nazi: by 1942 she was regularly helping members of the Résistance and consistently refused to have anything to do with Arab pro-Nazi magazines such as *Er Rashid*, which courted her. However, this perceived ambiguity was to make her professional life difficult after the Liberation and tensions were not dispelled by her sudden decision to join the Communist party.

The S.F.F. never became a mass movement, but it did useful work providing comforts for some of the 30 000 soldiers and prisoners of war from North Africa and the colonies, and lobbying to get them fairer treatment, which was much needed. It continued to operate until 1944.

A commission to write a book on the development of railroads in the colonies gave Odette new hope of leaving for Africa. Various delays occurred in setting out until, on the 7th of November, she and Marion were finally on their way. That night the Americans landed in North Africa and, since Algeria was now part of the war zone, travel was impossible. Odette was very bitter at finding herself trapped, as she saw it, in France and it was not until 1949 that she succeeded in leaving on her long-deferred expedition.

Unfortunately, by this time her relationship with the Musée de l'homme was decidedly strained and she was to have the usual problems with the authorities both at home and in North Africa. Among other things, she was exhorted to act with "*discrétion patriotique*" – not one of her strengths. She also found the change from military to civilian government disturbing, since she felt it put the local peoples at a grave disadvantage, as they were now dealing with an administrative system they really did not understand, rather than force, which they did, and it also made them much more vulnerable to financial exploitation.

In some ways, this third journey was a disappointment, because of the new bureaucratic snares, but also because of the changes to the world she loved. This sharpened her determination to record everything she could, with a sense that she was racing against time before the coherence of the culture vanished; this was to result in her most important work: *Arts et Coutumes des Maures*.

She settled down for a pleasant stay at Nouakschott at the headquarters of the *pistards* or desert patrol of whom she had a romantic perception, along the lines of the "brotherhood of the road". *La Piste Maroc – Sénégal* was the result, as well as another series of archaeological reports, which ensured that she and Marion Sénones were now recognized as authorities on the Sahara and the culture of the Mauritanians.

During the post-war years, Odette wanted to settle down to produce her major ethnographic work - *Arts et Coutumes des Maures* – but financial constraints meant that she often had to write for money, lecture or give radio talks, while Marion continued to paint and organize exhibitions and sales of her work. Odette also threw herself into an unsuccessful battle for better conditions for North African workers in France, particularly as regards education. She had a circle of North African friends, including the poet, Jean Amrouche, and his sister, the singer, Marguerite Taos Amrouche, and a young law student, Mokhtar Ould Daddah.

By the mid fifties, mining companies were beginning to take an interest in Mauritania and as Independence approached, the question of the country's status was much debated. The people of the south turned towards Senegal (independent 1960), the people of the north towards Morocco (independent 1956) and initially Odette strongly supported an independent Mauritania.

In early 1960, Odette returned to Mauritania for the last time, alone, to collect material for a major exhibition on the Sahara to be held at the Musée de l'homme. She stayed at Nouakchott as the guest of Ould Daddah and his wife, and completed her collection of artefacts for the museum. The journey was not an unqualified success. Malaria and bureaucratic snarls prevented her from travelling as she wished and she was increasingly disturbed at the changes she saw in "her" Mauritania. Furthermore, when she returned to France her part in preparing the Exhibition was barely acknowledged – she put it down to jealousy

By this stage, she had become convinced that Mauritania was too small and weak to stand alone and that the Mauritanians would find themselves driven into the new cities to live in a state of degraded poverty on the edge of foreign-owned industrial enterprises. She therefore began to proselytize for Mauritania to become part of "Greater Morocco" - since Morocco now began to have colonial aspirations of its own. This led to a complete rupture with Ould Daddah, who was to be President of Mauritania from its Independence in 1960 until 1978, and was to make it impossible for Odette ever to return to the country she so loved.

Odette also campaigned passionately against the French nuclear testing at Reggane in the Adrar, where four bombs were let off in 1960-1, pointing out that the desert was <u>not</u> empty, but full of Berber tribes, many of them settled in the neighbourhood and that if the tests were to go forward, the people should be moved or compensated. As usual, her words had no result, except to anger the French authorities, who were already suspicious of her support for "Greater Morocco".

It seemed like an answer to prayer when in 1961, the Moroccan Minister in charge of Arts and Tourism invited her to Rabat. There she was promised almost everything she had ever wanted: full support to continue her archaeological research, the opportunity to set up a Museum of the Sahara, facilities to hold exhibitions for herself and Marion, a villa, a contract, a stipend. ...Almost all of these things were to prove mirages.

In spite of that and in spite of Odette's imprudent angering of the Moroccan government by her outspoken political views, she continued to work in various capacities until the year of Marion's death - 1977 – when, aged 84, she was induced much against her will to retire on a pension. She produced the last chapter of *Arts et Coutumes*, which unfortunately remained unfinished, in 1980 and continued to live in Rabat until her death in 1991.

Mauritania

From the time of her first journey, Mauritania was to become the love of Odette du Puigaudeau's life. Romantic, she deeply regretted the intrusion of the modern world and the loss of an archaic pattern of society. Practical, she dedicated much of the second half of her life to recording everything she could of its material culture. Because, the country is still relatively unknown and its history over the past 150 years has been complicated, it is perhaps worth saying a few words to provide background for Odette du Puigaudeau's story.

Mauritania is largely desert with some mountain areas in the interior. During the Neolithic, however, in common with much of the Sahara, the area benefited from a considerably increased rainfall and water from melting ice sheets, and thus supported a much denser population, whose art work and artifacts Odette du Puigaudeau and Marion Sénones were among the first to discover and record. Since c.3500 B.C. the Sahara has become progressively drier and is now estimated to have reached roughly the state of drought that obtained 13,000 years ago.

The country takes its name from the ancient Berber kingdom known to the Romans as Mauretania - roughly western Algeria and northern Morocco. When Carthage was defeated in 146 B.C., the Berber rulers of Mauretania became clients of Rome. One of the last of these kings was the remarkable and deeply civilized Juba I of Numidia, who was raised in Rome by Julius Caesar and Augustus, and married to Cleopatra's daughter, Cleopatra Selene.

Together, they founded the city of Volubilis in Morocco and tried hard to introduce arts, education and trade, as well as Roman concepts of law and order. Hated for their Romanizing policies, Juba I transferred to Mauretania and founded the city of Caesaria (Cherchell in modern Algeria). After his death in 23 A.D., he was succeeded by his son Ptolemy, but twenty years later Mauretania was annexed directly as a Roman province and one of the Empire's main concerns was to achieve some control over the nomads' constant raids against trade routes and cultivated areas.

From the time Roman hegemony came to an end in the 4th c. until the 7th c. A.D., Berber nomad tribes from North Africa moved south, driving out the black inhabitants of the region, the ancestors of the modern Soninke, who were for the most part settled agriculturalists. Those who did not manage to flee beyond the Senegal River were generally enslaved; a pattern of raiding comparable to that, which has persisted to the present, in Darfur. This area of the Sahara was still considerably more fertile then than it is today. From the 8th century, the tribes moving west from Arabia, which overran the coast of North Africa and spread into Spain, also began to penetrate what is now Mauritania.

About 1050, the Lamtuna Berbers converted to a particularly fundamentalist form of Islam, which combined perpetual *jihad* with very rigorous Muslim orthodoxy. Known as the Almoravids, they conquered much of North Africa and began to spread south. Takrur in modern Senegal was converted and the powerful Sanhaja Berbers followed suit. This enabled the Almoravids to take control of the very lucrative desert trade routes, carrying slaves, gold and ivory out of sub-Saharan Africa. In 1054, they seized the caravan city of Sijilmassa and in 1076 conquered the Empire of Ghana, which gave them direct access to its wealth.

At about the same time, a new invasion of nomads from the Arabian Peninsula, led by the Beni Hilal and the Beni Sulaym swept across North Africa and began to penetrate Mauritania. For the next 500 years, both the Berber and the black inhabitants of the region put up a valiant resistance to Arab domination. The Mauritanian Thirty-Year War (1644-74) was the last concerted attempt of the Berbers to repel the Arabs, this time of the Beni

Hassan, and progressive arabization. One mark of this was the dominance of the Arabic language over Berber, particularly in the form of the Berber-influenced Hassaniya dialect.

The attempt failed and the Arab warriors came to form a dominant aristocracy with the original inhabitants relegated, by and large, to subordinate positions, exploited in various ways. Odette du Puigaudeau describes, for instance, the lives of the slave-fishermen.

The principal area in which the Berbers retained a certain status was as *marabouts* or holy men, often associated with one of the *sufi tariqas*, or brotherhoods, and they had a considerable tradition of scholarship in the field of Muslim theology. The Berbers were also often in a position to make themselves feared as warriors. The black population either fled south or was enslaved.

Mauritania emerged as a feudal society strictly divided by class and race with "white Moors" - the Arab aristocracy and "black Moors" an under class, essentially composed of the *haratin,* freed slaves, generally of mixed blood

French colonization from Senegal to present-day Mauritania, involved a very active effort to abolish slavery and prevent the ceaseless inter-tribal raids. Real change came in 1901, when Xavier Coppolani, a French Corsican, born in Algeria, was given the task of "pacifying" the tribes north of the Senegal River. He successfully played the warring tribes off against each other and also made alliances with some of the most important Berber *marabouts* of the Qadiriya *sufi* order, by offering them protection from attacks by the Beni Hassan. The combination of military and diplomatic pressure was successful. The emirates of Tagant, Trarza and Brakna accepted French rule in 1903-4. The Northern area of the Adrar resisted.

The resistance centred on Ma al-'Aynayn – Water of the Two Eyes – son of a famous *marabout* and himself a charismatic religious leader, backed by the Sultan of Morocco. In 1902, Ma al-'Aynayn, with the cooperation of the local people, decided to enlarge his family's hereditary *zawiya*, or religious centre, at Smara, making it not only his capital and a centre for the caravan trade, but also a holy city. It was the only city in the region not founded by the Spaniards.

In 1904, Ma al-'Aynayn declared *jihad* and formed a coalition of tribes, largely armed by Germany, to fight the French. Coppolani was assassinated on his orders in 1905. In the following year, however, the Sultan of Morocco accepted the Treaty of Algeciras, which gave the French control over much of the country. Ma al-'Aynayn decided to carry *jihad* north, but he was defeated and died at Tiznit some months later; he was over 80 years old.

Ma al-'Aynayn's descendants are still important political players in Mauritania and in the Polisario Front, the Sahrawi rebel movement currently demanding the independence of the Western Sahara from Morocco.

One result of Xavier Coppolani's policies and the French presence in Mauritania was the return of many, mostly sedentary, tribes to their ancestral lands north of the Senegal River, from which they had been driven by the nomad raids. Nevertheless, at this time, an estimated 90% of the population was still nomadic and the hierarchical society described by Odette du Puigaudeau was still intact.

After Independence in 1960, the flow from south of the Senegal increased. The capital was moved from the old French trading post of Saint-Louis du Sénégal to Nouakshott, at the time hardly more than a village. Immigration, economic policies, a certain amount of development and the drying of the Sahara led to a shift in the balance of power between nomad and settled and between different ethnic groups, and there have been severe tensions. Arab nationalist pressure to arabize the region, both in terms of language and law, has been countered by the Berbers and the black population alike and these tensions came to a head in the "Events" of 1989. Slavery is also still a major issue, in spite of being theoretically outlawed, as the organization SOS Slaves, founded by ex-slaves, makes all too clear.

The political situation of Mauritania after Independence rapidly became extremely complex, with tribal and personal, as well international issues, and goes some way to explain why Odette du Puigaudeau, who was not always diplomatic, found it difficult ever to return. For nearly 20 years, the country was ruled by President Mokhtar Ould Daddah, who involved Mauritania in an unsuccessful military attempt to annex part of the Western (previously Spanish) Sahara. Since then, there have been a mixture of governments, installed by military coup or elected, and the political relationships among Mauritania, Morocco, the Western Sahara and Algeria are still largely unresolved (2008).

Anyone interested in the life of Odette du Puigaudeau should read her biography, *Odette du Puigaudeau: Une Bretonne au desert*, by Monique Vérité (see bibliography), which came out in 1992, the year after her death. Monique Vérité spent much time with Odette du Puigaudeau in her last years and skilfully sets down both the story of her life and the legend that she liked to project.

The work of Odette du Puigaudeau is little known in England, because only her first book, *Pieds nus à travers la Mauritanie*, has been translated, because she was unlucky with her dates of publication during World War II and, perhaps, because her conservative point of view is unfashionable today. None of this should, however, affect assessment of her remarkable achievement in recording a largely vanished world.

Other Desert Travellers

The tone used by Odette de Puigaudeau when writing of her experiences, at least as it comes through in translation, can grate on the modern ear, combining as it does enthusiasm and condescension towards people perceived as "exotic" and "barbaric". It does, however, provide an enlightening demonstration of the changes in social attitudes since the 1930s, as Odette de Puigeaudau's own perception of the colonial experience was to change diametrically. In the latest edition of *La grande foire des dattes* this subject is commented on very perceptively in the unfortunately all too brief foreword by the Mauritanian anthropologist, Abdel Wedoud Ould Cheikh,

Sensibilities, seventy years later, have changed – and some of the changes she would certainly have approved of. But it is a mistake to dismiss Odette du Puigaudeau's work because of shifting fashions in style. *Barefoot in the Sahara* (1936) marks the beginning of her fascination with Mauritania and it is interesting to have an uncensored impression of the world that was to become her life's work: the recording of its material culture - and it contains much interesting information in its own right.

The style, hovering between romantic and flippant, is not unlike that of the glamorous Rosita Forbes, much better known in the English-speaking world. Her account of travel in the Libyan Desert and an attempt to visit the Senussi strongholds, forbidden to non-Muslims: *The Secret of the Sahara: Kufara*, was first published in 1921 – the same year as Rudolph Valentino's great success *The Sheik* - shares many of the same characteristics with *Barefoot in the Sahara*. Looking past these mannerisms and the irritatingly patronizing attitude to her long-suffering travelling companion Hassanein Bey, whose own account, *The Lost Oases**, came out in 1925, this book again is filled with valuable details and gives a rare picture of a still little-known world.

Something of the same criticism – romanticism and a perception of the people among whom she travelled as exotic and ineluctably "other" - could again be made of Freya Stark, whose work began to appear 1932, with *The Valley of the Assassins*, one of her most famous books, being published in 1934, but once more this is a reflection of the mindset of the period in which she wrote and that in itself is of interest. All three women were, in any case, writing for a general and not an academic audience. Isabella Bird's work, although intended for a similar market, does not share these characteristics, but she was writing considerably earlier, for example *A Pilgrimage to Sinai* (1886) or *Journeys in Persia and Kurdistan* (1891), and the expectations of a Victorian audience, as to both style and content, were very different from those of the 1920s and 30s.

The desert had been the subject of much more serious work, notably T.E. Lawrence's *Seven Pillars of Wisdom* which came out in various forms between 1922 and 1927, with a particularly complicated publishing history. It also has its moments of romanticism - although certainly no flippancy – but its intensions were entirely serious and very different from the works mentioned above, which largely aimed at entertaining. The same is true of Gertrude Bell, traveller, political analyst, Middle-Eastern policy maker and anti-suffrage campaigner, whose works, such as *Syria: the Desert and the Sown* (1907) and her numerous letters and diaries are completely different in style and in intention, sharing much more with T.E. Lawrence than with Stark, Forbes or de Puigaudeau.

---

* *Forthcoming in this series.*

Bibliography

A full list of articles by Odette du Puigaudeau and Marion Sénones are to be found in the biography:
Odette du Puigaudeau: Une Bretonne au desert, Monique Vérité, 1992 (reissued ed.Payot, Paris, 2001)

Books by Odette du Puigaudeau:

Pieds nus à travers la Mauritanie, Paris, Plon, 1936; Paris, Phébus, 1992
La Grande Foire aux dattes, Paris, Plon, 1937; Ibis 2007
Le Sel du desert, Paris, Tisné, 1940; Paris, Phébus, 2001
La Route de l'Ouest, Paris, Suisse, 1945; Ibis, 2007
Grandeur des îles, Paris, Juillard, 1945, 1989; Paris, Payot & Rivages, 1996
Mon ami Rachid, guépard, Paris, Albin Michel, 1948
Tagant, Paris, Julliard, 1949; Paris, Phébus, 1993
La Piste Maroc – Sénégal, Paris, Plon, 1954
Le Passé maghrébin de la Mauritanie, Rabat, ministère d'Etat chargé d'Affaires Islamique, 1962
Mémoire du pays maure, 1934-1960, carnets de voyage d'O. du Puigaudeau et de Marion Sénones, présentés par M. Vérité, Ibis Press, 2000

Arts et Coutumes des Maures:
  I *Histoire*, Hésperis Tamuda, vol.vii, Rabat, 1967 pp.111-144
  I *La vie matérielle*, H.T., vol.ix, Rabat, 1968, pp.329-427
  II *Costumes féminins*, H.T., vol.xi, Rabat, 1970, pp.5-46
  IV *La vie familiale*, H.T., vol.xii, Rabat, 1972, pp.182-224
  V *La vie culturelle*, H.T., vol.xvi, Rabat 1975, pp.185-211
  VI *L'artisana*t, H.T, vol.xix, Rabat, 1980, pp.169-188

Arts et Coutumes des Maures, Ibis Press, 2005 (reprinted from Hésperis Tamuda)

Selected Bibliography - Mauritania

Baba, Elemine Ould Mohamed, *De mémoire de Nouakchottois, chronique du temps qui passé*, Paris, Harmattan, 2003

Bales, Kevin, *Disposable People: New Slavery in the Global Economy*, University of California press, 1999

Caratini, Sophie, *L'éducation saharienne d'un képi noir: Mauritanie, 1933-1935*, Paris, Harmattan, 2002

Coppolani, Georges, Xavier *Coppolani: Fils de Corse, homme d'Afrique, fondateur de la Mauritanie*, Paris, Harmattan, 2005

Corral, José, *Ciudades de las caravanas: alarifes del Islam en el desierto*, Madrid 1985

Désiré-Vuillemin, Geneviève, *Histoire de la Mauritanie*, Paris, Karthala, 1997

Duboc, Général, *Mauritanie*, Paris, 1935

Marty, Paul, *L'Émirat des Trarzas*, Paris, E.Leroux, 1919

Mauritania: ciudades y manuscritos: exposición, Madrid, mayo-junio de 1981

Ould Cheikh, Abdel Wedoud, *Eléments d'histoire de la Mauritanie*, Nouakchott, 1988

Ould Daddah, Mokhtar, *La Mauritanie contre vents et marées*, Paris, Karthala, 2003

Ould Khalifa, Abdallah, *La région du Tagant en Mauritanie : L'oasis de Tijigja entre 1660 et 1960*, Paris, Karthala, 1998

Ould Saleck, El-Arby, *Les Haratins*, Paris, Harmattan, 2003

Segal, Ronald, *Islam's Black Slaves*, London, 2001

Shinqītī, Ahmad ibn al-Amīn, *El Wasît: littérature, histoire, géographie, moeurs et coutumes des habitants de la Mauritanie*, St.-Louis, Sénégal : Centre IFAN-Mauritanie, 1953.

Sow, Amadou Aliou, *La Mauritanie, mon pays natal*, Paris, Harmattan, 2003

Translator's note

ONE of the difficulties in translating this book was presented by the French spoken by the Natives in Mauretania. Their lingo has a charm of its own which could hardly be rendered adequately in English. For one thing, it has a peculiarly intimate and childish quality on account of the wholesale use of *tu* instead of the polite *vous*. I have done my best, translating their dialogue into a very simplified and somewhat broken English with scraps of the original French left in; and I hope in this way I have given some idea of the way they speak.

Another problem was how to spell Arabic names in an English text. In the transliteration of Arabic into Roman letters there is in any case considerable diversity of practice, and to avoid thorny ground I thought it best to follow the author exactly. This was not only the easiest way, but it seemed the most logical. Mauretania is a French country, and French maps are used in England. And if the author was followed in the rendering of place-names, it seemed best to follow her in the names of people and in the Arabic words that appear in the text. I have accordingly only anglicized a few well-known names such as Mauretania, Sudan, etc.

G. S.

Itinerary

Author's Preface

MY friend Marion Sénones has shared with me all the joys and vicissitudes of the journey which this book is to relate, and she shares no less the gratitude I feel towards all those who helped us on our way. In Paris we went to see General Gouraud, who received us most kindly, and gave us excellent advice and letters of introduction to the authorities of French West Africa, in which country he had had such great experience. Many others did no less, and out in Mauretania advice and help was supplemented with the most cordial hospitality.

The journey was accomplished without subvention from any source. We paid our way with our own modest means. So long as Breton fishermen fish in African waters it will always be possible to get cheaply to Mauretania—at any rate for those who can dispense with luxury.

We managed to bring back a collection of Neolithic stones and modern products of native handicraft. These have been given to the Musée d'Ethnographic du Trocadéro, to the Société de Geographie, or to various provincial collections.

We wanted to give ourselves some ostensible pretext that would serve to excuse our presence in a country which European women practically never visit. We accordingly chose to call ourselves reporters. Had we known the reputation enjoyed by journalists in Mauretania we might have hesitated to adopt the profession!

Certain reporters have indeed shown remarkable imaginative powers in their descriptions of the country. It seems that only a few days have been required for them to know all about the country, its landscape, its fauna and flora, its inhabitants and their manners and customs, and the Frenchmen who govern them, to say nothing of the scandals and dramas they manage to unearth. They have been mauled by lions or jackals, tortured by mosquitoes, shot at by savages, half-drowned in the torrential rains, or lost in the depths of forests or in the barren wastes of the desert. As a matter of fact they have always travelled with a cargo of European foodstuffs and with large escorts armed to the teeth. Then, fresh as daisies they have returned to France to curdle our blood with stories of hairbreadth escapes in a country from which they have only returned alive by a miracle, a country in which men—whether white, black, or brown—are one and all bandits.

But truth will out. The stories that have been told have been so outrageous as to defeat their purpose. In the end everybody has come to disbelieve them, and the only ones to derive any profit from them have been Colonials, who have been able at any rate to enjoy a good laugh!

What a pity it is to spoil a fine profession. Instead of being content to be reporters they have preferred to appear as heroes, and the part has not suited them in the least. Perhaps they have really been no more than unwilling martyrs, for many of them do not seem to have enjoyed very robust health. I can recall the stories of two journalists who went to Mauretania. One of them wrote that after a hundred and fifty kilometres by camel, riding in short stages and in the cool season, he had to stop half-dead with exhaustion, though he was in sight of his destination. The other wrote that, walking behind his camel, he had not the strength left to jump out of the way when the wind blew the camel's urine into his face.

It was on our return to France, after the pages of this book had already appeared in various periodicals, that we encountered the real dangers of Mauretania. One can avoid bandits. One can manage to get on with the Moors. One can escape the dangers of wild beasts, the sun and sand-storms. But one falls inevitably a prey to those who will accuse one of being a militarist, or to those who are themselves militarists and who will accuse one of just the reverse.

And then there are those who have been to the country themselves, and who must maintain their prestige as experts by finding everything one says to be wrong.

To give one example, we have been attacked for speaking of the lakes or *gueltas*, which are precious reservoirs of water in the mountainous region of the Assaba. It seems that officially these permanent reserves of water simply do not exist. At the end of the dry season we had the audacity to bathe in one and fill our waterbottles, as well as to eat its fish and the eggs of its crocodiles. Worse still, we were foolish enough to relate these facts, thinking in our innocence that the *guelta* was a geographical reality that it was not for us to question!

There are also those who maintain that the pacification of Mauretania is accomplished, and those who maintain that it is not. If you meet a band of marauders the first will be down on you at once. If you do not, your peaceful wanderings through the desert will offend the second. Amongst the latter are those guardians of tradition who wish to prolong the heroic atmosphere of the early days of French penetration into the country. These show no quarter whatever to the intruders—still less if they are women — who come unarmed and attended by a miserable escort to demean a land of mystery and danger.

These various critics are all agreed on one point: that we have had our heads filled with a lot of tall stories.

I have confined myself to telling what we have actually seen, heard and experienced in Mauretania, except for a certain amount of information derived from official documents of unquestionable veracity.

On setting out we had no prejudices about the country; we had taken no sides. Nor have we since. Mauretania is a huge country, half as big again as France, and shows wide diversity in its landscape, its people and their characters and habits. We have not sought to generalize, but to give a truthful account of what we found, hoping that the reader will be gripped as we were by the beauty of the Western Sahara and the poetic character of its people.

Chapter I

On the Slave-traders' Route

DECEMBER 11th, 1933. Thirteen days previously the *Belle-Hirondelle* had hoisted her pink-brown sails in the bay now far away in the north on which the town of Douarnenez looks down, contemplating its fishing fleet.

She was a beautiful boat with her sweeping curves, her small but well-built stern and her proud bows on which her name was carved and painted black on the white hull. She was beautiful, with the beauty of all that is perfectly designed for its purpose. She had become for the time being the centre of our lives, and we regarded her with childish pride, from her keel to her mast-head, where a little zinc swallow swivelled in the wind. The latter whispered or screamed in her rigging as she drove on, serenely or furiously, through the water.

We had crossed the Bay of Biscay with the mainsail reefed and with a new jib. For she had not come unscathed through the boisterous weather we encountered at the start. The tidal race by the Ile de Sein had cost her her jib and Cape Finisterre had torn her mainsail. The crew consisted of nine sailors and a boy from Douarnenez who, night and day, adroit and obstinate, maintained the constant struggle with the elements. With an oath or a jest they replied to the bufferings of the gale as they hauled in the sheets.

To every order they responded instantly, slipping and staggering with the pitching and rolling of the craft. After each evolution they swallowed a tot of rum, absinthe or wine according to the time of day. They spat, careless of their aim.

During a period of calm the captain wrote up the log in a careful hand with ornamental capitals. "9.0 p.m. struck topsail, 11.0 p.m. heaved to, close hauled. Sea rough. 5.0 a.m. clew of mainsail carried away. Strong breeze. . . ." etc. The Bay of Biscay was living up to its reputation.

What was she after, the *Belle-Hirondelle*? She was carrying a crew of fishermen who were out to catch cray-fish off the coast of Mauretania. They had far to go and were not to be deterred by bad weather. So the boat pushed onwards, throwing up sheets of glistening spray, her hull throbbing with the blows she took as she pounded through the waves. With nothing in sight we marvelled at this strange speed which left us always in the middle of the vast circle of the horizon and was only appreciable when one looked down at water rushing by.

She was also carrying two passengers, Marion Sénones and myself. We were not, like the sailors, there to earn our daily bread; in fact we were there for no better reason than that we were tormented by that old instinct of migration which slumbers somewhere in the souls even of civilized and sedentary folk. We wanted to go on a voyage—a real and beautiful voyage—with all that it might bring us, whether of joy or trouble.

The pacification of Mauretania had not proved easy. In fact an atmosphere of mystery and danger still overhung the country. The more luxurious means of travel offered by the shipping and air lines were altogether beyond our means—besides, that was not what we wanted. So we went the way of the navigators and slave-traders of former days, and still taken by the Breton fishermen today. And there we were on this solid, hospitable boat, which to us seemed full of nets, hopes, and adventures. The Breton fishermen I already knew, having often chatted with them on the coast of Brittany and at various other places between the Scilly Isles and Spain.

At Douarnenez we had got to know the owner of one of the fishing boats. We found him on the mole looking down at a boatload of provisions.

"Ah," he said, "so that's the way you want to get to Mauretania. It's no trouble to me. Not that there's any room. But if you like to make do as best you can . . ."

So on November 28th we duly embarked armed with four letters of introduction, two small revolvers, a Junior Kodak, and our heads filled with good advice. It was in obedience to the latter that we also took with us a quantity of woollen clothes such as would have seemed more suitable for a journey to Spitzbergen.

Our plans were simple, at least they seemed so at first. Landing at Port Étienne we were just to 'plunge into nature,' living with the nomads and adopting their manner of life. For we had no money to fit out a proper respectable caravan with all its modern camping equipment and 'boys' to carry it. When we had had enough of this mode of life we would look for another fishing boat to carry us home, or a ship almost as humble, carrying a cargo of bananas or monkey-nuts. But we did not bother very much about the return journey. After all, the important thing about a voyage is to start.

The boat was only 78 ft. long, and besides the crew of nine men and a boy she had to carry food and drink for three months, fuel for the auxiliary motor, spare sails and cordage, eight hundred nets, clothing, a dog, twelve rabbits, two dozen hens, and other miscellaneous stores and tackle, to say nothing of the motor itself and the tank for the crayfish. So there was indeed none too much room for the accommodation of two passengers.

Nédélec, the captain, did all he could, however, for our comfort. In the hold, which also served as saloon, general store-room and workshop, space was found for us. On the grating which covered one of the net-lockers a straw palliasse was laid, and curtains of tanned canvas were hung all round, tied by bits of cod-line. A row of barrels formed a step enabling us to climb in, while a case of calcium carbide served as a bedside table. The whole construction gave somewhat the impression of an old-fashioned carriage or a four-post bed.

No scrap of hull or bulkhead was visible. What was not covered by net-lockers was concealed behind barrels of water or drums of petrol. The lockers themselves were hung with great bunches of bananas, oilskins, coils of rope and netting, and strings of corks which looked like barbaric necklaces. A white cap hanging in a corner reminded us of our destination.

In the middle, between two benches, was the table, at which we squeezed, elbow to elbow, twice a day.

Every day eyes were raised to the calendar to which we gave our personal attention, tearing off the previous day's date as though the act brought us nearer to our goal.

The latter often seemed to us very far away, particularly when storms were raging or when the sailors, chatting over the nets they were making or mending, would tell us yarns of the great hot sand-dunes behind which the veiled Moors would be watching.

"Once to the south of Rio de Oro they fired on one of our boats—it belonged to Lanvoc'h—and they made a hole in the petrol tank."

"We, too, have been shot at," put in some of the others.

"Of course I don't know what you want to go to Mauretania for, but I should think twice myself before plunging inland."

"With the negroes near Dakar, at Sainte-Marie-de-Bathurst, it's quite different. As soon as we anchor in the fisheries they come out to us in their boats, full of fruit. They jump on board and pick up fish and shellfish as we haul in the nets. We only keep the crayfish for ourselves—that's only fair."

Marion and I, while busy winding cotton yarn on to wooden shuttles, dreamed of negroes carrying oranges and papaw, of wild dances under the coconut trees, of oyster pearls and swordfish, of giant turtles, in fact of strange men, beasts and flowers such as might be described in the travel books of ancient times.

With visions of exotic foods before us we contented ourselves meanwhile with the more homely fare provided on board, the good red apples of Brittany and country butter which the sailors would pass us.

"Help yourselves," they would say. "Take all you want. When there's no more we'll all tighten our belts together."

With their great rough beards our companions looked like pirates, but we found them, beneath their rough exterior, to be rich in that simplicity and kindness of heart which belong to seafaring men.

The little dog on board made friends with us too. She was a kind of diminutive spaniel, a dog that might more suitably have belonged to a country *curé*, for she had a modest air. She was called Bachturss, a corruption of Bathurst, or sometimes she was called Sainte-Marie. But such bold-sounding names were most unsuitable for a gentle, quiet dog who detested sea life and concealed her robust appetite beneath the false humility of a poor relation.

For thirteen days we had been living this simple life. Little by little the sea got calmer and its colour a deeper blue. Little by little the days got warmer. The hens began pickering about on deck, the rabbits played happily in the sunshine. At night the boat left trailing behind her a silver wake in which shone a myriad phosphorescent stars competing in miniature with the galaxy above.

At first Marion Sénones had been inclined to reproach me for having dragged her once again on one of those voyages which are so dear to my heart because, taking so long a time, they give the illusion of taking one so very far. But she had all the same to admit that it seemed at least logical to take a Mauretanian fishing boat to go to Mauretania. In the end she was quite reconciled to the manner of transport and became once more her charming self. She pored over novels of sea life, and won the hearts of the crew by sketching their portraits.

If I have begun this story at the thirteenth day it is not on account of any superstition, but because on this memorable day our hearts bounded, like that of Columbus and every other explorer, with that joy and excitement which surges up when, after long efforts, the goal finally appears over the horizon.

Throughout the previous day we had been skirting the Canary Islands. First Lanzarote with its clear-cut mountain ridge, like the teeth of a saw, grey-purple against the pale sky of dawn. Then Fuerteventura with its slaty mountains and their orange-coloured sandy slopes which towards evening melted into the light clouds on the horizon. Lastly, the summit of Teyde came suddenly into view against a golden background, and the sun set in a moment behind the Grand Canary.

Now the *Belle-Hirondelle* drifted lazily, waiting for a breeze, for the motor refused to go. With her idly flapping sails she looked like some great butterfly with its uncertain flight. A luminous mist clothed the horizon on all sides. The men were in sulky mood at the delay. Some were splicing hawsers, Julic and Quinnec were hanging up their nets to dry. There were nearly two hundred of them hanging from everything that could possibly serve as a prop. Tomorrow it would be the turn of two others to dry their nets, and the work would go on until the whole eight hundred nets were carefully dried, rolled up five at a time, and stowed away.

The mist was too delicate to resist a tropical sun for long. Suddenly towards ten o'clock it was gone and Africa appeared. It looked flat, worn and monotonous, eroded with rust and verdigris. It looked very old and not too beautiful, and the land was absolutely bare. But, just as it was, it looked wonderful to our eyes, for we knew that it was the embodiment of our dreams, the country for which we had come so far. The joy of something long desired and finally attained came to us as we contemplated that long thin sandy line of coast wedged in between the pale limpid green-blue sky and the crude ultramarine of the water.

That's what it looks like from the sea, we thought; but what would it be like inland? Inland it was to prove much the same except that the sand was pinker and covered with poisonous spurge, and, further in, with bushes with ferocious thorns.

Rio de Oro and its sister country Mauretania lay before us: the Trab-el-Beïdane, a million square kilometres of sand undulated with dunes and narrow valleys, cut from north to south by a chain of table mountains—Adrar, Tagant, Assaba. It stretched from the doubtful confines of Morocco to the definite boundary of Senegal, and from west to east from the Atlantic to the great deserts of the Sudan. To explore these sands men had given their energy, their youth, their science, and sometimes their lives.

For the riches of former times—gum, slaves, and the gold brought by the slow steps of camels through the scorching wastes—Portuguese, English, Dutch, French and Spanish had disputed the settlements along the coast, settlements which are today no more than heaps of ruins surrounded by tombs.

To conquer this country, French troops pushing northwards from Senegal had traced their passage in blood across the sand, the desolate country in which 500,000 nomads, some friends, some foes, strong alike in the faith of Islam and in the use of firearms, hid their faces in the folds of the dark blue *litham*, the colour of the sky at night. The conquest was necessary, but not for these sandy stretches in themselves. It was to unite Algeria and Morocco to the colonies in the south. *[The litham is a strip of cotton wound round the head. One end hangs down and is drawn across the lower part of the face so that only the eyes are visible.]*

It was to this country that we were now to dedicate a year of our lives, asking of it only that it should provide adventure.

The next day the *Belle-Hirondelle* sailed down the coast of Rio de Oro, the death-trap for the aviators of Air France. With any breakdown they would have the choice of two evils, either to trust to the Atlantic, in which Lecrivain and Ducaud went down in 1929, or to the still more menacing sands, risking captivity or even death. It was here, quite close to us, that Erable and Pintado were killed while their companion was bound to a camel and dispatched bleeding in the direction of Casablanca, where he died of his wounds.

Knowing its reputation our eyes turned instinctively to the sky.

"Look," cried Marion, "there goes one." And we watched it pass, lit up by the last glow of the setting sun.

Our companions looked at the scene with different eyes, thinking of their fishing. If they were given to reveries it would be of wrecks on the high seas, of shipmates washed overboard in storms, of nets carried away, and all the various adventures and vicissitudes experienced by this tenacious fisher-folk.

This evening we should see the Villa-Cisneros Light, and tomorrow the nets would be out.

Soon we came up with another fishing boat like the *Belle-Hirondelle*, from which a boat immediately put off. A little later ten sailors jumped on to our deck with such alacrity that it looked as though our craft was being boarded by pirates. They were fishermen from Tréboul, all pals with our men. With them the fishing prospects could be discussed. "There's not a great deal here, certainly," we were informed, "but it's not too bad either." And Nédélec decided to stay and see for himself.

They also brought us our mails, which they had fetched a few days before from Port Étienne, and which gave rise to great excitement; for the arrival of the mail is always a great event in the sailor's life.

Aided by their friends our crew now furled the sails, and the *Belle-Hirondelle* went to anchor near the other craft, the *Trébouliste*. Cries, orders, and humorous repartee mingled with the rattling cable as the anchor was dropped.

The ship's boy knew well his role on such occasions, and he scurried round collecting cans and glasses. For a meeting such as this on the 23rd parallel of latitude never passed without celebration, and gaieties continued till the early hours of the morning.

But these convivialities in no way interfered with the following day's business. They were indeed hardly finished when all were hard at work. Boats were lowered, nets got out, and the fishing started a few cables from the coast. Great care had to be taken of the nets, which were easily torn on pointed rocks or clusters of shell-fish.

The weather now was calm, but it often happened that to save ten thousand francs-worth of nets the fishermen were forced to risk their lives in their boats, tossed by the great rollers amongst the rocks and sand-banks of this dangerous coast. For it is particularly in bad weather that the best catches are to be had, as the troubled water bunds the cray-fish.

Marion and I were invited to go in the two boats. The men said it would bring them luck. At her anchorage the *Belle-Hirondelle* receded gradually into the distance and the coast-line rose before us. It was a strange coast, mournful, flattened, under the grey-mauve sky. Beaches appeared here and there between earthy rocks, striated horizontally in different colours, sulphur, orange and greenish-grey, and running through them were undulating lines, chalky and black. Massive dunes pushed forward like the bastions of a fort. As the tide ebbed sandy islets were uncovered, and these were immediately invaded by flocks of birds. On the beaches we could see traces of the jackals that hunt for fish during the night. The colouring of the landscape was very delicate and in its harmony reminded one of a Japanese print.

Nédélec pointed to the north and we saw Villa-Cisneros, a military post and fishing port.

"It was there," he said, "behind Point Durford, that Lanvoc'h took on board the Spanish prisoners who had been sent to Villa-Cisneros after the revolution of 1931. Twenty-seven of them there were, kings and queens all of them.... That was just a year ago. And Christmas night I passed his boat as he went south; but that was only a feint. After that he sailed north, I don't know where. They say it was Portugal. A good catch he got there, I'm sure. It pays better to handle kings than cray-fish. There are still two queens left there, who were too frightened to get into the boat.... At least, that's what they say."

They say many things at the mess table of a fishing boat and during the long evenings mending nets. And it pleased me, this legend of so many "Queens of Spain" waiting in an African donjon for the day of their deliverance.

The story we heard later was more convincing. On Christmas Eve 1932, the Governor had invited the political exiles to dine with him. The latter were free to walk about the place as they liked, and when the time for dinner came nobody appeared. The exiles had preferred the invitation of Lanvoc'h and had made off. Las Palmas was informed by wireless. Pleasant news to receive on Christmas Eve! There was no coal on the only warship that could have given chase, as there was no money to buy the coal. And, of course there was no coal on the day following. When finally the ship was ready to sail, Lanvoc'h was far away with his cargo.

For our part, however, it was neither kings nor queens that we found on the ill-famed coast of Rio de Oro, but our first Moors. They were watching us from the top of an old dune, scored by the wind. They stood like statues of bronze against the sky, draped in white and blue. Their faces were hardly visible between the folds of their black turbans. They were our first nomads, the first of those wandering people with whom we had come to live. Then they seemed to welcome us as they waved their rifles. But instead of taking us to them the sailors turned the boats quickly and headed out to sea. Indeed it was not too soon; bullets whistled through the air and splashed the water round the boats.

"And those are the savages that you have come to see in their filthy desert," shouted the coxswain furiously. "They never miss a chance to fire on our boats. At the lighthouse at Cap-Blanc three years ago they murdered the keeper, Panduff. Ah, the *canailles*."

Fortunately the nets had already been hauled in, and the bottoms of the boats were a seething mass of fish, crabs, and other sea creatures of all colours of the rainbow. Cray-fish were rare, so we would not stay long in these waters.

The grumbling went on: "It's always the same story. Shall we ever hear the last of those fellows? The evil's in their blood. And don't think it's only in the Spanish parts that the Moors are like that. In Mauretania it's much the same—at least inland. I know very well. There are lots of Bretons in the French ports along the coast and they all say the same. Nothing but stories of dog-bites and *razzias*, their troubles are never at an end. I swear if I were in your place, a young lady who could go where she pleased, I wouldn't poke my nose into that country."

All the same I knew that those barren sands had for him the attraction of the unknown, an attraction far too deep-seated to be shaken by a few shots from the nomads' rifles.

Nédélec took us to Villa-Cisneros on a morning as gentle and dreamy as a pearl. Africa's welcome was this time more cordial, the Spanish Governor and the French aviators doing the honours. Before their ragged tents the Moors greeted us with smiles, but at the same time something glittered in their eyes that was not altogether reassuring.

Crenelated white buildings were so grouped as to give the impression of quite an imposing village, but in reality these were only the barracks, the Spanish air port, the air port of Air France, a factory, a building concerned with the fishing, the Spanish-Arab school and a few huts. Beyond was nothing but the bare ground, as flat as if it had been carefully levelled for some purpose. It was dry and the colour of earthenware. In the distance the peninsular was shut off from the country beyond by little forts between which stretched thick barbed-wire entanglements.

And the country beyond ... it was immense with liberty, adventure, and the attraction of an ever-fluid horizon. It was the desert. And behind the barricade a caravan was waiting like some mysterious visitor....

***

A whole week we were trying our luck with the nets, the African coast, pale and melancholy, on our port hand.

Fishing was bad and Nédélec decided to try elsewhere, so on December 20th we had to say goodbye to the *Belle-Hirondelle*. One never leaves a ship without regret, nor could we our companions, whose life we had shared for three weeks. They had to push further south to the warmer waters off the coast of Gambia, while our path lay inland over the sands.

We landed at Port Étienne, passing the Coppolani and

Cansado lights. As we went through the surf to the long white beach our boat struck a piece of waterlogged timber, the relic of some schooner that had foundered on the coast. Among the three kilometres of sand-dunes, four little groups of buildings were scattered, surrounded by barbed wire, their roofs crowned with old pots. There was also a third lighthouse and a few little forts. Here and there was a group of miserable tents. There were no bushes, and not a blade of grass, for the locusts had just passed.

Some Moorish fishermen approached. They were clad in cast-off European clothes except for their turbans of dark blue cotton. They greeted us in a strange language and took charge of our baggage, which consisted of a trunk with rusty fittings, some mouldy suitcases, a bundle of sabots and oilskins, and lastly our palliasse, which was shedding part of its stuffing. Marion and I walked behind. We were just a little disconcerted by the astonished though friendly looks that were being turned on us by some colonials.

The local name for Port Étienne is Nouazibou, meaning the jackals' well, though there is no well there of any kind. In this place one easily understands why the Moors have only one word, Trab, for country and sand. How could they even imagine a country that did not consist of sand? Looking into the distance, all we could see was the white powdery sand covered with dunes, with here and there earthy rocks sticking up chiselled by the sand-laden wind into fantastic shapes. Even these rocks were only made of compacted sand.

One of the first posts established by the French at the frontier of Rio de Oro, Port Étienne is now too well known, since it has become a regular port of call for passenger planes, for me to describe it once again. Everything has already been said concerning its military significance, its aviation, its fishing and its marauding bands, its ambition to become a great fishing port and its failure to do so. Perhaps the government of Mauretania, which sits at Saint Louis in Senegal studying its budget deficit, considered that there were better claims on its meagre funds than the doubtful need for wharves and basins of concrete for the few vessels that bring water and food to a place that in itself lacks all resources.

What really interested us were not so much the places as the people. We had come to see the Moors, and on their side they seemed only too ready to be friendly, though their advances consisted chiefly in pursuing us with the request for alms. "*Bonjour—Madame—cadeau*" they repeated in a single breath as though it was one word. As we walked about we had quite a following: a horde of naked children and also women draped from head to foot like antique statues in their *malahfas*. The latter are made of *guinée*, an imported cotton stuff, and dyed with a greasy colouring matter, dark indigo, which stains the hands when touched. The women did not beg; they demanded. The men, more mistrustful, looked at us from the distance, and turned their heads away from our camera.

Little by little we won the confidence of these people, and even managed to get into their miserable tents. Sometimes when passing we would be asked in to drink the customary four cups of sugar-saturated tea, which we did, squatting on the matting.

We began to make friends. One was the *dioula*, a wandering trader who had come to the place to buy sugar-loaves, tea and cotton stuff, which for centuries had been the chief articles of exchange. These he would sell or barter at the camps inland. Another was the beautiful Aïcha, who had been brought from the south by a husband who had subsequently cast her off. She had been waiting for two years for the passage of some caravan which could take her back to her father's tent from which she would get married once more. Another was Ahmed-Saloum, the owner of the *lanche* which was to take us south to Memrhar, where we were to be joined by an escort as soon as we had received permission from Dakar to go into the country. A *lanche* is a one-masted boat with a lateen sail.

We were eager to find out all we could of the country we were going to.

"Over there you have the big camels, the cows, the sheep. Plenty of good milk. Over there, fine tents of wool. Here, you see, is nothing. No pastures for animals. Nothing but scrub everywhere. You go where you like, do what you want, you walk, you stop. Nobody there to see you, nobody there to tell you what to do. You are free; understand? That's it: free. The Beïdani too, he is free."

Thus they spoke under their ragged tents. In a place where soldiers, officials, fishermen and visitors established some sort of European life, the Moors remained what they really were, nomads. To earn money they were drawn into civilized activities, but they showed a common solidarity before the masters they had to serve. They might sometimes like their masters, but always they preferred the open country out behind. They would look with indifference on motor cars, aeroplanes and wireless sets, their minds far off, enjoying in reverie the grand liberty of the nomad's life.

The nomads who came here for supplies were for the most part Berbers, descendants of the people who had, long ago, conquered Spain. These were poor and miserable, but their richer cousins in Fez and Agadir still retained some relics of their former glories.

At Port Étienne they had twice been conquered, and now they had to pay tribute to more warlike tribes as well as paying taxes to the French administration. Many became sailors, labourers, mechanics or 'boys.' In contact with a strange civilization they seemed bereft of all will-power. All the same they managed to make ends meet, paying their taxes and their Arab suzerains.

These people were easily recognized by their Berber traits: short thick-set bodies, flat broad faces edged by black beards. We also got to know their chiefs, *marabouts* of the Ahel-Grâa and Barekallah, who handled the rifle as well as their Musulman beads. While the warriors who proudly called themselves Hassan Arabs, that is to say sons of Hassan the Conqueror, were exclusively warlike tribes. Of the latter, the Ouled-Delim had resigned themselves very reluctantly to French rule. On their ill-fed camels the chiefs of units would come from Rio de Oro to make submission and haggle over the tribute which they knew so well how to extort from their own vassals. They were wild and noble-looking men, and under their turbans, or *aouli*s, their cruel watchful eyes glittered like those of a jackal in a trap.

Sometimes after drinking their tea they would pass the time in dancing. The turbans when removed would reveal dark curly hair. The dancers would shake with an ecstatic trembling, and their long *draa*s, the tunics of blue cotton draped over their outstretched arms, would flutter like impatient wings. To the rhythm of the tom-tom, beaten by an old woman on an empty pot, they would keep for long periods in a state of exaltation, but all the time on their foreheads was written the fatalism of their race, the resignation which held them here uncomplaining only because Allah, whom they called Moulana, willed it.

The owners of the fishing fleet also belonged to the Ouled-Delim tribe, the only warlike tribe which provides sailors or submits to any sort of work, though they grumbled enough at serving Christians for the meagre pay of four to eight francs a day.

The men, however, who did the work of cleaning, salting and drying the enormous *courbines*, so abundant in these African waters, were black slaves whose ancestors had been carried off in slave raids in Senegal or the Sudan. These fishermen (the Imraguen they were called) lived in straw huts all along the coast. By the administration they were called *serviteurs-nés*. Any sale of slaves was, of course, severely punished by the authorities when discovered, but much could happen in the hinterland which never came to light.

To set foot in Mauretania is to step backwards twenty centuries to biblical times. Master and slaves shared the same poverty or wealth, were covered by the same goatskins at night, drank tea out of the same glass and smoked the same pipe. Nevertheless these were real slaves that could in fact be bought, sold, liberated or killed at their masters' will.

In Morocco, France had given the slaves their freedom, but with the latter came the anxiety of providing for the morrow, unemployment and economic depression, so that they begged their former masters to take them back into their families as they were before.

The slaves of Africa know no worries, nor insurances, nor pensions. Their home is in the same camp from their birth to their death, and if the master should give them their freedom, they prefer to stay with him. In this condition a slave is called a *hartani*, the plural being *haratine*.

Far from perfect though Moorish customs may be, we must be sure we have something better to offer before we abolish them.

Once in a while the mask of servitude would fall and we would catch sight of a flash of fierce pride, revolt and hope. Many of these men belonged to the dissident tribes which had carried out the great *razzias* of 1924 and 1927, holding up aeroplanes that made forced landings in Rio de Oro, and killing without hesitation anyone they might chance to find who, wandering in the neighbourhood of Port Étienne, had ventured too far from this base.

One evening, when we were visiting a European friend who was friendly with the Moors, a boy entered, who was a perfect specimen of the proud beauty which graces the adolescents of the desert. His *aouli* framed a marvellously noble face of a perfect oval, in which were set the large black eyes. Crossed over his blue *draa*, white muslin bandoleers carried a Moroccan dagger in chased silver, while the cartridge pouch was of red leather.

He was the doctor's servant.

His right hand covered his heart while he invoked the blessing of Moulana on the master of the house who was a father and mother to him, who was kindly as the rain, great as the sun, who . . .

But his master interrupted: "What do you want?"

At this invitation the young Mohammed began a long story all mixed up with praises and supplications. For a long time (and he must have been about seventeen) he had wanted to marry, and the lady of his heart (who was twelve) had that very day come to Port Étienne with her parents. The father demanded a dowry of 500 francs.

For in Mauretania it is the husband who pays the dowry, the amount of which varies with his social status. Europeans say that the Moors sell their daughters, but the Moors say that French women buy their husbands, and each despises the custom of the other.

"Five hundred francs, a hundred *ouguïa*! What can I do, I who have nothing. So I come to you because you are rich, powerful and generous."

His master seemed to hesitate, then changed the subject.

"You saw the Ouled-Delim tribe which came in yesterday to make submission?"

Mohammed's face clouded.

"Yes. They paid the tribute, rifles and camels. But there's been no rain in Rio. The cattle are hungry; they have to bring them to French pastures."

At the base of all diplomacy, whether concerned with submissions, raids, or anything else, the rain always played a big part.

"It's not only for that, Mohammed. The French are going to make a big war on the Ouled-Noun, and your relatives the Ait-Lhassen themselves are talking of making submission."

"No, no," cried the youth. "The Ait-Lhassen never submit, never pay taxes to the *Roumis* [*a word used to denote a Christian*], never. My tribe too great warriors. *'Lhamdou 'llah* (thanks to God)."

And Mohammed, the blood in his cheeks, his hand clasped on his dagger, forgot his fiancée and the 500 francs. But he got them all right next day.

The marriage was very beautiful. In the middle of the night, in spite of the beat of the tom-toms, one could hear the cry of the young bride, and next day her *malahfa* could be shown at the threshold of the tent with its proof of her virginity.

They were also capable of great devotion when the power and personality of a man touched them and offered a fitting subject for the admiration of their warrior souls.

The boy who waited on the fishing authorities, who had been born in Adrar, was vassal to one of the tribes of the Hassan Arabs. Quite young the hazard of nomad life had brought him to Port Étienne. He was gentle, devoted, and an excellent cook, and only got angry when his master called him a 'philosopher.'

"*Non, Monsieur,* Sidi not 'make eggs.' (*Sidi pas 'fait les oeufs'*). Not nice to say that, Monsieur. It is only ostriches that 'make eggs'."

And Sidi drew his *aouli* across his nose and retired with dignity to the kitchen, his apron flapping against his bare legs.

One day when we were gathered round the table, conversation turned on the Adrar, of its conquest, and of General Gouraud, who had just arrived at Dakar on his way to Bamako where he was to unveil a statue of Archinard.

Sidi stopped dead, his mouth wide open, a dish of cream in one hand, his other on his breast,

"What is it, Sidi? Are you dreaming?"

"*Non, Monsieur,* Sidi never dream. But if you speak of 'Gélinal' Gouraud, Sidi lose his head."

It was true that, in the esteem of Sidi, Gouraud came immediately after Moulana and his prophet.

"*Oui, Monsieur*" he went on, "I know him *complètement*. When all my relations is killed in war with the French, the soldiers find me in the scrub, lost. They take me to 'Gélinal' Gouraud, and he makes me 'boy' to him. I was little, too little to wear *boubou* . I serve coffee, Monsieur, to 'Gélinal' Gouraud. Ah, *mon vieux*, he was great, 'Gélinal' Gouraud, *fort et bon complètement*. Ach!"

The death of his father, his uncles, and his elder brothers, and the humiliation of defeat were all effaced by admiration for the great soldier.

Thus little by little we got to know the Moors, who are cruel and hospitable, proud, yet flatterers, grasping and generous, beggars because, sharing the little they themselves have, they find it natural that others should share with them, who are capable of admiring their conqueror so long as he is a man they can respect, who are accused of trickery because the heart does not always submit, even while the hand pays tribute....

We were off once more on the African seas, which northerners will always imagine blue beneath a brilliant sky. But this time the water was a tumult of jade, flecked by silver where the 'white horses' broke. The east wind at times brought squalls of heavy rain, and at others pink sand from the desert. In the sky were flying streaks of purplish cloud.

The Bay of Lévrier is wide and cuts deep into the coast. Port Étienne had disappeared, and nothing was visible but the horizon all round. In the middle of this circle was our little Canary Island *lanche*, buffeted by the wind, its large sail tugging at the yard.

The after part of the boat was covered in by a kind of awning of coarse canvas; forward was a great heap of blue rags. At the helm was Ahmed-Saloum, his face hidden, all but the eyes, by his *aouli*. Alert in the bows was a turbanned negro, half naked under a large piece of threadbare fur. Marion Sénones and I were tucked away under the awning, getting what shelter we could amongst our baggage. We did not put our heads out until, towards evening, the boat was peacefully sailing through calm water in the Bay of Pelicans.

Brahim, an Ouled-Delim boy, woke up. The heap of rags stirred, and a tall, disdainful-looking Moor disengaged himself dressed in a new tunic, greasy with its fresh dye. He was going to Tenaloul to get together a merchant convoy. The second sailor looked up showing his face, something between that of a pirate and a sheik, glowing with the beauty of young nomads. Then from under an old sail a woman appeared dressed in rags, with a baby three years old, her granddaughter. The latter was dressed with extreme simplicity, having nothing on but a silver bracelet round each ankle. Probably this attire seemed to her insufficient, for she started screaming in the glacial wind which blew clean through our woollens. But she screamed in vain, for it is not the fashion in Mauretania to clothe young children, whatever the temperature or the circumstances.

Everybody stirred and stretched, murmuring *Elhamdou lillah!* . . . *T'arek Allah!* . . . God be praised that we, earthly wanderers, had been preserved from the fearful jinn which inhabit the waters. But fearful as these spirits were they had to be braved, as there were worse things still on the tracks inland, marauding bands who watched along the Rio frontier for small defenceless caravans.

Each wound round his head the long strip of cotton and tightened the belt that held the harmonious draping of the tunic. On their crossed bandoleers they fastened the red pouch full of cartridges and the silver dagger. And the little Moorish pipe stuffed with acrid tobacco passed from mouth to mouth.

The *lanche* sailed gently on towards the beach, while thousands of birds flew screeching round. When we were quite near the shore, Messaoud, the fisherman-slave, hauled down the sail, climbed over the gunwale, and jumped into the water.

When he had hauled the boat as near the water's edge as it would go, he started to carry the Moors ashore on his shoulders, for they were his masters since they belonged to warlike tribes. Then he took the old woman, and since the baby would not be parted from her grandmother, he took her too, carrying her by one arm, she struggling the while and looking like a little brown frog.

A tent was rigged up on the desert coast, and soon a brushwood fire was crackling and water boiling for the tea. The peace of an Arab night descended. The men turned towards Mecca under the first star and prostrated themselves, making the symbolic gesture of pouring the fluid sand over their upturned faces, and the grave words of the *salaam* drifted eastwards across the sands.

Paris was very far away and we did not think of it. This was what we had come for and we were wholly absorbed by it. As soon as we had received permission to proceed inland from the Governor-General of French West Africa, we had set off for Memrhar, an Imraguen village, where three warriors under the command of an old chief were to meet us and escort us to Nouakchott. That was as far as we had planned.

But for the moment we were there with our little revolvers and our abundant confidence, in the middle of the Ouled-Delim, a half-subjected people forming a fraction of a large refractory tribe. We had been told that they were good fellows who had for long been employed at Port Étienne, but they also told us that in 1935 some cousins of theirs, employed as sailors in the French *lanches*, had run off to take part in the Moutounsi raid in which Lieutenant Mac-Mahon was killed.

The loyalty of tribes to the Government depended a good deal on the weather. Rain in the Rio pastures meant insubordination, while in the south it meant submission. This year the Rio pastures had been dry, but no one could know how long the drought would last.

Brahim came and sat near us. Now that we had got away from Port Étienne he dropped his somewhat crafty manner of the well-drilled 'boy.' Once more he was wearing a *draa* like the others: coming into his own country he became himself again, a nomad of the scrub.

"You not afraid?" he asked. "Listen and you understand. Beïdani a good fellow. Only makes trouble when angry too much with being poor and paying taxes. European wants to take all, take all Africa. Make people pay for pastures, for wells, for everything. Sometimes there's no way to pay. When you can't get enough to eat one way, you get it another. If you make no money you make battles to get the necessary, *le tout-c'qu'y-faut*, and after you run and hide in the Spanish country, *forcément*."

At Port Étienne, the Beïdane profess to despise our neighbours, the Spanish, but Brahim gave us another version.

"Spaniards, there are good and bad, like everywhere else, *forcément*. But I'll explain it all, so you understand. You saw my chief at Port Étienne. Made submission, gave rifles and camels and all. Commandant looks at him same thing as if he was a slave. If my chief goes to Cap Juby, the Spanish demand nothing. He makes presents and salutes Spanish very politely. The war is over. Good. They make friends and forget the bad, like Beïdani does with Beïdani. Understand? Spaniard not so strong as Frenchman, but very good for submission."

Then Brahim returned to the subject of the moment.

"No, you no reason to be afraid. We do all we can for you. Take you to Memrhar. Good fellows the Imraguen. After that you see all Mauretania, and that is beautiful altogether. *Cà, mon vieux, c'est beau complètement.*"

And to seal the pact which he was making on behalf of the country and its nomads, Brahim, the Hassan warrior and French 'boy,' produced from his cartridge pouch two little carved rings of silver, very worn, which he held out to us in the hollow of his brown hand.

After the *salaam* of dawn, Messaoud, the negro, carried us all on board, and we made off, encircled once more by the screaming birds as we sailed out of the Bay of Pelicans.

A bitter wind blew off the land and we shivered in the dull morning light, which lit up the sombre landscape which had been the scene of so many tragedies. For since remote ages many had been the galleys and ships of every description that had grounded on the sand-banks which Messaoud, leaning forward at the stem, pointed out to the captain, Ahmed-Saloum.

The gloomy landscape told upon our spirits, but towards ten o'clock our thoughts were diverted by our arrival at a point southwest of Arguin, where we landed again. Climbing in turn on to Messaoud's shoulders, we were set down on the soft wet sand which sucked at our footsteps. We walked up to the dry slopes above the beach and sat down among the bushes, watching with the keenest interest the preparation of our first Moorish meal.

First of all our companions, from Ahmed-Saloum down to Bettah the baby, drank murky water from the spout of the teapot. After that came the green syrupy tea of which it is the custom to drink four glasses. After the second I had enough, but Marion, more determined, managed three. Brahim attended to the stew, and when it was ready we helped ourselves to handfuls of a horrible mixture of rice, meat, and sand.

We did not realize that the time was soon to come when the teapot would seem to us always too soon emptied, when rice, pawed by dirty hands, would be a most welcome change from the *méchoui* of tough mutton cooked in sand and embers, and when we would gulp down water from the common cup without a thought of those who had drunk before. Life in the scrub was soon to make us forget, in the simplified existence it imposed, the precepts of civilized table-manners and hygiene.

We passed the Island of Arguin, a ruined fortress and reservoirs whose possession Portugal, Holland, England, and France had disputed for four centuries. Once it had been a flourishing place, until ruined by the Compagnie du Senegal. The chief remains of its struggles were the tombs which covered the end of the island. Where the sandy shore had been eroded by the sea, skeletons had been uncovered. Of the bloody conflicts which envy and jealousy had fomented this was all that now remained: stones, bones, and broken bricks made in former days by Portuguese slaves.

As we rounded the high rocky headland of El Freh, which is joined to the mainland only by a narrow ridge of sand, we left behind us the desolate landscape with its mournful memories. We now entered into a veritable kingdom of birds. They wheeled and circled above us, or, alighting, formed a feathery mantle for some earthy rock worn by wind and sea. Next they would form a great undulating island on the surface of the water. There were birds of all shapes, all shades of grey, and of every kind of flight. The flamingos were pink and very graceful. The solemn pelicans kept apart from the smaller birds, the snipe, gulls and cormorants.

From time to time we made efforts to find out where we were. We studied our map and tried to compare its outline with the configuration of the coast. The crew were able to name every island or promontory that we passed, but that did not help us much; for French geographers had so Gallicized the names that we were unable to find on the map those our companions pronounced. Or sometimes completely new names had been given by some official in the colonial administration. Finally we gave up the attempt, and settled down simply to enjoy what we saw.

And there was plenty to see both in the boat and out. Little Bettah delighted us as she watched the gestures of her grandmother and attempted to imitate them. From her we would look up to see the line of a shark as it swam past the *lanche*, to see the bushes of spurge which made up the scrub inland, or to see the first dromedaries on a sand-dune silhouetted against the sky. And all at once, rounding a cape, we came upon a *lanche* like ours, sailing towards us.

It was some of the Imraguen making for Port Étienne. The two boats brailed up their sails and drew alongside. The interminable salutations that passed between the men sounded like a litany.

"*Labès*: how are you? ... Well, thanks to God. ... How are your children? ... Your family? ... Your friends? ... Your camp-fellows? ... Your cattle? ... *Labès alikoum, 'hamdou lillah*! They are well, God be praised! ... May he prolong your life! May he raise you in rank and confound those who envy you!"

Each question and each wish were repeated several times, in fact the whole proceedings lasted a good quarter of an hour. We then learned that Cheikh-ould-Mouknas was camping at Tenaloul and was waiting to join us.

Their *lanche* was full of dried fish, and a negro handed an armful to Messaoud in exchange for half a sugar-loaf, the deal being witnessed by a swarm of flies.

Suddenly a small brown hand lifted the corner of a piece of sail-cloth, and a Be'idania was revealed squatting among some sacks. She was the wife of a warrior returning to her tent in Rio de Oro, and her face was not covered like those of the *marabout* women. She had bold and yet caressing eyes, her teeth glittered in her dark face, a barbaric necklace was wound round her neck; her hair divided into many little plaits was adorned with beads and shells. When the boat shoved off she waved us adieu and we caught sight of an arm loaded with bracelets.

It was on the shore of an island, Gouchneh, that we passed the last night of the trip. It was a peaceful night, and sitting by our little fire thinking of the bareness all around us—the bare islands, the empty sea, the desert coast—I recalled the words I had heard not long before:

"Nobody there to see you. Nobody there to tell you what to do. You are free.... The scrub is beautiful: *Y en a beau complètement, la brousse.*"

On a low dune some yellow flowers, '*bananes de Maures*' they are called, exhaled their scent of cyclamen. To the west two other islands stretched parallel with ours, Iouili and Tidra, to the east the land covered with bushes. In more troubled times the place would not have been so peaceful, for when raids take place it often happens that caravans take refuge on Gouchneh, which can be reached from Foumotric only by wading knee-deep through the water.

Raids, however, were not far off, as Sid-Ahmed was soon to learn, and we too for that matter. He had reached Tenaloul the night before, having done the last part of the journey overland.

The next day we reached Memrhar. The shore here was a long white beach which ran down in a gentle slope far beneath the sea. It was of fine sand shifted easily by the waves so that the coastal scenery was constantly undergoing transformation. Crabs, red and purple, brandished their single white claw. Pelicans, gulls and flamingos fished in the water for their food.

Memrhar is some two hundred kilometres south of Port Étienne and some five hundred north of Saint Louis in Senegal. Between it and these latter was nothing but islands dangerous to navigation, pink sand, grey-mauve spurge, and the desolate charm of nature when she offers nothing to man, nor makes any demands upon him either.

The village consisted of a few huts, round like beehives, and some brown tents. Naked children played about under the swarms of flies. We could hear the monotonous sound of pestles which were pounding fish debris for the evening meal.

Some negroes dressed only in tight-fitting leather shorts were bringing in their nets suspended on poles which they carried two by two. On the left of the village three humble wooden crosses recalled the massacre of some Spanish fishermen.

On the right, resting on some porpoise skulls, were three worm-eaten cases full of books. An old *marabout* had left them there before he died in order that their dust should one day be incorporated in the wind and the sand.

News travels fast in Mauretania, both by sea and land, and we found the Imraguen waiting for us on the beach at Memrhar. As soon as our boat was anchored they ran down into the water, looking like bronze Tritons. With great white smiles they seized hold of us, and as we went ashore mounted on their shoulders we had the flattering impression of being carried in triumph to some savage people.

The tom-tom was beaten, as at Reguïba, making a great noise, and the half-naked slaves, who had never set eyes on European women, seemed to be transported by a Dionysiac joy quite out of proportion to our modest arrival. One of the women beat a big drum while a baby slung on her back slept peacefully in the midst of the din.

Excitement rose all the afternoon to attain its climax in the evening when the Imraguen danced in mime a warrior parade, using their drivers' sticks to represent rifles, after which they went on to dances of seduction, the obscene gestures of dogs, and the death of a bull killed by a lion.

Towards the end, a distribution of tea, tobacco and sugar spurred them to a final frenzy and definitely established our popularity. The fact is that occasions for rejoicing are rare in the lives of the poor Imraguen.

They formed a race apart, despised, unclean. They were derived from a cross between the Berbers who had come to the country and the mysterious aboriginals they found there, together with an admixture of negro blood from the slaves sold all along the coast. Their origin accounted for their very definite physical type: thickset bodies, astonishingly wide, short faces, with pronounced features and sad eyes. They were quite unlike all other Mauretanian types.

They were treated as pariahs, and they kept well away from the French posts and from the great *marabouts*. As vassals or slaves they had to serve the Arabs and Berbers, whom they had to pay for the right to fish or to graze their cattle, and even for the right to draw water from the brackish wells.

Masters they had everywhere, although the law of the *Koran* stipulates that no one should pay tribute to several men. Only nature was kind to them, nature which had so richly stocked the

Villa-Cisneros, the Spanish Military Post

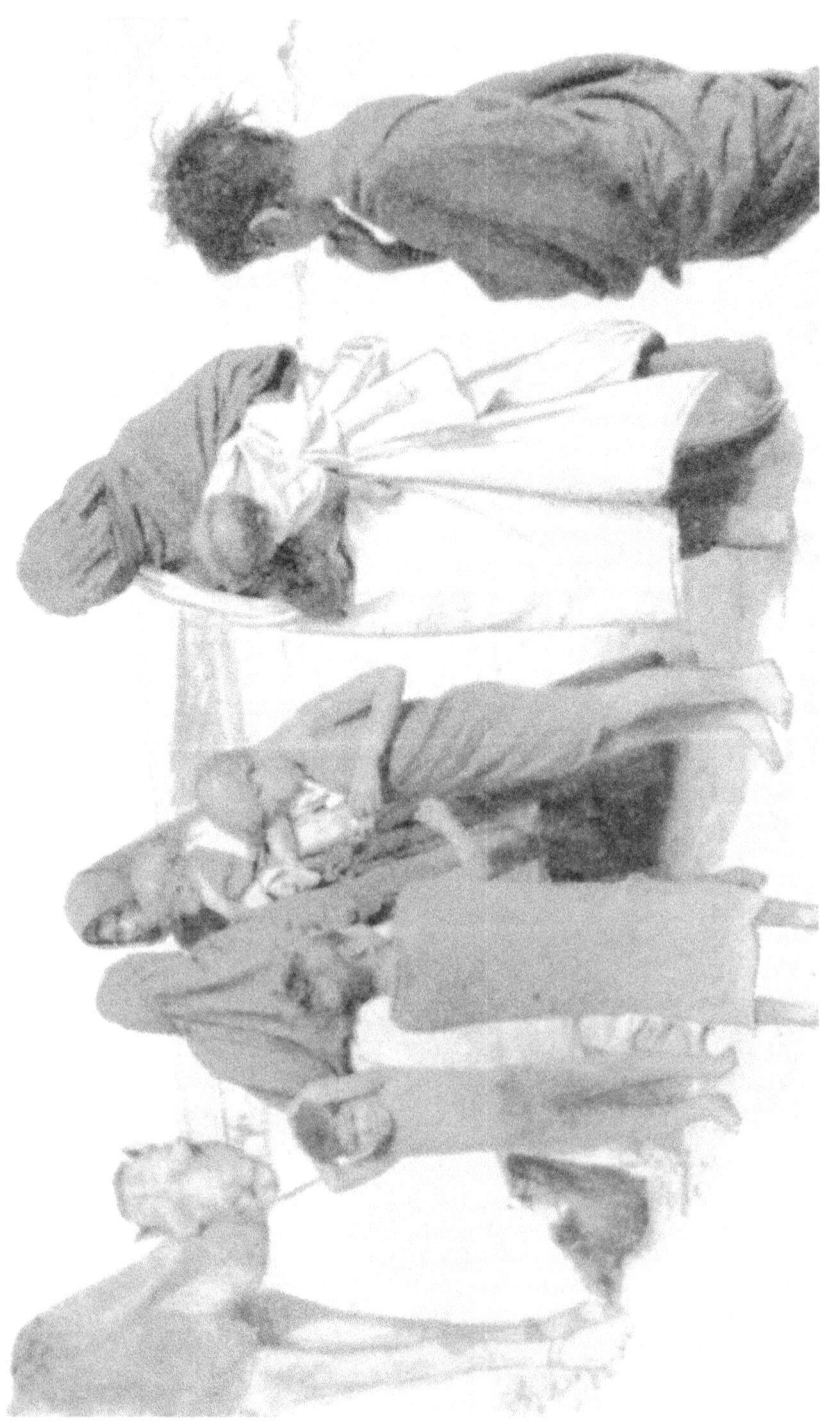

Nomads on the Beach at Port Étienne

African waters with fish, and on land had made the *titarek* to grow abundantly, a sort of broom whose fibres could be used for making nets. The latter were coarse seines, weighted with lumps of clay and with floats of light spurge-wood. Amongst the fish, *courbine* and mullet were plentiful, the latter particularly at new moon. Fish was dried in the sun, and caravans of small asses carried it to Saint Louis and Nouakchott; mullet roe was sold at Port Étienne. Unsaleable débris, heads, skin, and crushed bones made the diet of the fishermen.

We used to watch them waist-deep in the water setting their nets in the shallows or hauling them ashore with their catch. They were armed with sticks to beat off sharks or jackals. Boys seven or eight years old, their eyes oozing with ophthalmia, their bellies and legs swollen, would already be at work helping their fathers. These would be the masters. For they had slaves who would then gather in the fish and carry it from the beach to the huts where the women would prepare it for drying.

To permit this enterprise taxes and tribute had to be paid. The tax paid to the French authorities was 600 francs a year. The various annual tributes to the tribes were as follows: five pieces of *guinée*, the dyed cotton stuff, to the Ouled-Séïd, three pieces to the Ouled-Mohammed-Laleub, thirty pieces to the warriors of the Adrar, half a piece to the Ouled-Lap, etc., down to two and a half metres to the Ahel-Graa. The price of twenty large fish was five francs, so it may easily be imagined that hard work had to be done for all these obligations to be met.

While we were camping there Memrhar was a peaceful spot, but it sometimes happened that warriors would come from far to claim arrears of payment. Then woe to the vassals who possessed nothing. If they could not pay they were chased with heavy sticks out into the scrub, from whence they were brought back famished and terrified a few days later. The warriors would then watch them from the beach, seizing the fish as it was brought in. They took possession of the best huts and the most good-looking of the women. When finally they rode off into the scrub on their great camels or *méharas*, they left nothing but famine and desolation in the wretched camp.

The Imraguen are shrinking in numbers from a variety of causes: destitution, the flight of some to Rio de Oro, and the inflexible law which decrees that infants shall be killed at birth if born of an unmarried woman.

When we pointed out to the warriors that by enforcing this law they were blindly destroying a source of revenue to themselves, they simply shrugged their shoulders with indifference.

"You are quite right," they would say, "but what can be done about it? It has always been like that, and we cannot change things. The Imraguen, they are *lhamm*, meat, and their lot has been written. Let the will of Allah be done! *La illah ill Allah*."

On January 10th our escort arrived at Memrhar, mounted on magnificent camels. It consisted of Cheikh-ould-Mouknas, prince of the desert, dressed in white, accompanied by three warriors dressed in blue. The cloud of sand that rose as they trotted up melted into the gold of the dunes in the glare of the setting sun.

The foaming camels knelt down before us, roaring with impatience. Tied to the croup of one of them, a racing *azouzel*, was a black sheep that belched blood from its open throat. The *azouzel* is a gelded camel, while the *fal* is a stallion. The former is the better for racing.

With their daggers, their white scarves crossed over their chests, and their deep blue *lithams* concealing all but the large cruel eyes, these Moorish warriors seemed to belong to an unknown country and a forgotten age, reminding one of the rough yet noble chivalry which their ancestors brought to the Christian world.

Looked at closely, Cheikh was really like a brigand. To reassure us, no doubt, he had pinned two Sahara medals on his burnouse. He was as cunning as a usurer, but compliant, and he always gave himself the airs of a *grand seigneur*. He had been to Paris to the Colonial Exhibition, from which visit he had returned with a picturesque vocabulary, an intense admiration for a country in which so much water could be squandered in public places, and a taste for the photographs of dancers on cigarette cards. He regretted the Folies Bergeres:

"Petits pantalons de Paris, ah! Never break!"

All the same he preferred life in the scrub.

We immediately began to make arrangements for our journey

inland. The most important thing, of course, was the distribution of the rations. They had been ordered in advance from an intermediary who had reasons for wishing to please Cheikh. They were exorbitant in price, as also was the pay of the men and the hire of the camels, but we knew nothing of that and were delighted.

Under the tent, the light of a rag-wick lamp burning fish oil lit up Cheikh's curved features and sharp eyes. A Palestine shepherd held open the leather bags, and we counted out assiduously the loaves of sugar, the leaves of tobacco for each, and measured glass by glass the rice and tea. We seemed to be back in biblical times measuring the bushels of grain with which one bought a king's daughter.

We never knew whether Cheikh was pleased or not, not even when later at Nouakchott he accepted in silence the presents we offered him. We laid the pieces of *guinée* timidly before him without his deigning to touch them or even to look at them. At that time we did not yet know that a Moor is never satisfied, the pleasure at a gift being balanced by an equal desire for more.

When the bags of our escort were filled they wandered off to other occupations, while the curious spectators who had gathered round continued in preaching tones and with endless repetitions to comment on the great display of riches they had witnessed.

Suddenly the event occurred which was always latent in the designs of Allah. A distant cry rent the night air; it was repeated nearer and taken up by other throats. Instantly the Beïdane understood. A hand put out the lamp, and a subdued voice enjoined us to remain where we were without moving or speaking. We heard the thud of naked feet running over the sand, orders, counter-orders, arguments, lamentation of women and sobbing of children. Finally, through the tumult of the camp we were able to make out the cry of alarm, which was repeated a hundred times by an old woman half-mad with fright: "*Razzi! Razzi!*" It was a raid.

We were alone there with a young woman who was hugging her sleeping baby. Before the tent the sea lapped gently; under the peace of the stars was the wild commotion of men.

Marion Sénones chose this moment to ask me calmly whether after all we should not have done well to have followed the advice of General Gouraud: "Never trust yourselves to the

Moors. Never journey alone with them, however civilized some of them may seem."

It was a happy moment to choose to say such a thing! Here we were at the mercy of the Ouled-Delim, whose unsubjected relations watched every week in Rio de Oro for the aeroplanes of Air France! In a flash I saw again the hostile faces, with their cruel oblique eyes, of the Ouled-Delim, who had come to make submission at Port Étienne. To make submission indeed! Yes, until the next rain should make the northern pastures green once more.

Outside the noise was greater than ever, augmented by the sound of quarrels. And our escort, where were they? A few weeks later, when we had got to know the Moors better, we should have known that, having got their pay, they were exercising their droit du seigneur in the shadows of the huts with some pretty slaves. It was in this posture that the alarm found them.

Buried in the dark tent that seemed to us like a trap, we finally came to the end of our patience and decided to fly to the beach, but we were hardly outside when a sombre group barred our passage. It was Cheikh and his men, their muskets in their hands. The commotion had now subsided.

We asked what had happened, and learnt that an old slave had been out in the scrub looking for her stray sheep when she was seized and questioned by two strangers, their faces concealed by their *aouli*s. Managing to get away she gave the alarm, showing her torn clothes to substantiate her story. A search was made, but nothing was found but indistinct tracks in the sand. No doubt the presence of four warriors in the village had daunted the marauders. Perhaps they would return with reinforcements. To meet this possibility a watch was kept all night.

At dawn, just as we had finally got to sleep, guarded by Cheikh, a fusillade woke us up with beating hearts. The firing, however, turned out to be a celebration. The wife of Lhassen having been so frightened during the night had 'got little one' somewhat prematurely, and her husband was going round the straw hut firing off his rifle in honour of the little warrior that had just been born.

Later, at the French post of Boutilimit, we learnt from official telegrams that we had not trembled for nothing. It appeared the notorious cousin of the 'Blue Sultan,' Brahim-Salem-ould-Moïchan, nicknamed the Unseizable, had been marauding less than a hundred kilometres from Memrhar. He had destroyed the caravan of a Port Étienne merchant on its way to Atar, the very caravan that the unfortunate Sid-Ahmed was due to convoy. Thirty camels had been stolen as well as a quantity of goods. What could not be carried off was burnt on the spot.

As always, the marauders had come down from the north, and their route had lain along the coast. Who had told them of the caravan's departure? Perhaps the Ouled-Delim chiefs had taken revenge for the humiliating way in which the Commandant of Port Étienne had refused to accept their emaciated camels and rusty rifles.

On their way south the marauders had been able to get further information as well as provisions from relations who had for a long time been established in French territory. After the raid Brahim-Salem went to a cousin whose son served as 'boy' to the French merchant whose caravan had been destroyed. The latter was sleeping in his tent unaware of his misfortune. Brahim gently woke up the boy, who was sleeping next his master.

"Tomorrow," he said, "you will tell the *Roumi* that I, the Unseizable, have sacked his caravan and that I have been here and seen him asleep. The law of hospitality forbids me to kill an enemy under the tent of one of my tribe. But let him take care: if ever I catch him in the scrub, or in the camp of another tribe, I will slit his throat as I would a sheep's."

And he rode off, making wide detours to confuse his tracks.

Brahim-Salem certainly knew of our presence in the vicinity, for it was a thing that had never happened before for two European women to travel in the scrub alone with the Moors, and it had naturally been the subject of a lot of talk around the camp fires. Our capture would present the possibility of ransom, quite apart from the value of our luggage and the satisfaction of giving trouble to the hated conquerors.

But his scouts had reported that Cheikh-ould-Mouknas and his three nephews had already reached us, and they were men with whom it was wise to reckon. So the marauders directed their predations to small, unarmed vassal tribes in the neighbourhood of Akjoujt.

Their ravages did not pass unnoticed by the authorities, and the commander of the native camel corps called up his tribesmen, or *goumiers*, and they set off on their fine mounts to give chase. They rode for a long time without rest, when finally one morning the tracks they had been following could no longer be discerned. The fugitives had perceived the enemy, and weighted as they were by their spoils had not attempted to ride further, but had concealed themselves, camels, baggage and all, behind the tufts of thorny bushes, half burying themselves in the sand. In this position they waited patiently until the *goumiers* with their red scarves had disappeared over the horizon towards Rio, after which they proceeded leisurely by a different route. The whole manoeuvre was discovered later by the tracks in the sand.

As for us, we considered ourselves lucky. For our itinerary might so easily have taken a different course. Had we ventured inland further to the north, we might have learnt at our leisure to serve the Moors instead of being served by them.

Chapter II

The Dunes of Fear

The scrub, *la brousse,* is that immense expanse of land swollen by pale pink and pale yellow dunes, with here and there red-brown *sebkhas,* or dried-up salt-marshes, and white valleys or *gouds,* which undulates between the waters of the Atlantic and the bare sandy desert of the North Sudan. A wall cuts across it, at least the Moors call it a wall, *Dhar*: the chain of mountains in the east.

The French part, as measured by Europeans, is 850,000 square kilometres. But the nomads know only that to cross it by camel many days are needed, many days of solitude and silence, and that only Moulana can foresee the chances and mischances that will fix the number. For the scrub is full of hazards, dangers, and evil spirits.

This scrub, the Trab-el-Beïdane, occupies the whole of Mauretania. The Beïdane wander over it driving their beasts from pasture to pasture. Its population is about one to every two square kilometres, and, since it is not spread out but grouped in camps, the empty spaces are enormous.

The area is divided into eight administrative districts controlled from eighteen posts. These are for the most part linked by roads to Senegal which carry a certain amount of motor traffic, but those of the north, Akjoujt and Atar, are reached only by camel along the caravan routes.

The morning of January 11 we dressed ourselves in *sirouals,* and in blue *draa*s over white *draa*s, finally winding the dark blue cotton *aouli*s round our heads. We were at last starting out to lead a nomad's existence, with all the difficulties which are the manifestations of the inscrutable will of Allah, and the slowness and silence which make one reflect upon it.

We were due to start at dawn, but only four camels were led in by the men. The two other animals had wandered from the pasture during the night. The pasture, it may be added, was no more than a place where the thorny bushes of the scrub were slightly more abundant. Ali had gone after them. He was following their tracks and would soon be bringing them in if that was the will of Moulana. But a camel can wander far afield in the course of a night, even though hobbled.

Cheikh seemed anxious, for it was a bad place to confide camels to the care of Moulana. Marion and I, too, were upset at a hitch occurring so soon. But it was only the first of many we were to endure.

To pass the time we began a detailed inspection of our camels. They were splendid: well-built animals with elegant heads, their coats beige or somewhat redder, soft and curly. But we were not yet alive to the beauty of camels. These big lumpy masses on long fragile legs, with their coffee-pot necks in front, seemed to us perfectly ridiculous. Probably the dread of having soon to mount them accounted for a good deal of our antipathy.

As a matter of fact they were really dromedaries. But Europeans have decided—in Mauretania at all events—that dromedaries are called camels, and there is no use running counter to usage so firmly established.

At last in the middle of the afternoon the stragglers were brought in by Ali, who, however, did not seem to be in any hurry.

The camels promptly obeyed the '*Chott* . . . *Chohtt*' of their masters and knelt and squatted. Till now they had been as quiet as could be, but they were no sooner in this position than they set up the most hideous row. It was something between the belling of a wounded deer and the bellowing of an enraged bull, and to it was added the belching from their gaping mouths, showing half-toothless jaws and half-masticated food. Suddenly they all stopped at once, but we had no sooner sighed with relief than they started afresh. The least thing sufficed to provoke them: a saddle, or *rahla*, a little too far forward or the reverse, a strap a shade too tight or too loose. Camels protest on principle. They bellow when loaded or when unloaded; they bellow when started or when stopped; they bellow when you want them to turn or to go straight on; and you think yourself lucky if their last meal is not spat in your face. They are like those sulky benefactors who grumble while helping you, unable ever to give succour with good grace.

We had never seen the caravans usually provided for Europeans, and imagined that ours was rather a grand affair, though we

Administrative districts and military posts of Mauretania

were conscious of a certain lack of unity in our equipment. The many-coloured *tisoufren* (plural of *tassoufra*, a large sheepskin travelling bag) with their long fringes jostled scouts' haversacks and sailors' kitbags; our sun helmets, now discarded, adorned the hind-quarters of our camels; while the common tin kettle, whose primordial utility we were yet to learn, was tied to Cheikh's. Ali and Hassan took charge of the *guerbas*, the goatskin water bottles, full of brackish water, which reminded us unpleasantly of the drowned dogs that float with their swollen bellies turned towards the sky as they drift down rivers towards the sea.

To complete the preparations Ahmed disengaged a flayed sheep from its crust of flies and secured it, bleeding as it was, on the top of our most beautiful *tassoufra*. Cheikh, escorting Europeans who had certainly never learnt to eat at a sitting sufficient for three or four days, had judged it necessary to bring ample provisions. In the country through which we were to travel two hundred kilometres to Nouakchott, the wells had water and the pastures were still green. This meant that marauders might come there in quest of fortune, and accordingly the more peacefully minded nomads left the place to them, seeking other pastures themselves in more secure regions. Only the Imraguen, who had no choice, nor as matter of fact much to lose, stayed where they were camping along the coast.

Our baggage anyhow was sumptuous compare to what it was later when experience had taught us to simplify everything.

The painful moment at last arrived. We had to mount. Hassan looked after me while Ahmed saw to Marion.

"Not very difficult," said Hassan. "You put your foot, *le ton-pied*, on leg your camel, and then on her back. That's it."

I swayed forwards then backwards, and then found myself with a final push sitting down in a sort of hollow two and a half metres from the ground.

Hassan passed me the bridle and a stick which he called a *tebbou*, and then went over to his own mount. Not finding on her back an authority capable of deciding her course, my own camel began turning round trying to decide which way to go, at the same time emitting a series of rending cries. The worst of it was that I could see Marion, as powerless as I was, being carried off in the opposite direction.

Imraguen Fishermen with their Nets

Finally, however, we all got together and the caravan moved off. Fortunately the camels were sociable creatures liking to be near each other. So all we had to do was to concentrate on not falling off, while our camels followed those of our companions, who rode in front keeping a sharp look-out and holding their loaded muskets across their knees.

We went at a slow steady pace, and before long there was nothing in sight but the endless undulating sand, a pinkish ochre, on which was growing the violet-grey spurge. Here and there were clusters of almond green leaves, starred with yellow flowers, which spurted with poisonous sap as the camels bit at them.

At last we were really out in the scrub, bathed in silence and dusk. This was our first night in it, and a beautiful night it was. We stopped at the top of a sandy hillock on the top of which a bush was growing. The camels were relieved of their burdens and hobbled with twisted grasses, after which they calmed down and wandered off quietly in quest of pastures. After that our warriors prepared the camp, showing us all the consideration of the best of hosts.

We had brought two others along with us: Bouhibé, one of the Aït-Lhassen, and Messaoud. The former was travelling fifteen hundred kilometres from South Morocco to pay the price of a camel at Nouakchott, while Messaoud was a slave rejoining his Imraguen camp. Both were taking advantage of our escort to secure protection, particularly Messaoud, who knew well that a slave was a valuable piece of movable property, tempting to any bandit. As we came along, he kept beside the camels which his humble station would not permit him to mount, walking indefatigably, a stick across his shoulders, his *siroual* rolled up round his waist to give greater freedom to his limbs.

Besides his proper master, a slave was supposed to serve people of quality wherever he might find them, and Messaoud was quick to make the tea or the *méchoui*. It was certainly a simple cuisine: a joint of mutton was cut off and buried in sand and embers, and when it was cooked it was beaten with a stick, like a carpet, to get rid of the sand. As for carving and eating, we had to manage as best we could with our teeth and our nails.

When it was ready the tea, flavoured with mint, was poured out. Cheikh blessed it, murmuring *Bismillah*, and as our warriors were well brought up they sniffed noisily and drew deep sighs of comfortable relaxation. Four times, according to ritual, Hassan broke the loaf of sugar, tasted the infusion and, holding the pot high, filled the glasses with great precision and handed them round. But Ali got up and carried off his portion, concealing himself behind a bush.

"He is ashamed," explained Hassan. "For him not possible to drink, nor eat, nor smoke, nor laugh, nor sing, nor listen to singing, nor look at woman Beïdania in front of Ahmed who is big brother for him. Same thing in front of his father, *devant le son-père*, and same thing for brother in front of his father. *Forcément*, you understand, if little brother can joke before big, he no more ashamed, no more obey nor nothing."

"Not much good being a little brother, Hassan," I answered.

"Oh yes. He get many presents, get a camel with Ahmed when he marry. And when his father die he stay with his mother, and when she die too, he get the tent for himself."

"And Bouhibé," I asked, "he's comrade for you?"

"Not know him. . . . No. . . . He come. . . ."

"But he has no baggage. Do you feed him from your rations?"

" Yes, *forcément*. When fellow has nothing and is good fellow, the Moor always does like that, he share."

And he lit his pipe made from a mutton bone, which passed from mouth to mouth to the last puff of acrid smoke. It was the time for talking, and Bouhibé described lyrically the splendours of the north where he had a garden. The others laughed heartily at the idea of having a garden with walls around it. They teased him about it.

"You are like sheep in a sheep-fold. You, what you want with garden?"

"Altogether beautiful, my garden, *y a beau complètement*, and my wife he eat it."

Cheikh's Olympic laughter rose above the others. Bouhibé was hurt, and said it was time for the *salaam*. They all went out and bowed down towards Mecca, sprinkling the warm sand over their faces to symbolize ablution.

Then everyone rolled himself in his burnouse, the hands still clasping the rifle. Hassan went out to take his turn on watch at the top of the hillock, and nothing further could be heard in the immense peace but the deep breathing of Cheikh and the distant cry of a jackal.

The next morning, while we were waiting for the return of the inevitable stray camel, Ahmed pointed to the east.

"Beïdani coming."

Immediately we heard cartridges being slipped into the muskets.

At first the Beïdani did not seem any more pleased than we were at the meeting. While exchanging the customary benedictions he kept his rifle ready in case of need. But this was not to Cheikh's liking and he made him put it up, at the same time he offered him some tea. All the same he kept watching him out of the corner of his eye.

For suspicion lurked everywhere in that country. Rounding any obstacle the thought was always present: what might there be on the other side?

Cheikh would talk to us about his exploits amongst the dunes.

"You see those dunes there beyond the blue trees? That's the place where I, Cheikh, killed one of the Northern chiefs who had done much bad. Killed Beïdane, killed French. Stolen many camels. After Lieutenant Mac-Mahon was killed, I watch a long time. I know all the tracks and all the wells."

Cheikh's eyes were keen as on that day when he had won his medal. He lived through the scene again as he bent over his rifle under a bush with long white thorns similar to the one that had served him as cover. His eyes were lit up with a wild light, his nostrils quivered with the memory of his victory, while his eloquent hand traced out the scene. He described the surprise of the enemy, his complete defeat, and the prowess of Cheikh, the old chief of the Ahel-Gazel, whose shot never missed its mark.

"*Forcément*, one day I got a shot at him standing near a tree with his men who make tea, *qui faire le tout–qu'est-c'qu'y-faut pour le thé*. He not know I come with forty men. I aim quietly. I shoot first shot, it break his arm; I shoot second, break his shoulder; I shoot third, break his leg; I shoot, break his head. Ahahah! I shoot and I shoot and I shoot. And he there is dead, *mort complètement*. Ahahah! and my men shoot on the damn swine and kill fourteen."

Cheikh put down the musket with which he had acted the scene. His whole body was shaken by his great laugh, which was famous from Port Étienne to Nouakchott, till the tears came into his eagle eyes.

"Look at your camel," he went on, "the hole there under his ear is bullet from that battle."

But it seemed to us that his enemy must have been very tough to have broken into so many pieces before being killed *complètement*.

"After that many bad men come from North. Three hundred rifles with Mohammed-el-Mamoun. Pass by here, but too much fear for Emir of Trarza and French camel corps. So make off to Brakna and steal camels a lot, then clear out home to Rio de Oro. ... No, not good here. Only me, I too strong, too good head, good powder. No need to be frightened with me. Great bandit, me. Got two medals."

Cheikh, in spite of his military distinction, was in many ways of astonishing simplicity. Thus all the baggage which the younger ones did not want to carry found its way to his camel: the mutton, the kettle, the leather water-bottle; and his was the oldest and dirtiest *tassoufra*. Even his camel was the least good of the lot. Its harness was incomplete, and what there was was tied together with bits of rag.

But that did not matter; he was Cheikh, the chief, and he carried himself on his unworthy mount much as Don Quixote might have done, with his helmet-like turban, an end of which floated in the wind looking like a plume.

In the camp at night he would sit with us around him and settle down to mend his tattered burnouse.

"Give the needle," he would say. "Give the thread."

And we would obey, like the others, the patriarch under whose protection we were.

Later he would give back needle and thread and the scissors with which he had trimmed his moustache, and taking out his beads he would turn them over with his fingers while he talked to us of Paris, particularly of the Exhibition which had been visited by eight hundred men in a single day!

While he was there he was naturally the target of every camera, which he turned to what advantage he could.

"I say to the Frenchman: 'You give five francs or I hide my face in my *aouli*!' But Frenchwoman too pretty. No way to make pay for photo, never."

Good old Cheikh! So shrewd and yet so childishly vain, so devoted, so ragged, and so proud. He ordered us about as if we were his own daughters, but would never have allowed the least departure from propriety from anybody. He watched over our welfare and our safety—yes, really he was like a father to us.

Each day passed like the one it followed. We crossed wide *sebkhas* of blue salt which from the distance looked like lakes. We climbed up the soft-sanded dunes, and came down the other side in a pink cascade. The spurge had given place to *talhas, iguinins*, and acacias. Midday and in the evening we stopped near some bushes, eating always exactly the same: a piece of mutton between two series of four glasses of tea.

The only question that gave us cause for anxiety was whether the contest between our skins and our saddles might not prove too unequal. Our sores got larger at every stage and after a little while carbuncles appeared.

One day, however, we were riding close to the sea and the waves frightened our camels, who began to trot. How delighted we were with them! At last we were delivered from that slow, tiring, and even sickening pace, which was all we had known till then. After that we decided to trot all the time in spite of Cheikh's protestations, for he preferred to wear out our seats rather than risk wearing out the camels.

But where were they all: the brown tents we had been promised, the calabashes of camel's milk, the tom-toms of the feast? The scrub was deserted, emptied by fear. Since that first meeting on the second day the only person we had seen was an old shepherd at some wells. The latter consisted of some twenty *oglats*, round holes half full of manure and magnesian water. The shepherd watered our animals and filled our *guerbas*. After selling us a small sheep he gave us a greyish nauseating liquid to drink made of sour milk and dirty water. Pointing to his zebu-cows I asked for some milk.

But Hassan answered me: "Bull's milk, no way to get it, *y a pas moyen gagner.*"

I did not insist. Hassan seemed to have some reason. So the cows went off carrying with them the only clean beverage one could possibly hope for in such a place.

Indeed Hassan had his reasons, as I found out at the wells of Lemsid.

For hours we had been riding through a prairie of tall dried grasses. On the horizon the white dunes grew gradually larger. As always, one was puzzled to know why that sad flat landscape was so seductive and so noble. Perhaps it was its essential purity and that atmosphere of contemplation which weighs on all the people and all the things of Africa.

Tired and thirsty we reached Lemsid. The wind had cut the dunes into an amphitheatre of hills superimposed in successive levels, and had deposited a blackish dust on the summits, which were thus darker than the slopes. The impression was strange and unreal, suggesting a landscape in negative.

In the centre of the amphitheatre was a camp of nomads gathered round the wells, who were wandering towards Nouakchott. There was also a large herd of zebus, hundreds of goats, sheep and grey asses. The slaves gathered eagerly around us. Women trailing their long veils in the sand approached with their naked children, attracted by the incredible phenomenon: European women in the scrub, and without any men of their race.

Once more I asked for milk, and once more there was no way to get it. "*Y a pas moyen gagner.*" This time it was explained. Little bull, *petit-le-boeuf*, was not there, so that "the bull he not want to give his milk."

I did not grasp the explanation and continued to insist and implore. Finally a slave showed himself anxious to oblige me.

Never again did I anywhere in Mauretania dream of asking for milk in the absence of *petit-le-boeuf*.

The slave went up to a cow, tied its legs, lifted up its tail, which he tied with a twist of grass to a horn. The cow lowed and shook herself; when, however, she calmed down he tried to milk her, but all she did was to kick. He then proceeded to caress the teats with quick light movements, but as this too was without avail more radical measures had to be employed. So he next focussed his efforts beneath the tail, blowing with all his might through that gateway through which *petit-le-boeuf* is in the habit of making his entry into this vale of tears. He blew and he blew until the veins of his neck and forehead stood out beneath the black and silky skin. He blew devotedly at the behest of an ignorant, capricious Christian woman. The cow turned her head, seeming somewhat surprised, and released a few drops of milk. I had by this time little wish for the poor slave to succeed, but by now he was thoroughly warmed up to his work, and he persisted in his alternate ticklings and inflations, obtaining a few drops each time. At the end of a quarter of an hour he was able to offer me, with a triumphant smile, a few mouthfuls of milk, full of hairs and sand, which the most elementary politeness obliged me to find delicious.

Marion was able to enjoy the scene. Having asked for nothing she had no need to drink.

Not far from Lemsid, just as we were camping, a Moor mounted on a white camel rode up in the dusk.

He saluted Cheikh, whom he already knew, and so that his intentions could not be misconstrued he put down his musket, leaving it to the care of a young half-caste who followed him. The latter was his *hartani*, a liberated slave following his master by choice. Both dismounted and the *hartani* spread out a sheepskin for his master in the circle round the camp fire, and then squatted behind him holding the rifle between his knees.

The new arrival was a Trarza prince, cousin of the Emir Ould-Deïd. He was going to Memrhar to receive tribute that was due to him, and to inspect his flocks and herds. The fire lit up a handsome face framed by a sparse beard, a face that would have fitted any oriental legend. His neck was elegant and supple, while his wrists and ankles were graceful almost to the point of femininity. His fine hands were spread on his knees.

Gravely and without gestures, his eyelids lowered, he exchanged the long Moorish salutations with Cheikh and his nephews.

"Labès.... Are you well? ... Quite well.... Are you very well? .

.. Very well indeed. . . . How are your sons, your friends, the friends of your friends, your tent, your camels, your slaves? . . . May Allah be praised, and may he give you peace!"

Your "tent" really means your wife, whom it would not be proper to mention.

The visitor drank his tea in silence, offered his pipe, and then began telling us that firearms were speaking between the sea and Atar, that raiders were threatening his herds and that they had even attacked some French lorries not far from Akjoujt. But all was related very calmly as though a warrior could not be moved by such things.

This attack had taken place six days before, five hundred kilometres away from the place where we, through this chance meeting, were informed of it. News travels astonishingly quickly through the solitudes of the desert.

The skirmish had not been without casualties amongst the Senegalese sharpshooters and the Beïdane who were acting as escort. They were: five wounded and one killed. As for the enemy, they made off and their losses were not known.

Incidents such as these were the final efforts of unsubjected elements. The conquest of Southern Morocco was soon to put a stop to them for good.

Having told us all the news, the prince rose, invoking once more the blessing of Moulana the All-powerful. Then mounting—all white on his white camel—he rode off into the dark.

The new moon rose suddenly, welcomed joyfully by our companions since it was the divine signal for the ending of the Ramadan, the period of fasting. After this hard week's travelling they would arrive tomorrow at Nouakchott just in time for the Little Feast, the Aïd-el-Seghir, which they also call *Fatreh*.

It was, however, not the ending of the fast which pleased them, for according to the custom of the Moors when travelling, they had in any case broken the Ramadan. They reaped no advantage by doing so, as the days lost had to be made up during the course of the year. In fact it made the fasting a more severe penance to have to observe it while others were enjoying the pipe and the *méchoui*.

But tomorrow they would be taking part in the *Fatreh* and

making merry with the rest. They would even be the Kings of the feast, those who come from far. They would have stories to tell, and money tied in their *aouli*s, and possess the attraction which all novelty exerts on the native curiosity of nomads.

In the clear morning from the top of the last dune we looked down on an immense stony plain, colourless, blinding with the light it reflected, which stretched for miles and miles right to the uplands of Akjoujt.

To the west the brick-red ruins of the old post were silhouetted against the sky.

In the plain below us was the new military post, massive, square, grey and austere, a sort of fortress.

As we got near the post everything was blazing in the midday sun. Bushes with sad slender leaves tried in vain to give shelter in a garden. Here and there *chevaux de frise* and barbed wire, and the skeleton of an aeroplane shed, threw cruel metallic reflections.

This was Nouakchott, our first post in our journey across the scrub. In it we enjoyed hospitality, champagne, gramophones, and a good clean up. We were lodged in a sort of military hut, a *case de passage*, kept for travellers. It was luxurious in comparison with some we were to enter later. It had a door and shutters to the windows. The lieutenant in command of the post had pitchers of brackish water brought to us, and a great Moorish bed-cover of soft black lamb was thrown over the old mattress.

It was indeed luxury, and yet, although we had only been eight days in the scrub, we somehow felt rather out of our element. Strange that the life of the nomad had so gripped us that its interruption should upset us!

The noise of a quarrel broke in on our siesta and drew us into the courtyard. The lieutenant was trying to appease two angry rivals—the two chief prostitutes of the village, each of them a mistress of the tom-tom.

Dressed in loin-cloths and veils and loaded with pinchbeck jewellery, they railed at one another, making gestures of malediction. Their faces might have been beautiful but for the artifices which were intended to adorn them. Maryam had painted a red square round her right eye and a blue circle round the other, while

Bonheur's forehead carried an Arab inscription and flowers were painted on her cheeks.

We listened to their ragings and I managed to make out that each objected to the other's beating the tom-tom for the fête, because "Commandant know she whore too much, and make trouble to muck up everybody." As if there was not plenty of room in the place (and plenty of clients too, white, brown and black) for two tom-toms in front of two hospitable huts.

The wives of the Senegalese soldiers were laughing from the thresholds of their huts. "Beïdania women no good," they said.

Only the raised cudgel of the police sergeant obtained a moment's silence. He was an old negro wearing an unspeakable English cap. The lieutenant then gave permission for both women to play the tom-tom, which permission would be withdrawn at the least dispute.

But it was the sergeant who had the final word: "If you not good, me break your head." And the two women walked off full of dignity, but with menacing looks, rolling their opulent haunches under the folds of their loin-cloths, with their dragging steps caused by their ankles being weighted with silver.

The evening air was freshened by a sea breeze.

The *Fatreh* was in full swing. The slaves were dancing to the sound of drums. Bonheur and Maryam had recovered their smiles and their seductive glances. The French merchant and the native *dioula* were selling loaves of sugar and green tea whose aroma would later be mingling with the sand-laden air. Fires were burning before the mud huts and the brown tents.

The young men played *kora*, a game in which a leather ball was hit from one team to another with curved sticks. The half-naked men looked magnificent as they ran, with their blue or white *draa*s twisted round their bodies or floating out behind them and falling in archaic folds. At the end of each game the winners would throw their sticks in the air and the *you-yous* of their women would join with their own shouts of triumph.

Older men, beads in hand, would prefer to squat on the mattings, drinking tea as they conversed. In one tent Cheikh was playing draughts. The draughtboard was drawn in the sand, while bits of stick and lumps of camel dung served for pieces.

Thus the *Fatreh* passed; and so was it over a large part of Africa that night. Men and women danced and sang, ate and prayed, for the Ramadan and its days of penance was over with the coming of the tenth moon.

Chapter III

The Great Tents

ONE evening at Nouakchott a man arrived on a great white camel. He was grave and quiet and held himself very straight. The setting sun coloured the folds of his long tunic, and his frizzy hair was encircled in a halo of golden light. An escort of young warriors surrounded him, while behind him on the croup of his camel rode his *hartani*, carrying his musket and his cartridge pouch. He himself carried nothing but his black beads and his leather *gri-gris*, the latter being cases to hold verses of the *Koran*. His nobility had no need of external signs; without any display one knew at the first glance that he was the chief.

Slowly he saluted us, his hand on his breast, abandoning his kneeling camel to the care of his *hartani*. Our interpreter told us that it was Mohammed-Fall-ould-Sidi-ould-Mohammed-Fall-Ould-Deïd of the tribe of Ahmed-ben-Daman, and that he prayed Moulana to bestow peace and nothing but peace on the two Christian women who were travelling like strong men across the Trab-el-Beïdane. Moreover, that he would be greatly honoured if we would accompany him to Tin-Deila where were the tents of his father.

We gratefully accepted, being delighted by the proposal, and we passed the evening eagerly packing our *tisoufren* and tracing our route on the map, marking in the line of wells which ran from the grey Nouakchott to the rose-coloured Boutilimit.

Our fourteen companions were Trarza warriors with their *haratine*, or freed slaves. They had black curly hair, and their smiles thinly disguised the cruelty of their enigmatical faces. They were dirty, ragged and magnificent, and they had a knack of throwing their *draas* over their shoulders like Roman togas, or hitching them up round their bodies like Greek shepherds.

For two days we had been following winding tracks over the pink sand through the great dunes covered with thorny bushes the colour of verdigris, or over the white dust of narrow valleys where, as we reached a well, some negro slave would drive off his cattle to make room for us.

In the middle of the day and at dusk we would stop before some miserable tents, similar perhaps to those inhabited by the Hebrew fathers of old, and were nourished by the same fare that Abraham offered to the traveller: camel's milk and lamb roasted in the embers.

Soon we should be under the tent put up for us by Sidi-ould-Mohammed-Fall, the dispossessed elder brother of Ahmed-ould-Deïd, Emir of Trarza.

In the evening over the tea, we would listen to the stories and descriptions which Ahmeddou, our own attendant, translated for us.

"Mohammed-Fall is happy *complètement*," he would explain, "because you come to his camp. There, there are fine tents, plenty to eat, plenty of sheep, and Mohammed-Fall, who is grandson of an Emir, will give you all you want and all there is, *te donnera le tout c'quy-a*: give you *faro* (bedcover of lamb's skin), give you cushions, the necklaces, the carpets. You and sister for you, you choose. You stay long time, long time, and after that Mohammed-Fall take you to Boutilimit and still further. He give you fine camels, warriors, a *hartani* to wait on you and all you want, *le tout-que-tu-demandes*."

Sitting on an old sheepskin, with all the dignity of Solomon on his throne, Mohammed-Fall acquiesced nobly.

The idea of his giving us a *hartani* was certainly tempting. Ahmeddou knew how to wind his turban like a seneschal at the court of Saint Louis, but he was not much good at harnessing a camel and securing the leather bags on its back. No doubt he could have done it better if he had chosen to, but it did not interest him. Marion, whose head was already a little turned by these lavish promises, began to think that Ahmeddou was not quite sufficient to sustain our prestige.

But what pleased us far more were the good camels promised, geldings whose trot was swift and sure. Those which had carried us to Nouakchott were tired. The stony ground had cut their feet, and fatigue had softened their humps.

Every night we dreamt of wise men and princes of the East, and the Queen of Sheba, and of vast treasures being poured into our laps, and we rode forward to Tin-Deila as to a Promised Land.

Camping in the Scrub

Mohammed-Fall

The sky was a delicate grey. Between the flying shadows of the clouds a ray of sunshine played on the soft almond green of the leaves and rose-coloured dunes. Our camels sensed the approaching camp and broke into a lame trot.

It began to rain, and at this season rain was unhoped for. Armeddou explained to us that it was a special favour of Moulana, and that the Moors, who had no dates for their years, would say in recalling births, deaths or migrations: "It was the year when the two women-the-Europeans came to us. The rain was with them and it was a lucky year."

The men sang and laughed, happy to be back at their tents once more among their wives and relations. Mohammed-Fall was thoughtful and said nothing.

Suddenly, when rounding a clump of gum trees, we encountered a group of perhaps fifty warriors sitting motionless on their camels waiting for us, their rifles in their hands.

Volleys were fired in salute, rending the silence.

Behind the warriors was a crowd of men and naked boys. There were old men with pale bluish hair, the *marabout* weighed down with years and amulets, a *goumier* with red scarf, the doctor, blacksmiths, masters and slaves, in fact every able-bodied man of the population. Everyone was excited, the camels too. Fathers looked for their sons, brothers sought brothers, and friends their friends. Long and punctilious salutations and benedictions took place. The young men touched the hands of old men, palm against palm, after which they reverently carried their hands to their own faces.

When greetings were over we all turned towards the camp. Silence descended once more, but it was soon broken by a shrill voice which floated up into the now sunny sky. The singer was one of the minstrels or *griots* of the camp, a woman named Barka, veiled in dark blue, who hung on to the back of a warrior's saddle. She sang the praises of the Emir's family and of the well-beloved son who returned after long travelling: The song ran something like this:

> 0 Thou who art nowhere to be found,
> Who art like nothing else,
> I pray thee not to harken to the desires
> Of the enemies of him whose praises I sing.

The horses, the night and the desert know him.
When triggers speak
He does not listen to the bullets,
And when he fights it is the enemy who falls.

We make thee welcome.
Thou art brave, thou art terrible, thou art
courteous and generous,
Thou art Mohammed-Fall, son of Sidi,
son of Mohammed-Fall,
Son of Mohammed-Habib.

A tom-tom rumbled in the distance.

This mixture of military parade and family reunion was very moving. Marion and I were very proud to have taken part in it. We drove our camels into the front rank, and were very annoyed when two little grey asses came out of the bushes and blocked the narrow track which wound its way through the thorny scrub, and obliged the triumphal procession to stop while they passed.

The camp came into sight. It was much like others we had already seen and the hundred we were to pass through before reaching Kiffa. In front of the tent that had been set aside for us was a crowd of shouting negroes. The strident *you-yous* of the negresses whose bare chests were adorned with amber and glass beads, the clapping of their hands, and the roaring of the camels almost drowned the dull beat of the tom-toms. In the midst of the frenzied slaves two warriors were dancing. The dance was in imitation of a battle, and they threw their rifles above their heads and caught them again as they sprang into the air.

We should like to have stopped to watch the spectacle, but in Mauretania it is incumbent on people of quality to be in need of rest after a journey. So to preserve our dignity we had to go straight into the tent and squat on the matting and skins.

Mohammed-Fall and his father sat opposite us on the other side of the tray on which glasses were set all ready for the tea. Around us were twenty warriors, and outside them a circle of *haratine*, and beyond them again a thick hedge of slaves. All were staring at us with curious eyes.

Some women pushed their way through the ring of onlookers and approached Mohammed-Fall, bowing before him till their foreheads touched his outstretched hand. They were his sisters and half-sisters, the daughters of his nurse and his nurse's husband. They were the only women who had the right to come before him in public. Moorish families are very complicated not only because of the frequency of divorce, but also because milk makes relations as important as those of blood.

If Sidi's wife had been present, Mohammed-Fall could not have remained there; nor could he have appeared with his own wife before his father. Moreover, if some tactless person had spoken to him of his mother-in-law or of his wife, decorum would have required him to retire, veiling his face. With suchlike complications the simplest thing was to keep all the women, the cause of so much trouble, in their tents.

Sidi was a fine courteous old man, a dignified representative of the senior branch of an illustrious family.

In 1905, together with his brother Ahmed, he assassinated his uncle Ahmed-Saloum I while he was sleeping, and became Emir himself for a short time till he was obliged to fly to Morocco.

It is only fair to add that Ahmed-Saloum I had killed his cousin Amar-Saloum, who had killed his nephew Mohammed-Fall, Sidi's father, who had killed his uncle Ali-Diombot, who had killed his brother Ahmed-Saloum I, who had killed his brother ... which is as far as I can go.

To be Emir of the Trarza meant an income from Moorish and French sources together of a hundred and fifty thousand francs. Such wealth as that would certainly be an obstacle to long life.

With Armeddou interpreting, Sidi offered to kill a camel for our dinner. To this Marion answered politely:

"There's no need for such a sacrifice to make us realize that you are a great chief; a sheep is quite enough."

So after the tea mutton was produced: first the liver, kidneys and feet, served in a filthy calabash; then the *méchoui* itself, black with cinders and sand, which was placed, not on a silver platter, but on a *lebda*, the mat of leather and fur which goes between the saddle and the camel's back. We all set to to devour it as quickly as possible. From time to time one of our hosts would courteously hand us a particularly choice bit. Slaves and children disputed the bones and the fat.

It was not altogether an edifying spectacle, but the calabash of rice, which was brought on to finish the meal, provided a still worse. For the warrior's hands, with which they mauled the rice, were blue with the inevitable dye of their clothes. The rice got bluer and bluer as they pressed it into lumps, like making snowballs, before putting it in their mouths.

Marion and I watched Mohammed-Fall with the distress of all illusions lost. We could still picture him leading his caravan, or with his companions prostrating himself at the summit of some dune in the final *salaam* at night. The evening before he had ridden before us in the moonlight looking like a veiled light. But now, having finished his rice, he was scraping the grease off his hands with an old knife and rubbing it into his feet.

When the repast was over everyone retired, having first wished us a pleasant rest. We were feeling quite ready for one, but a moment later a warrior came to tell Armeddou that Sidi was waiting for us in his tent. The message was of course clothed in many civilities:

"*Essalalam aleikoum!*"
"*Aleikoum essalam ! Labès?*"
"*Barekallah! Labès.*"
"*Elhamdou lillahi!*"

Sidi wished his messenger to say that now that the Christian women had come under his tents, they had come as to their own home.

Sidi's tent, made like the others of brown wool, was very big. White cotton hangings covered the inside on three sides. The furniture consisted of some chests. Between the bits of matting on the ground some spaces had been left so that one could spit into the sand.

We sat beside our host and drank tea. His youngest son, a baby, played with his white beard. A little to one side sat his wife Fatimetou, who must have been about sixteen. She looked at us in silence. A new cotton veil, shiny with purplish dye, enveloped her. She was beautiful with long voluptuous eyes, secretive air, and her delicate hands stained red with henna. But at the least gesture, her displaced *malahfa* revealed arms as stout as thighs and her graceful body moved as though heavy with milk. She was indeed a very beautiful woman.

"*Essalam aleikoum!*"

"*Aleikoum essalam!* May peace be with you." This time we were at the tent of Mohammed-Fall. It was much like his father's, and there was the same tea and his wife was drawn in the same rounded curves. A'icha, like Fatimetou, was an Emir's daughter. She looked with the same interest at us, the first Frenchwoman she had ever seen; she had the same dignified manner and the same way of rubbing her teeth with the aromatic stick of *adress* wood and of wiping her nose with her fingers and then wiping the latter on her clothes.

Mohammed-Fall called in his sons to present them to us, holding out his hand towards them with a Christlike gesture. Through an opening in the tent a ray of sunlight fell on his forehead.

When we had thoroughly exhausted our small Arab vocabulary we returned to our own tent. Marion was sleepy and I was anxious to attend to certain vermin. But we had hardly set about our respective occupations when Sidi arrived followed by Mohammed-Fall and all their escort. Renewed courtesies, contemplative conversation, and tea. The tom-tom had once more taken up its wild refrain in a cloud of gold-coloured dust.

Armeddou made us understand that it was now the right moment to distribute sugar and tea to the dancers.

After that had taken place some of our guests departed, and we had again hopes of being left in peace. But they soon returned and remained with us till it was time for the evening meal, and we all gathered round the tea, the *méchoui*, and the calabashes of milk.

The herds, driven in from the surrounding pastures with the first shades of descending night, filled the camp with their lowing.

The ninth series of four glasses of tea had been served in Sidi's tent. He was giving a soiree in our honour. The tent was full of people—warriors, *haratine*, and slaves.

In the middle Barka was singing, her head thrown back, her mouth protruding beneath the veil which she held up to the level of her eyes, but which quivered with the movements of her lips. She sang the *Fagkou*, with a shrillness and intensity as though from the centre of that tent she sought to inspire men with courage right to the confines of the desert.

Fools are the cowards who fear death,
Death which never comes except at the appointed hour
As well for the brave as for the fearful.
Folly, folly to hope that destiny could ever forget.

Between the verses and the refrains her slender fingers plucked at the strings of the primitive harp or *ardine* which had been handed down from time immemorial with the music, the traditions and the people themselves, following the tracks from Egypt.

There was also a small simple kind of lute on which Barka's husband, Souidate, played, accompanying her song.

Men must be strong;
Men must be gay, so they may be courageous.

Together they sang the hymns of the prophets; then the glory of their chief, the strongest, the handsomest, and the most illustrious, he who from his youth had been accustomed to praises, he who was the eye of his tribe, the friend of the great, the protector of the small, he who was generous to poor minstrels.

There is no god but Allah!
La illah ill Allah!

Slaves wearing amber and silver ornaments were grouped behind the musicians, and they clapped their hands in unison with the plucking of strings and the beating of calabashes. A barbaric odour emanated from these people, the smell of the Moors, composed of sweat, leather, tea and spices. And the perfume of the yellow flowers of the *tahla* floated in with the lowing of the cattle on the night air.

Barka went on singing, but now her face was unveiled, and with the hand thus freed she could accompany her song with gestures.

From the *ardine* between her knees and Souidate's *tidinit* surged forth a flood of quick light notes in complicated rhythms. Her hands, her bracelets, the tresses of her hair, the draperies of her clothes, all entered into the music which was of rhythm rather than of melody. Barka herself seemed the embodiment of rhythm. Although she was sitting she seemed to be as much dancing as a leaf in the wind.

These minstrels are the joy and poetry of the desert; the troubadours of this Mauretania, biblical and mediaeval. *Griots* belong to the lowest caste but one, despised—yet formidable. How indeed could gifts be refused to those who, according to their whim or interest, could humiliate you with their mockery or sing your praises across the plains? Sometimes attached to a chief, sometimes as free lances, but always nomad, they amuse, flatter and console. They are confidants and clandestine messengers. Lovers and betrothed whisper in their ears vows destined for the objects of their passion, and it is one of their order who conducts the bride to the nuptial tent. Of course all is paid for, sometimes in camels, sometimes in *guinée*, greasy with its blue dye.

This evening Souidate and Barka had no other thought than to 'do beautiful things for the Christians.' They sang *El Bial,* which is a love song, and *Z'rac* meaning 'Resignation,' by the poetess El Khansa, who lived in the second century of the Hegira, and *Zeïni* by Omar-ben-Khalssum, who was born before Mahomet.

Before we separate,
I pray you stay awhile.

For a long while we sat listening to them and watching their deft fingers as they played. Finally Barka stopped and, drawing once more her veil across her face, went off to her tent. Then all was silence but for the thousand distant rumours that make up the desert night.

To terminate the soirée Armeddou conveyed Sidi's salutations to us and his hopes that Moulana would keep us for a long time in his camp.

As soon as the dawn broke we were wrested from our sleep by

slaves bringing us tea. They were followed by visitors.

Mohammed-Fall made us a present of a painted leather cushion and announced that he had to leave immediately for the *Mahssar*, the Emir's camp, where he was to pay his respects to his uncle Ould-Deïd. Unfortunately, Moulana looked unfavourably upon him, for the superb camels that he had wished to give to his well-beloved European visitors were at that moment far away in distant pastures. Here he had only inferior camels that had arrived at the camp the day before, but he would of course choose the two best for us.

'The words of the night are not those of the day.' Armeddou understood perfectly and began to pack our *tisoufren*.

Fortunately there was a boy of fifteen who had to go to Boutilimit, where he was to get employment with the French; and of course it was necessary to give us a *hartani* to look after the camels that were lent. Thus we were not to be without escort.

While our thin camels were being saddled—oh, the beautiful mounts we had dreamt of!—slaves were taking up the matting and dismantling the tent.

But we did not mind, as we were already thinking of the scrub that was waiting for us and that would never dismiss us. It was waiting for us with all its subtle charm made of long days of endurance, the primitive joy of danger, and the uncertain promise held out by things unknown.

We set out light-heartedly enough, but what the scrub had in store for us was not so charming after all—a long series of delays and irritations caused by our escort. Baggage came untied, saddles shifted, orders were not obeyed. In the mornings the camels would have strayed and were being looked for by a slave, but the real reason would be that our men had been talking half the night and wanted to sleep. This meant starting out in the heat of the morning. And so it went on—lying, trickery and obstinacy until our patience was well-nigh worn out.

Besides the varieties of acacia that we already knew —the *talhas* with their long white thorns and the *sadra-el-beïda* (the white tree) bedecked with silky flowers like pompons, yellow and sweet-smelling— we also found the *iguinin* whose prickly branches were so dense as to cast a dark shadow, though I never saw any leaves on it, the *adress* from which the Moors cut the aromatic sticks with which they rub their teeth, and the calotropis or *tourdja* with its mauve flowers surrounded by pale velvety sheathes. Their winged seed is used as tinder. We also saw new kinds of gum trees, the *tamat*, the *amour* and the *aouerouar*, from the last of which is drawn the real commercial gum.

The last rains had been in September so that the grasses were already dry and discoloured. There was *hechich*, *sbat*, the long *markeba* which is plaited to make matting, and the bitter *colocynth* or gourd plant.

Between the grassy tufts the ground was covered thickly with *initi*, hairy thistles, crocuses, and prickly plants that caught on to one's clothing and on to the coats of the camels and whose tiny poisonous prickles stuck in us everywhere.

For all its freedom, there is a tyranny of the desert, made up of a thousand little annoyances which pursue one day and night, from which one is never wholly delivered even in the hours of sleep.

Bustards flew heavily out of the glades of gum trees. Light gazelles, the colour of the sand, ran swiftly in the large circles which, it appears, bring them always back to their starting-point. Small hyenas and jackals made us aware of their proximity at night by their useless howling. As for snakes, they are abundant only in sensational reports. In the course of a whole year's travelling in the scrub I only saw one, a long viper sleeping in the shadow of a thorny bush.

We rode from well to well, from camp to camp, without either pride or joy, surrounded by our meagre escort, our pace varying with the inclination of our camels.

When we halted, Armeddou would install himself in the best place, give useless orders, and talk at length of his taste for long journeys at five francs per day. He would make plans for the future, in which our roles were cast for us. The *hartani* asked us for needle and thread so that he could patch up his ragged clothes. The young warrior would disappear mysteriously to the tents of the camp by which we had stopped. As for us, we would resign ourselves to waiting patiently until some slave would come along and take pity on us.

The only work which Armeddou considered it expedient to do was to flatter us and the race to which we belonged.

"You and sister for you have good heads. Ach! Too much good."

By which he really meant that we did not know the way to make ourselves obeyed by the Beïdane, and that they could with impunity snap their ringers at us, which he found very agreeable.

"Before the French, you and sister for you, no way to make this journey. Even two or three Beïdane, no way. Meet *razzi* from north and be killed *forcément*. Always must go many men together, with rifles. The French, they do big things."

And that was true enough. For the pacification of Mauretania, which required a hundred years of patient diplomacy in face of the trickery of the Moors, and the bravery of many a soldier in face of their cruel fanaticism, was an undertaking which must be respected even by those who do not approve of imperialism. It is true that the French were acting in their own interests, defending both Senegal and the Sudan against the incursions of warlike tribes, but at the same time they were protecting the Berber *marabouts*, the Zenagui and the terrorized black population.

The cruel law of Mauretania, the right of the strong, prevailed through the whole country, even down to 1900.

This vast extent of scrub and sand would never lend itself to colonial immigration or exploitation. But it now forms an indispensable peaceful zone between the agricultural peoples of Senegal and the marauding tribes of the north, which cannot, according to the agreement of 1900, be pursued by the French beyond the ill-defined Spanish frontiers.

***

Suddenly in the evening of January 26th we came in sight of Boutilimit, the administrative capital of the Trarza, founded in 1904. In the distance it looked like a romantic fortress lifted high up on a great dune inflamed by the setting sun. The valleys below, emerald green, streaked with blue and grey, stretched like a sea beneath.

It looked quite close, but it took us another two hours to reach it, crossing the undulating country dune by dune. Finally, we reached the wells of the last valley in the middle of enclosed fields of millet, Moorish tents, and straw huts for the black soldiers.

Naturally the arrival of two Frenchwomen made a great stir.

The Europeans, who were waiting for us in front of the monumental gateway surmounted by crescents, surveyed our caravan with some surprise. They candidly inquired where was all our baggage and our camp beds. And they were astonished that all we asked of them were cigarettes, cold drinks and their cordiality.

Prisoners at work stopped dead, staring at us, balancing on their heads the regulation load of two bricks of *banco* or clay with which the houses are built. Moors, who were waiting for I don't know what, on the steps of a terrace, stopped scratching for a moment.

And the next day our arrival was set as the subject for composition in the *Médersa*, the only French school at that time in Mauretania.

One solitary school for a country half as big again as France! One could hardly count the few native village schools in which the teachers were hardly more erudite than their pupils. As a matter of fact, since writing this, a second *Médersa* has been established at Atar.

At the *Médersa* of Boutilimit the sons of tribal chiefs, about a hundred of them, ranging between the ages of eight and twenty, studied the Koran, French, and Arabic, under the instruction of an Algerian teacher and an old *marabout*. No fees were charged. A certificate was given after four years of study, after which the pupils could, if they wanted to, enter the native school in Saint Louis.

The first prize for the French composition concerning ourselves was won by Mohammed-ould-Yadali, whose work was indeed a curious document, the product of Arab imagination.

To make his heroines more impressive, he had left out our guides and had provided us with muskets and silver-mounted daggers. He spoke of "masculine audacity," of our "act of competence," and of the "members of the country applauding a difficult and tireable journey." It ended with this conclusion: "This story proves the intellectual and physical force of France, and her superiority over all other countries." As the proverb says, great effects can come from little causes.

The regular poets, who could be seen in meditation inside their tents, with their long graceful hands crossed over their knees, were on their mettle, and each day our many-coloured interpreter would bring us some lyric which he would translate for us.

Mohammed-ould-Yadali was rewarded by us for his eulogy by being given the rôle of page. Faithful and smiling, he would wait for us at the gateway of the post to accompany us on our walks.

Other children, whom we would find playing round the tents and mud huts, would greet us gaily and would join us too. Those belonging to the *Médersa* could be recognized by their shyness and their clean tunics. The others would beg, artlessly and obstinately, like those at Port Étienne. "*Atteni tank, Madame*" they would say, "give fifty centimes."

And they would refuse ten-centime pieces if we offered them.

They questioned us endlessly: Why did we come? Were we going tomorrow? At the new moon? In a year? Where would we go after Boutilimit?

The Beïdane children are very charming with their beauty, confidence and grace, till they reach the age when they grow too bold and have to be chased off as one would a flight of grasshoppers. But if they did not annoy us we delighted to watch them playing about together, their bodies were so harmonious, free and supple as young goats. Naturally I speak of those who had escaped hereditary disease, tuberculosis, ophthalmia which blinds so many beautiful eyes, and all the manifold results of malnutrition.

"You come here, Madame. *Tu viens! Attention!*" And the slender arm of one of the children, encircled by a silver bracelet, would hold aside a thorny branch. A small hand would be thrust in ours where the path was difficult.

When they were tired they would become suddenly very good and quiet, turning on us their dreamy eyes, while the older ones would put their arms round the shoulders of the little ones with that curious caressing tenderness in which even the roughest of warriors would now and again show a surprisingly voluptuous gentleness.

Griots Playing in Sidi's Camp

With our youthful escort we visited the camp of the schoolboys, the *banco* quarries, the European gardens cultivated by prisoners, where French vegetables are grown, the market, full of flies and stinking with bad meat, and the prostitutes' quarters where they spent the whole day doing their hair, mixing their cosmetics and perfumes, and pulverizing the leaves of henna with which they dyed their hands. An Ahmed or a Sidi would proudly point out a mother or a sister: "It is beautiful woman."

And we went to the wells where we would get news of the country around. Two small grey asses wound up the long cord of twisted leather to the shouts of *Arré! Arré!* from their driver. The old pulley would screech as the *delou* came up bringing lukewarm water from a depth of eighty metres. The delou was a large bag of sheepskin sewn to a wooden circle. The water was poured into a trough for the camels to drink. *Oooh! Ooooh!* The asses would stop and return to the head of the well, while the *delou* plunged down again to the water. Then *Arré! Arré!* and they would pull it up once more. And so it went on all day: a monotonous task, slow and rhythmic, like all work in the desert.

What our little friends liked best of all were our visits to merchants or smiths, for there they could enjoy the spectacle of vast wealth, and have the illusion of taking part in those deliriously exciting things: purchases and sales.

In spite of the threats of the Moorish or Negro *dioula* a crowd of children would invade the narrow little shop, greedy to set their eyes even for a moment on the pieces of purplish *guinée*, blue *roum*, English and Japanese cotton stuffs, Dutch *madras*, tiny flasks of strong perfumes, loaves of sugar, Indian boxes containing green tea, bags of rice, millet and monkey-nuts, and goatskins stuffed with dates from Adrar which are sold in slices, cut through skin and all.

On the walls hung metal teapots and tin kettles, round brass trays, wooden saddles ornamented with poker-work patterns, big bags of painted leather with fringes, red cartridge pouches, pipes made of blackened iron inlaid with silver and brass, Moorish padlocks, and bundles of cord made of baobab fibres or *talha* fibres or of some animal's skin with the hair left on.

It was a marvellous sight for nomads accustomed to possess nothing. For us, however, it was rather sad to see the goods of so many nations and so few French products. Indeed, we were forced to make the same observation again and again during our wanderings in the Sudan, and in Senegal as well as in Mauretania. They say that to develop colonies is to open up new markets. For others perhaps!

The merchants and their customers used a system of weights and measures of their own: the hollow of the hand, the handful, the two hands together, the loads carried by ass or camel, the length of the hand, the pace, the cubit or length from elbow to fingertip, a man's height. Longer distances were measured in stone's throws, the distance a voice could carry, or day's journeys.

The monetary unit was the five-franc note of French West Africa, which the Moors called *ouguïa*. For one *ouguïa* and a half one could buy a padlock in carved brass, or a pair of sandals, or a gri-gri of red leather incrusted with brass. For one *ouguïa* one could buy a pipe in the form of a cigarette-holder together with a case for it, or two or three silver rings, or a painted and embroidered portfolio with many pockets. A good *tassoufra*, however, cost as much as four. The price of a three-pound sugar-loaf was four francs, green tea forty francs a kilo, and a packet of 'Job' cigarettes seventy-five centimes.

Mohammed's greatest moment was when we paid for anything: He would seize the money we proffered and would hand it to the *dioula* himself, partly for the pleasure of handling even for an instant a thing so fugitive and so rare, but also out of consideration for us. It was considered undignified for people of quality to pay except through the mediation of a servant.

Among the children there were always one or two that the others looked down on.

"It's nothing, him," we would be told. "It's son for the blacksmith."

The smith, or *mallem* and his wife or *mallema* belonged to no tribe or country. They were also called Yhoud, because according to tradition they were descended from the Jews of Adrar scattered by Boubakar the Conqueror.

The smiths were the artisans and artists of the Trab-el-Beïdane. They understood the art of working in wood or metals, of tanning and dyeing leather, making saddles, chests and padlocks, and also of chasing daggers and setting jewels. The richest of the Arabs and Berbers, for whom all manual work is shameful, have smiths permanently attached to their camps.

Like the *griots* and the doctors the smiths are indispensable and yet despised.

"*Mallemin* stealers, *Mallemin* infidels. *Mallemin* no good." Perhaps, but *Mallemin* make very pretty things!

All the country's industry is in their able hands, and the ablest of them are, I believe, to be found at Boutilimit and in the great camps of the Trarza.

We were continually finding pretexts to go to the tents of Ali or Baba-Ahmed for the pleasure of seeing real activity among this indolent and casual people.

I would order a silver ring like Fatimetou's or some bracelets of ebony inlaid with silver. Or if my sandals were worn I would get Ali's wife, Aminattou, to make me a new pair, pretty ones with red straps. And I ordered a fine yellow *tassoufra* for travelling.

Mimouna would open a chest and get out the bracelets I wanted. These bracelets were always worn in pairs. Aminattou would cut with deft precision the imprint of my foot in the supple leather, using an old broken knife; and with her white teeth she would chew the strips of leather for the straps to make them supple. Then she would tie them in complicated knots which served as ornament. Meanwhile Baba-Ahmed would set to work to cut a ring for Marion with his primitive tools, which he would do in the time we took to drink four glasses of tea.

They never worked in gold, stigmatized by the Prophet as the great corrupter, the unclean metal, the mere contact with which could cause the death of a Musulman.

Then there was the bargaining. Holding up their fingers Baba or Ali would indicate the price: "Five *ougui*," that is to say twenty-five francs, but this figure was rapidly reduced to "*cinque francs demi*," by which was meant one and a half *ougui*. Even so we were just a little overcharged.

But however hard the bargaining, we left good friends, Baba saying: "You come tomorrow. My wife make you pretty portfolio.

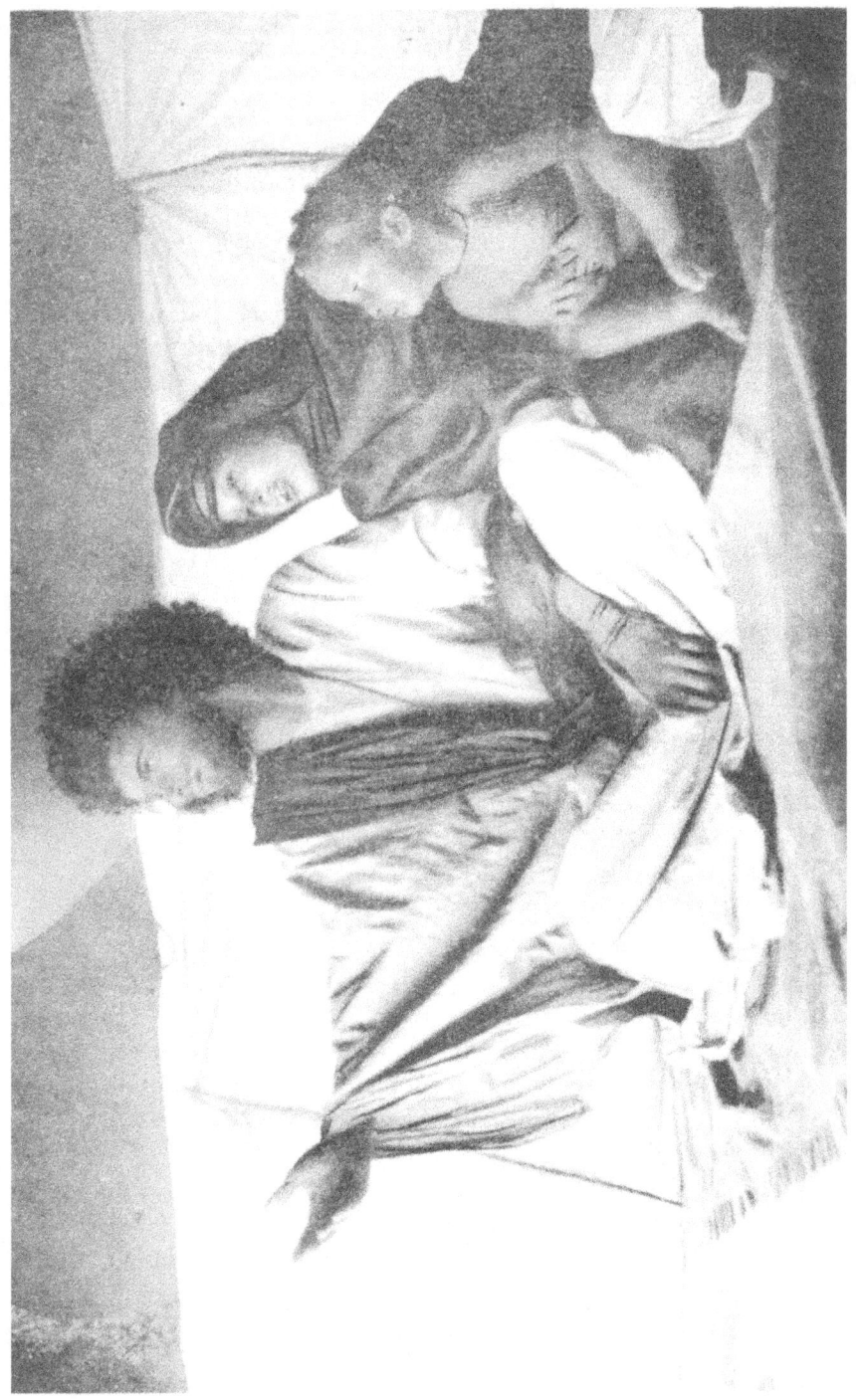

Mohammed-Fall in his Tent

Mon femme y faire joli-le-portefeuille pour toi"

He would send his youngest son to show us some red leather *gri-gri* or a string of ebony beads. "'*Zeine ate*," he would say, "Very pretty, Madame. You buy." But while playing the salesman he would wander round our room to see if he could pinch what we had bought the day before, so that they could sell it to us again on the morrow.

"My father, he make pretty things. He say you come drink tea in his tent." With that, he would leave us.

At the end of last century, when the French were just beginning to penetrate into the country, a great figure stood out among the native population, that of Cheikh-Sidia of the Ouled-Biri tribe, the spiritual chief of the Trab-el-Beïdane.

He was descended from those 'Berbers with the *litham*' who came from the Maghreb with Boubakar eight hundred and seventy years ago.

They were men of God, but also men of the sword, and their empire included a multitude of people, black and white, from Spain to Timbuktu, till in the end they were in turn conquered by the sons of Hassan, Oudeï and Delim, and their Arab warriors.

Inch' Allah! And they resigned themselves to their fate, abandoning their arms for the books of the saints (except for a few tribes, such as the Ma-el-Aïnin, who still kept both) and assuming over their new masters, marauders and illiterates, the religious and intellectual authority of the *marabouts*.

But though there was a certain give and take between these two elements, an acute conflict persisted. Besides the natural difficulties of the country the *marabout* and Zénega tribes had to contend with the cruelties of war and pillage. They had to pay one warlike tribe to get protection from another; also to have access to the wells and to the pastures, and for the right to grow millet and gum in the south or to gather dates in the north.

The *marabouts* were rich, possessing great herds and many slaves, the only forms of wealth recognized in the desert. These were often stolen, but as the *marabouts* were the mouthpieces of God, and as the Spirit has always its revenge, the most saintly among them were begged for their blessing on the eve of battle. These latter were accordingly not despoiled, but the lesser *marabouts*, the country priests, humble shepherds mumbling prayers and making amulets of shells or claws, were constantly being raided.

Then Cheikh-Sidia decided that something must be done for his people. He was already powerful, being the refuge of the weak and the terror of the strong, and it was he who set free the B*lanche*t Mission when they were held prisoners in Adrar. He now decided that the only course was to meet force with force, and that the only people strong enough to put an end to the evil deeds of the warriors were the French.

It happened that the French, who had successfully defended their commercial interests in the Sudan and in Senegal against these same warriors, had just reached the stage where European nations are ready to bestow the benefit of their civilization on people who have no need for it and in fact possess another.

So Cheikh-Sidia approached Coppolani, promising him his moral support in Mauretania. At the same time he secured Coppolani's favour for his successful religious tours in Senegal and the Sudan. Together the two men planned the peaceful occupation of the Trarza in 1902.

Boutilimit then became a political centre. In Cheikh-Sidia's spacious tent submissions were negotiated, and also alliances and diplomatic marriages which were to set the seal to advantageous reconciliations.

In the north the warlike *marabouts*, the Ouled-Bousba, R'Guelbat, and Ma-el-Aïnin had proclaimed a holy war which lasted over thirty years, but French pacification advanced steadily though resistance increased as our troops pushed upward to the north.

On May 12th, 1905, Coppolani, too trustful of these Moors he loved, was assassinated at Tidjikja by a fanatic belonging to the Ouled-en-Nour, the Sons of the Light. His revered name is still on the lips of all the white-bearded *marabouts* and all the old slaves of the southern districts.

In 1924 his friend Cheikh-Sidia died, and his tomb near Boutilimit is the goal of many pilgrims.

At the time of our stay in Boutilimit, where not so many

years before Coppolani had established his rule, the two sons of Cheikh-Sidia were carrying on the work of their father. Abdallahi was the religious leader, while his brother Isma'il was the *Cadi*. They collaborated with the French commandant of the district, whose twenty-three years in eastern Sahara had given him some experience.

The Beïdane's name for the latter was 'the Shrewd,' *le Rusé* which said a good deal for his understanding of their intrigues. The two *marabouts* had grown up beside their father, friend of the French, and had known Coppolani, protector of the Berbers. Between them and the Commandant, the policy of Franco-Moorish friendship was well secured.

Quite soon after our arrival, Abdallahi-ould-Cheikh-Sidia invited us to his tent, which could be seen from the terrace of the post on the summit of a dune near by.

Once again we crossed the valley of grey clay and the grazing lands of *tilimit*, the long grass which had given its name to the place.

The climb was stiff in the soft sand. We passed a few tents pitched in the shade of some flowering acacias. Right at the top, outlined against the sky, we could see Abdallahi's camp.

Sitting on the right according to custom, Abdallahi was waiting for us with his respectful attendants. The Moorish tent of brown woollen stuff was lined with many-coloured silken hangings. Abdallahi himself possessed a sort of majesty very different from that we could perceive in Mohammed-Fall and his father, Sidi. Apart from their being of different race, the nobility of Abdallahi was that which emanated from a noble spirit and from goodness of heart.

He wore no gri-gri over his white *draa*. His religion was in his soul; the only outward sign of it were the black beads wound round his naked arm. Between his clipped hair and his short Berber beard his face was wide, smiling and tranquil. Such was the son of the man whom Mgr. Jalabert, Bishop of Dakar, regarded as a saint.

With a paternal kindness of manner Abdallahi made us sit down beside him on the thick woollen carpets from the north and the cushions and furs which covered the matting.

Ould-Aïda, heir to the Emirs of the Adrar, came forward to act as interpreter. Until his turn came to be Emir, he was making himself useful in more humble ways after having received a schooling at Saint Louis, where he had acquired a rigorously academic French. He never said *oui*, but always *certainement*, which sounded more distinguished!

"Abdallahi greets you. This is his favourite poet, Boumediane. This other man is his brother, the *Cadi* Ismaïl; and all these young people are his most remarkable pupils, his *télamid*. They are the sons of chiefs of various *marabout* or warrior tribes of the country. Some of them are black, as you will have noticed, for on the far side of the Senegal River there are noble and Musulman tribes, and the influence of Abdallahi extends as far as Guinea. He possesses the best library in all Mauretania, and every father regards it as an honour to send his son to study under him."

During this speech Abdallahi regarded us with an amused look. Then he spoke:

"France is certainly strong since she can now allow her daughters to travel across the scrub which has known hitherto such troublous times. Indeed, Frenchwomen can write like *marabouts* and travel like warriors! *La illah ill Allah!*"

Slaves the colour of night set large brass trays at our feet laden with dates, biscuits and cigarettes. They poured camel's milk into crystal glasses, and soon from the silver teapots rose the cool perfume of the mint-flavoured tea.

It was good to be in that tent in the soft filtered light. The lower orders, *haratine* and slaves, stood in dark silent groups. There was no noise, no childish pride, no forgotten crimes or vain promises. All was dignity, cleanliness and quiet courtesy.

Abdallahi told us of his far-distant ancestor Marabot Mekka with whom had started the reputation for miracles enjoyed by the Ouled-Biri tribe.

Marabot Mekka possessed the science of the sacred books. He was a just man and lettered, but at the same time a herdsman, and the day that his finest cow disappeared from his herd he set out with a black slave to search for it.

He journeyed for several days following its tracks which led to the camp of some Euleb warriors.

After greetings, tea, and some general remarks of no importance, Marabot rose, asking whether, with the permission of Allah, they had not seen his cow.

No. They had seen nothing. Besides, they knew the marks on the animals of every tribe, and if they had found it they would have brought it back to its owner.

But Marabot Mekka had his ideas concerning the fate of his cow. Murmuring *Bismillah* to ward off evil spirits, he said to his slave:

"Souilem, my son, you who looked after the cow, call her, and may Moulana give us his blessing."

Souilem called and called again, turning to all the points of the horizon. But the cow was not so far.

From all the mouths which had eaten of its meat and from all the stomachs that had digested it, the sound of lowing came forth. The sandals made from the hide lowed, as formerly the cow herself had lowed in the pastures when she led the whole herd towards Souilem. The saddle-covers, which the *mallema* had hardly finished sewing, lowed too; so did the new straps, the cords of plaited leather, the belts, bags and waterbottles, and even the horns which the chief's wife had kept to make a pair of bracelets. And the children lowed who had sucked the raw fat, and the old dog who had gnawed the bones.

The Eulebs threw themselves on their knees, imploring forgiveness, and promising a tribute of one sheep per tent which their descendants are paying to this very day.

"And the sons of Marabot Mekka," continued Abdallahi, inherited the gift of working miracles right down to my father, Cheikh-Sidia, because they were just and respected the sayings of the Prophet. There are many *marabouts* in Mauretania. There are men of God who live a life of fasting, who drink no tea (that alcohol of the Moors), who know nothing of gunpowder, tobacco or women, and who give all their goods to the poor. Those you will not see: they hide themselves like hermits, entirely absorbed in their meditations. But if Moulana grants it that you go to the north, to show also in that country that Frenchwomen are strong and bold like men, then you will see great sages, the Chorfas, sons of the Prophet, the Tadjakants, sons of Solomon, the Kountas, who were one of the first tribes to become allies of the French. For the great Musulman universities in Mauretania are at Chinguetti in Adrar and Tichitt in the Tagant."

Then Abdahallahi offered to show us his father's library, and we all went to a humble-looking hut built of *banco*, which gave no hint of the treasures its walls contained.

One of Abdallahi's suite took a heavy key which was hanging round his neck, went up the three crumbling steps and unlocked the door. Shutters were thrown open, and the evening sun lit up two bare and rather dilapidated rooms. In them were the wooden chests covered with leather, studded with heavy nails and bound with iron bands, which contained all the wisdom of Islam.

Hundreds of rare books were there in sumptuous bindings: Moorish Korans and also Moroccan, Tunisian and Egyptian, and many books of philosophy, poetry, and law. Four generations of the family had laboriously collected them. There was a most precious Koran of the thirteenth century of which Abdallahi was particularly proud. It had been brought from Egypt by some of the disciples which his great-grandfather was constantly sending over all the Musulman world.

Abdallahi's disciples took the books out of the chests and pointed out to us the ornamental capitals and mystic illuminations. Their faces glowed with pride: all these books belonged to their beloved master, and it was for them as well as for him that they had left their families and their countries.

The sun set. And through the open window we could hear the voice of children chanting some *Sourate* in the women's tent.

It was the time for prayer, and we left the library. Each disciple slipped off his impure *siroual* from under his tunic and they all surrounded their master, prostrating themselves with him, then kneeling, the body leaning slightly to the right. Sand was poured over upturned faces and outstretched hands.

We retraced our steps down the steep path leading down into the valley, which was by now full of grey and green shadows in the twilight. In front of us, against a purple background the fortress of Boutilimit reared its crenelated walls.

And going down the side of that dune smelling sweetly of acacias, and with the distant murmur of prayers behind us, I felt for the first time since I had set foot in Africa a temptation to stay where I was instead of pushing further into unknown country, to live here quietly and enjoy its peace.

I turned and looked back. There at the top of the dune, with a little black slave hanging on to his white *draa*, stood Abdallahi waving us a gesture of farewell, a slow gesture like a benediction.

***

As on every Saturday after the siesta, there was great animation in the courtyard of the post. The Court of second degree would be sitting presently, and amongst the crowd in their blue or white *draas* one could see all the notables of the place.

Chiefs of tribes had come for justice, perhaps concerning some matter of taxation or concerning rights to wells or gum trees. They argued volubly in shrill tones, reinforcing their points with sweeping and dramatic gestures.

Abdou-Galilar was there, who managed the affairs of Abdallahi-ould-Cheikh-Sidia. He had a mysterious past, a boundless vanity, and a head like the African hawkers who offer carpets round the cafes of Montparnasse. He was producing some letters from an embroidered leather case. They were written in a feminine hand.

"My dear friend, *la marquise*. . . . My great friend, the wife of General . . ."

These were naive admirers whom he had imposed upon during the Colonial Exhibition, making them suppose that he was the greatest *marabout* in Mauretania.

"I who am educated ... I who am a veritable European in my knowledge of civilization. . . ."

Nevertheless today he looked worried, and with an afflicted air he confided to us that his poor mother was about to die of starvation. This information could not but surprise us considering his wealth. But he went on to explain:

"Yes, it is indeed very strange. In this country there are kinds of devils who get hold of a person, as they have with my mother, persuading her that she can no longer take nourishment, that all food is dirty or poisoned. They torment her night and day until she dies. My mother is in a miserable situation."

It was perhaps on the advice of these same devils that Abdou-Galilar engaged in a clandestine trade in arms and slaves, an activity that was a few months later to bring him before this tribunal, this time not as a curious spectator but as the accused.

Abdallahi had come with his brother Ismaïl, the judge. He was standing to one side, surrounded by his disciples, talking to the principal of the *Médersa*.

The latter acted as his interpreter when he turned to speak to us. This time he was able to say things which the law of hospitality forbade him to say to us when we were visiting him in his own tent. He told us that Mauretania was at the same time the poorest colony and the most heavily taxed. The trade in gum and dates was crushed by taxation, in spite of the fact that the French had promised to respect the *Koranic* custom according to which taxes must not exceed the fortieth of the capital.

Flocks and herds formed the principal form of capital with the Moors. And in the Trarza, for example, on a sheep worth between six and ten francs, the owner had to pay a tax of sixty centimes, that is to say, sometimes as much as a tenth of its value. To save the Government's face, a Trarza sheep was gravely valued at twenty-five francs in the *Livre Vert* of Mauretania. The same with cows and camels, and in every administrative district.

Orders came from above and from far away. Local officials were powerless to do anything. They had only to resign themselves to the role of tax-collectors whose chief occupation was to go round assessing the herds, whose owners hesitated to sell their stock at the low prices prevailing even to get money they badly needed.

Abdallahi told us also of the need for schools and doctors, and for relieving the increasing indigence of the nomads.

"The doctor here has been touring for the last fortnight. When he is at Nouakchott or at Mederdra, four or five days' journey away, the tribes here have no one to turn to except his native assistant, who knows just enough to give injections against syphilis— but they can't all be syphilitic! When the doctor is here at his base, he's not much use to his patients at Mederdra and Nouakchott."

The principal scourges of French West Africa were venereal diseases, ophthalmia, tuberculosis, and smallpox. The Moors believed in doctors and did not hesitate to allow themselves to be given injections or be vaccinated. Thus in the dispensaries and during the doctor's tours something was done to combat disease and alleviate suffering, often much to the credit of the doctors, who were badly equipped and seconded. Some of them indeed were in the highest degree capable and self-sacrificing, like the young major at Boutilimit, who was on the go unceasingly all over the Trarza, animated by a spirit of devotion worthy of a more fruitful field.

For the whole of Mauretania there were no more than half a dozen French doctors, assisted by a handful of native assistants. And from this number one or two must be eliminated on account of incapacity or indifference.

During our stay in the country one of the military posts had two doctors successively. The first went mad in the middle of an operation on a native soldier. His successor gave orders that he was not to be disturbed at night even for a compatriot, and he boasted that at his last place his interpreter used to report fictitious epidemics in regions where game was abundant!

To make up for this deficiency many officials, both military and civil, deprived of all professional help, would procure medical handbooks and organize a little infirmary on their own, fulfilling the functions of doctor as they had to those of builder, judge, and many others.

And not without a little bitterness, Abdallahi added in his grave voice:

"I have too much respect for France to think that so great a nation could be content with conquering a country and imposing taxes, without giving the benefit of her civilization to those who have placed all their hopes in her."

What could I answer? That the Government had to maintain a police force and dig wells? I knew too well that the police were only paid five francs a day for themselves and their camels, while those digging wells got seven and a half. On the other hand, the nomads of the Trarza alone had paid a million francs in taxes in a single year.

I also knew that in some of the bigger towns in the south the bureaucracy was clumsy and expensive. No, it was not easy to find excuses.

A sudden stir and the patter of feet towards the Residence announced that the Court was sitting.

Sitting at a long table in a small dark room were the Commandant of the Trarza, the *Cadi* Ismaïl, a Revenue official, the schoolmaster, and two Moorish assistants.

Near them was the interpreter, very tall and thin, with a falsely deferential air. He had the graceful figure and aristocratic bearing characteristic of the well-bred Toucouleurs. He wore a very ample *draa* of white *basin moiré*, with fine Sudanese embroidery up to the waist. The free end of his black turban, thrown across his shoulder, accentuated the proud carriage of his small shaved head. His features were delicate and clearly drawn, their expression cunning and mysterious.

The crowd of curious Beïdane pressed round the two doorways, while the boldest edged their way into the Court. In the latter the atmosphere was soon stuffy and smelly to a degree that was hardly bearable.

What a pleasure it was for them, these sons of Abraham, to listen to the interminable pleadings, to watch while chicaneries were disclosed and rivals humiliated; or even to see their comrades, who yesterday carried their heads too high, today obliged to bow them to the dust! *La illah ill Allah!*

The native guards used the butts of their rifles to clear a passage for witnesses or accused. The latter remained impassive before their judges, resigned in advance to whatever might be their fate. After all, nothing could happen except it was the will of Allah, and if it was his will it was useless to make supplications to anybody, not even to him the Unique and All-wise.

Proceedings began with the dispatch of several cases of no particular importance. One would come protesting, with the aid of vigorous gesticulation, that he was only a poor man, that God was witness of his poverty, and that his last assessment had given him many more sheep than he possessed.

Another would complain that his slave had run away on a moonless night, and had gone to another camp, over there, far away; and he stretched his hand theatrically at the end of an arm laden with greasy stuffs, pointing to the north-east, which is the north of the Beïdane, pointing eagerly as though he expected Governor, *Cadi*, and all the rest to rush out in pursuit of the fugitive.

The slaves of the interpreter were secure in the millet fields in the neighbourhood of Bakel. But he seemed quite at his ease when he told the plaintiff contemptuously that *serviteurs* were free, according to French law, to go where they pleased, and that he, the plaintiff, if he did not wish to see the inside of a prison, had better stop talking of slaves in a French court of justice.

Then there were cases of fraud and robbery which could always be counted on to provide the indispensable recruits for the transport of the *banco* bricks and the watering of the gardens. Indeed, what would happen to the vegetables if all subjects were suddenly to become honest and virtuous? But thanks to a merciful providence there seems little likelihood that this source of cheap labour will ever become scarce!

There was also a weeping woman, the wife of a *marabout*. She was covered in veils and looked like an antique mourner.

Her husband had left her since the previous Ramadan—over a year before. He had left her without having even pronounced the irrevocable formula "Thou art three times abandoned," after which the woman, henceforward forbidden to her ex-husband, is free to remarry. But this one, what would become of her if her father-in-law did not help her? Her own father would have nothing to do with her. "You are still married according to the will of Allah," he would say. "Go back to your husband."

Unfortunately for her, however, her *malahfa* was somewhat transparent revealing certain evidence that she had not thought it necessary to give. Ismaïl quietly asked her how long she had been pregnant. To this she was too ashamed to make any reply, and clutching her veils about her more tightly than ever she forsook her cause and left the Court.

Although the Koran allows them four wives, the Moors have adopted a monogamy which is in reality a polygamy by succession, considering the ease and frequency of divorce.

The next plaintiff was also a woman, but she was far from being ashamed of herself. She came in clattering her painted wooden sandals on the floor, a strong will written on her small brown face with its bluish shadows. She was no wife of a *marabout*, whining and hypocritical. She belonged to a warrior tribe and made herself plain, coming straight to the point. A widow, she had already been to complain of an official who ill-treated her, Zeïnament-Abdallah, and those of her tent. Now she was at the end of her patience, and if the Commandant—the blessing of Moulana be upon him—did not remove the culprit, she would go and kill him herself, with her own hand loaded with heavy silver rings, which would not tremble at the task.

The women of the warlike tribes are like that. They are not so given to the murmuring of *La illah ill Allah*! but are the daughters of those who in former times used to take their place in battle alongside their men, loading their rifles for them. And today those married to native soldiers do not hesitate to follow their husbands when they are campaigning.

The heat in the small dark room got more and more oppressive. The curious spectators, crowded round the doors, shut out the fresh air. For a moment the interpreter cleared them away and we had a glimpse of the bright sunlight and a few breaths of good air, but they were soon back again, crowding the more eagerly as the climax of the afternoon had now approached.

This time it was a crime, a real crime, the kind that makes people shudder, yet excites the keenest public interest, all the world over. It was a murder.

Ahmed-ould-Boudia had killed Mohammed-Bilal and had

then thrown the body into a well, where the native sharpshooters, Bakari Kamara and Moussa Coulibali, had discovered it long after, together with a sharpened stick of hard wood (such as is used for a goad by the cattle drivers) with which the crime had been committed.

It was indeed a serious crime, but it would very likely never have come to light had it not been that the victim's brother, having first received a hundred sheep and then fourteen as blood-fine, or *dia*, had denounced Ahmed-ould-Boudia to the tribunal in the hope of obtaining the rest of his flocks.

It was after all very convenient for everybody, this French justice, even for the accused.

Formerly, as soon as the Emir had made his inquiry, arrested the accused, and appointed the *Cadi* to try the case, the accused or his family had to pay a fine of four hundred pieces of *guinée*. Moreover, both parties would have to give presents to propitiate the *Cadi*.

On this subject I was told a charming story, which in the style of the old fables might be called: *The Cadi, the Cow, and the Skin of Butter*.

A plaintiff sought to reinforce the rights of his case by giving the *Cadi* a skin of butter. The latter assured the donor of his goodwill. The other party, knowing himself to be guilty, considered logically enough that his innocence should naturally be more expensive than that of the innocent. So he gave a bull and, as a result, was acquitted. The plaintiff complained bitterly.

"It was not my fault at all," said the *Cadi*, disavowing like Pontius Pilate all responsibility, "but the fault of the bull, whose horns disembowelled the skin of butter."

The Moorish administration of justice had been indeed both cumbersome and costly. After the first judgment by a *Cadi* one had the right to appeal; but the appeal would be heard by a court of seven judges, which considerably increased the costs.

When a man was convicted of assault, he would be fined ten pieces of *guinée* (worth about five or six hundred francs) for a blow, up to three hundred pieces for inflicting serious injuries. Murder, however, could only be paid for in kind, a life for a life.

Even so, when a man was condemned to death he had still the chance of a reprieve. But it was a complicated business. Beïdane and slaves would be seen hurrying in all directions across the Trarza on their camels and their asses. They would go to the Emir, to all the *Cadis*, to the camp of Cheikh-Sidia, and to the camp of the condemned. Days and nights were spent in travelling and negotiating. Finally, the elders of the tribe would decide whether the criminal should be executed or whether it was a suitable case for a reprieve.

If he was to be executed the whole family went to the Emir's camp with a slave who was to carry out the sentence by cutting the man's throat. In fact the family, after all the expense of fines, presents, and all the rest, had in the end to furnish the executioner.

The French, on the other hand, had not only cut out all the expense, but had even carried magnanimity to the point of standing the cost of the execution—a luxurious execution, moreover, with rifles in the place of an old knife.

These reforms in judicial procedure, however, did not suffice to console Ahmed-ould-Boudia, who stood with lowered head between two soldiers, facing his judges.

"Why did you kill?"

The answer came slowly, almost inaudibly, with a gesture of impotent resignation: "It was the will of Allah!"

"Mohammed-Bilal was an old friend of yours, even distantly related. What happened between you that led you to throw him in this well? "

"I did not do it on purpose. . . . He fell into the well."

"Then why did you pay a *dia* of a hundred and fourteen sheep to Lobbat, his brother?"

"That was something else. I never paid a *dia*. Lobbat fought me because he wanted my sheep. I gave in because I wanted to marry his sister-in-law, Moulkountia."

"Really. . . . The wife of Mohammed-Bilal?"

"It was not I that wanted it," went on the prisoner. "She wanted it. She had wanted it for six years. Me, I wanted her sister, but Moulkountia stopped me marrying her. She said she loved me more than her husband. And once she even asked me to kill him.

It's not my fault. I didn't kill him. It was Mohammed's fate to fall into the well."

Looking at his lined face, in which glittered his crafty eyes, his ragged beard, and his crooked limbs clad in dirty rags, it was hard to believe that Ahmed-ould-Boudia could be the object of such a passion. But a man may have other charms than those of beauty: for instance, flocks of fat sheep and she-camels providing abundant milk, or a tent as big as that of a *Cadi*. And these were all lacking to the dead husband.

"Where is this Moulkountia?" inquired the Commandant.

"*Monsieur l'administrateur*" answered the interpreter, "she has fled to her tribe in the Tagant."

"And her sister?"

"She has disappeared with her."

"And Lobbat?"

"He could not be found. He is supposed to have gone with this family and his herds to the Adrar."

"*Ah! Diable!* ... Then bring in the other witnesses."

There were only two of them: the two native sharpshooters who had fished out the corpse. They came in, holding the goad between them with naive pride. Having saluted with their free hands they began to tell their story, both speaking at the same time. They gave a great many details, some of them true, some invented for embellishment. Their fabrications were quite devoid of malice: they had no grudge against Ahmed-ould-Boudia. Their sole and quite understandable motive was to make the most of their evidence and of the proud situation in which they found themselves in thus collaborating with the French administration of justice.

Nevertheless, what it all boiled down to was that they had found a body with a hole in the head, and a goad which fitted the hole.

So there was no reason as yet for Ahmed-ould-Boudia to despair, for the designs of Moulana are impenetrable, and Sidi had made off into the desert with all the witnesses. This Sidi, this son of a dog, was as a matter of fact the most important witness as it was he who had actually seen the crime, and for three goats had told the whole story to Lobbat.... But all things come to him who waits, and with the permission of Moulana Ahmed would soon be able to find Sidi, for as there were no witnesses he must now be set free. And when he found him, Sidi's life would not be worth much.

But Ahmed was not set free. On the contrary he watered the tomatoes of Monsieur l'administrateur, carried bricks and emptied the closets, while further inquiries were made. The latter dragged on for weeks and over thousands of kilometres, but in the end the witnesses were found.

Finally one morning a volley of bullets put an end to the prayers which Ahmed-ould-Boudia was muttering, as well as to his coveting other men's wives, and his plans for vengeance against traitors who do not hesitate to betray a man for three old goats.

***

I should have liked this account of our travels to have been more rigorously composed. Had the material been methodically sifted and set out according to a predetermined plan, the reader might have found, chapter by chapter, the story of all the castes in Mauretania, whether noble, religious or servile, the whole being built up so to speak on the huge surface of the desert, and against a suitable background of manners and customs. But our journey was itself far from being a well-planned methodical affair. We were wandering much like the nomads themselves, with our chief object to experience what the day brought forth, more or less at the mercy of seasons, droughts and rains, and the various accidents and chances that might occur. I did not want to be false to the spontaneous quality of my events, so I have let this narrative take the shape in which we lived it.

Another point which weighed with me was that any methodical description of these various peoples would tend to gainsay their essential oneness. The religious chief, the Emir, the slave: all have much the same needs—the same hunger and thirst drive them to the same pastures and the same wells. They drink from the same vessels and carve their meals from the same sheep. They cannot be dissociated without distorting the biblical picture of the Trab-el-Beïdane. God is everywhere, so is the *marabout*; fear is everywhere, so is the warrior; suffering is everywhere, so is the slave.

One day, in the courtyard of the post of Boutilimit, I met Ahmed-Ould-Deïd, Emir of the Trarza. Behind his obstinate forehead, framed by greying curls, was a mind full of memories of revolt and murder. His thin mouth had given orders for the most merciless slaughter. His brilliant, predatory eyes, which peered out from beneath bushy eyebrows and added a cruel glitter to the deeply lined face, had witnessed the death of two uncles, victims of the dagger. Other deaths too: that of Lieutenant Leboul, and those of two Moors belonging to a French patrol who were surprised in their tent, rolled in the matting on which they lay and burnt alive. . . . Yes, these nervous hands were good at killing. This big, thin muscular body had been many times in flight or in pursuit, always tireless, while men and camels were worn out with fatigue.

From the age of thirteen he had struggled to usurp the Emir's place. He had fought French and Moors alike, sacking, stealing, and assassinating, in the Trarza, in the Adrar, and in the Tagant, weaving intrigues, betraying his allies.

But the Moors respected him: he was strong because he had succeeded.

In 1909 a volley of explosions broke over the dune to the east of Boutilimit. It was Ould-Deïd and his men, tired and ruined, who were burning their cartridges before the tent of Cheikh-Sidia. They had finally accepted the advice of the great *marabout* and were suing for pardon, for the *aman*. Half of the band crossed the valley and went up to the military post, and Ould-Deïd, with fury in his heart, threw down without a word at the feet of the Governor, Gaden, his arms and those of his men, which had been tied in bundles.

Gaden knew the Moors. Confidence is a sign of strength, and they respect strength. So he showed his confidence in Ould-Deïd, returning his rifles and ammunition and ordering him to bring in the rest of his warriors that had been left behind at Cheikh-Sidia's tent. There were a few who refused to make submission, but these Ould-Deïd killed with his own hand. The others followed him.

There was no room for him in the Trarza, where Brahim-Saloum had succeeded his father, the assassinated Emir. He accordingly wandered about as a nomad warrior in the service of the French, for he had decided that it was with the latter that his best interests lay. In 1911, he fought in the Hodh with Colonel Patey. Two years later at the head of his men he accompanied Colonel Mouret to Smara. Many were the *razzias* he repulsed, working off his warlike ardour on his hereditary enemies, the tribes of the north, the Ouled-Delim and the R'Gueibat. In 1932, after the ambush of Moutounsi, he and three hundred riflemen pursued Mohammed-el-Mamoun, a relation of the 'Blue Sultan.'

And in the end Ould-Deïd reached the goal for which he had striven, becoming Emir of the Trarza. In 1930 Brahim-Saloum, now suffering from illness, bowed to the wishes of the District Commandant, and he too gave Ould-Deïd the aman. His sons were too young to succeed him, and in order to avoid further conflict he married his daughter to Ould-Deïd before he died. The tribes accepted the son-in-law as their Emir. Brahim-Saloum's sons were sent to Timbuktu; Sidi, Ould-Deïd's brother, then in Morocco, renounced his rights of succession; and finally the Government at Saint Louis ratified the choice of the tribes.

One cannot ask Moorish history to conform to moral principles.

Ould-Deïd was now living peacefully and respectably in his camp, the *Mahssar*, which was situated sometimes at one well, sometimes at another, between Boutilimit, Nouakchott, and Mederdra. His one care was to collect his tribute from his subjects and to get all possible concessions from the French authorities.

When I saw him he was sitting on the edge of a terrace, surrounded by his court of warriors and freed slaves, waiting for an audience. Dressed in white, with many amulets round his neck, he was slowly fingering his beads. He was an edifying sight with his *Légion d'honneur* on his breast. He was indeed a man not without nobility. He was a bandit certainly, but coming of good bandit stock, and his work had been accomplished on a grand scale. The atrocities he had committed attained such a perfection of horror that we could not help feeling a spark of admiration for him, as for some Homeric hero. In fact we were beginning to get used to the Mauretania atmosphere, full as it was of the grandeur of legends of antiquity.

Chapter IV

At the Emir's Camp

OUÔTCH!... lourrrtch!... lourrrttt!... Châhh! Chchâââh!...
Our three camels ran down the dune of Boutilimit raising a heavy cloud of pinkish sand. At the bottom they felt more assured and, stretching their necks towards the west, fell into a steady rhythmic stride over the hard grey clay of the valley. We did not need to guide them: they themselves avoided the thorny barriers round the fields and the cords which ran along in the sand far from the tents, like cables running along the sea-bottom to a ship's anchor.

Mine was the finest, a large pale blond *azouzel* whose lines were both powerful and graceful. He had four teeth (on account of his age), a sure foot and a subtle instinct. His long regular stride never faltered. He got up or down without making a noise, listened calmly to the firing of rifles or the beating of drums, remained stationary as long as one liked, and obeyed more promptly when spoken to in a soft voice.

In fact he was just the sort of camel for *razzias*, pursuits, and ambushes. He was the Emir's own camel.

As for the latter he was detained at Boutilimit, and would rejoin us in the evening, with his warriors, *haratine* and slaves, at the wells of Iboulkham where some of his vassals were camping.

For a week Ould-Deïd had been engaged in diplomatic contest with the Commandant of the Trarza on the subject of the salt-workings of the Dahar which of old had been under the Emir's suzerainty, but had then been confiscated by the French.

At first he had treated Marion Sénones and me with his fiercest looks, but then he noticed the great consideration with which we were treated by the Commandant, and that made him reflect. The French are a very curious people! After all it might even be possible that with them women were creatures of some importance. Perhaps even the esteem of these two travellers was not to be disdained....
Was their experience of Moorish hospitality confined to that of his dispossessed brother, Sidi, and of Abdallahi his rival?...

One fine morning his cruel lips relaxed into a thin smile. An interpreter informed us on his behalf that if so far we had been well entertained in the Trarza, in the future we should be better still; and that he, the Emir, would be delighted if we would accompany him to the *Mahssar*, which at the moment was quite close to Boutilimit, only five days' journey by camel. Then the Christian ladies would see that he, Ould-Deïd, was powerful, rich and generous far beyond all his rivals.

This invitation was to us a godsend. The Commandant gave his permission and confided us to the Emir's care as if we were his own daughters. Abdallahi offered us camels, but the Emir was annoyed by this and frowned. Had not he as good camels as anyone of the Ouled-Biri tribe? . . .

There were a number of men at Boutilimit who had their eye on the job of serving as guide to us. They would come and pay their respects to us every day, preferably at the time for drinking tea. For the sake of our dignity it was necessary for us to have a personal escort.

All would have been perfect if the carbuncle, from which Marion had been suffering since Souelguia, had proved amenable to treatment. But it obstinately held out, and, as there was no question of Marion's sitting on a saddle, I had to go alone.

Accordingly I was not in the best of spirits that evening as I trotted between my two guides, Armeddou and M'Hammed-ould-Touif.

Yes, Armeddou was with me once more, with his pock-marked face, his laziness, his obsequiousness, his tedious stories, and his great sense of his own importance. We had sent him away a hundred times, but he waited for his chance day after day in the courtyard of the post, begging, promising to go away, but staying all the same, and trying to play on our pity. Finally it was arranged that if I took him on this trip he would then return to Nouakchott. So I was full of hope . . . but so was he!

The qualities that made me choose M'Hammed might have led me to reject his candidature had I possessed more wisdom or experience. He was a young man, one of the Ouled-Daman tribe, and a cousin of the Emir. He was a warrior of the pure Arab type who, according to his humour, the circumstances and the surroundings, could look like a pirate of the desert or a picture of Christ. He photographed well. His gracefulness and kindness—his artfulness, it might be said—had made him the spoilt boy of the post where little else was asked of him. He had a good deal of vanity, taking great interest in his personal appearance. His *aouli* of dark blue *guinée* would shine like satin, while his *draa* would be cleaner than those of the other Moors. Shooting at close range after many hours of waiting had won him the reputation of a hunter. He spoke French fairly well, having taken part in the Colonial Exhibition in the role of camel driver. That may seem a modest rôle to European eyes, but not to a nomad's, nor, incidentally, to those of some of the female visitors to the Exhibition, who, in ecstasy before everything exotic, regarded M'Hammed and his three companions as fallen princes worthy of all the favours they could bestow on them.

"European women," he would say, "*Femmes l'Européen* make too much fuss."

And after a woman aviator had attempted suicide in his honour, M'Hammed returned to Boutilimit, convinced of the superiority of his race and impatient to marry a nice fat peaceable woman who would fulfil her conjugal duties without manifesting the least pleasure, like any well-brought-up Beïdania, and who finally would resign herself to divorce when desired by her husband without claiming anything beyond the number of camels stipulated by custom.

The success in Paris of this Don Juan of the desert gave us a little uneasiness, but his compatriots assured us that French women did not run this sort of risk in the Trab-el-Beïdane. A Christian woman is unclean in the eyes of the Saharan Musulmans, who are much stricter than their brothers in the north, or at any rate more anxious to avoid scandal. In Paris M'Hammed did not need to fear the censure of his tribe. In his own country nothing could be hid and "it is better to commit ten sins before God than one before men." And then there was also the fear of prison which is, after the *Koran*, the second wisdom of the Moors! But whatever may have been their motives we never had the slightest cause to complain on this score of the men who escorted us: never an indecent gesture or a coarse word.

With the Women in the Emir's Camp.

M'Hammed sang nicely, which certainly advanced his cause with us. Another of his virtues was always to appear on the scene, smiling, his hand on his heart, just at the right moment to render some little service— to bargain over the price of dates, carry our parcels home for us, or mend a sandal. In fact, he had made himself useful on so many occasions that he had succeeded in drinking far more glasses of tea in our company than the other three candidates together. To these merits must also be added the fact that his rivals were not too prepossessing.

A third bandit was to join my escort next day. He was Bendir, the son and brother of prostitutes. He had not been able to set out with us because he had not yet secured a camel, or perhaps it was for some obscure reason of his own.

It was almost night when the Emir and his men caught us up at Iboulkham.

We were in a little valley full of *oglats* amongst the thorny scrub. The stink of a rotting ass which had fallen into one of these wells reminded us what deathtraps they were.

It was an unsuitable place for the effusive greetings which, as usual, followed our meeting. The cries of men were mingled with those of thirty camels frightened, as was their wont, by the presence of wells.

Finally the troop broke up. Ten warriors and *haratine* remained with me. It was now quite dark. The Emir rode on with the others to lead the way to the camp we were making for. From time to time he called a long ' Ioôh,' or lit a heap of branches on the top of a hillock. We followed his calls and beacons, chanting in an undertone as do nomads all the world over when they ride over a sleeping world under the starlit sky.

From old habit, learnt in the days of general distrust and *razzias*, humble people avoided camping at wells. When travellers passed, the least that might be demanded of them would be the three days' hospitality, milk, and a change of camels which were due by a vassal to his overlord.

A messenger had informed the vassals of Ould-Deïd of our intended visit, and even before we arrived we could hear the dull beat of the tom-tom across the night. Fires were blazing and *méchoui* cooking. On the sand, carefully swept clean of its *initi*, two tents were ready, one for the master, the other for his guest.

An illustrious journalist has related how when he visited the Emir at his *Mahssar* the latter himself attended to the camel, making it kneel for its rider to dismount. I myself was not honoured in this fashion, nor am I altogether convinced by the story of the said journalist. For the Emir is far too proud to accept a task given usually to young people or servants, while on the other hand he is far too polite to do anything which would suggest that his guest was incapable of managing his mount. And I cannot help suspecting that the journalist's camel was the car belonging to the military post at Boutilimit.

With great dignity we retired, the Emir and I, to our respective tents. Besides my personal escort, at least half a dozen of the Emir's men shared my tent. It would have been ungracious of me to protest, for they were only performing a duty of politeness. The leader of this contingent seemed to be Selmou, an old friend of Ould-Deïd and a companion of his heroic days.

The rites of Mauretanian receptions were duly gone through. Darker than the night behind them a crowd of shadowy figures danced and shouted at the opening of my tent, dimly lit up by the flickering camp fires. The flocks were brought in, and the lambs, who had been picketed to the tent pegs all day, jumped bleating to their mothers who sought them. Slaves brought calabashes of milk, the tea and *méchoui*. Women, not daring to enter the Emir's tent, crowded under mine, where the warriors were more accessible.

After we had drunk all the tea the little children shared the *ouarga*, the wet tea-leaves sticky with sugar. Every mutton bone was gnawed successively by the warriors, the women, the children, the slaves, and the dog. Then Armeddou resumed his role of master of ceremonies, explaining to me that the Emir could not visit me on account of the presence of the women, but that it would be proper for me to go and pay my respects to him because he was doing such great things for me.

Squatting in the middle of his men, Ould-Deïd seemed to be expecting me. A white sheepskin was spread for me opposite him.

A *hartani* immediately set down the tray of tea between us, and Armeddou had the honour of breaking the sugar and meticulously filling the little glasses and handing them round, in strict accordance with propriety and precedence. He was suitable for the task, being a guest and neither too old nor too young. It must not be given to a person of importance, but neither to a young person of no authority. As for M'Hammed, being related to the Emir he could neither eat nor drink in his presence, and he stood behind me very humbly covering his mouth with his *aouli*.

With Armeddou interpreting, the conversation began. Greetings, on account of their great length, were very useful, but finally they came to an end and less conventional topics had to be found.

"Is the Christian lady not too tired?" "No, God be praised, she is not tired.... She asks if Ould-Deïd is not tired." "No, really I am extremely well, *elhamdou lillahi!* ... Is she satisfied with her camel? ... Is there nothing that she wants? ... I am very happy that you are coming to the *Mahssar* and hope you will stay long."

Then Armeddou plunged into a lyric description of the *Mahssar*, this 'great capital' which outshone the camp of Sidi as the round moon outshines a star.

The Emir was once more absorbed in the sombre meditation which he never left for long. The empty glasses having been set down for the fourth time on the brass tray, I retired with all the proper formulas of leave-taking.

If the conversation had been a little stilted in the Emir's tent it was by no means so in mine.

Beside each of the warriors fluttered the dark blue veils of the women and all round there was subdued babbling and shy laughter. Now and again with an affectedly coquettish gesture a small hand would readjust a fold or draw in the *chandorah* around the brown faces lit up by caressing eyes. Their front teeth showed up a brilliant white as they stuck out in front, almost horizontally, which they were made to do by the strange laws of Moorish aesthetics. Some naked babies cried with cold.

It happened that the husbands were away, collecting gum down in the south of the Trarza, so their wives were at full liberty to entertain their noble visitors, whose attentions were flattering and whose wealth was enviable. They had already managed to get some scraps of sugar, a little tea, and a few pinches of tobacco. But what they were really after was *mesk*, and their cajoleries were redoubled. *Mesk* was their name for the violent perfumes which one found in the shops at Boutilimit and which mix so deliciously with the rancid butter which the women use to grease their hair each month when their coiffure is renewed.

The prettiest whispered with Selmou. She was the first victim. Without taking his eyes off her, Selmou fumbled in his cartridge pouch and brought out a tiny flask. He threw his wide tunic across her and they were silent. Only a delicate hand could be seen clutching at the little bottle. Then the couple got up and went off slowly to the *adress* bushes which scented the night with a balm-like odour.

One after the other the rest of the couples glided furtively out of the tent. The last glow of the fire lit them up as they passed. The little naked children went off to sleep in the warm cinders around.

I took advantage of this moment's solitude to examine the folds of my tunic and the pleats of my *siroual* which were the favourite haunts of lice.

Some of the days of February in Mauretania are as mild as those of June in the Ile-de-France. The first morning of our journey to the *Mahssar* we rode across pastures that were green once more. Scattered about were round trees like the crab-apple. The blue sky was half covered with small white clouds. Butterflies were flying over the scented acacias. An old slave, returning from the wells with a she-ass and her foal, stopped to let us pass, and greeted us with a sign of benediction like a peasant in France.

The Emir himself smiled to see me spur on my fine blond *azouzel*, racing the young warriors. The pure, keen air made us feel that we must play, race, and be fraternal, free and joyful.

Some straggled behind, rejoining the caravan later at a trot, to be greeted with playful banter. M'Hammed, whom I had not seen since the night before, came up last of all. His camel had got lost and he had spent a long time looking for it trying to pick out its tracks from the others. It is strange how easily camels get lost when women are beautiful and husbands absent! The other member of my escort, Bendir, had not yet appeared.

Armeddou made disdainful strictures: "Men of Boutilimit always amusing themselves. That, it's no good for big journeys."

As the sun rose higher we left the green pastures behind us and were in the scrub and the dunes once more. The steep slopes of the high dunes had been cut into crevices by the torrential rainstorms. Three months earlier torrents had been rushing over the dry sand which now we trod, cutting the sinuous ravines which caused the camels to stumble. We had to dismount and lead them.

The Emir had ridden off with his men to a camp where he had some tribute to collect.

A gazelle started out of a thicket and dashed off, drawing Armeddou after it. The latter saw a good opportunity to prove that in hunting a Euleb was as good as any Ouled-Daman.

But a moment later a bustard gave M'Hammed an opportunity to maintain his reputation.

As a result I was left alone and I dragged along painfully, losing my way to right and to left. Finally the Emir, tired of waiting for us, began to be uneasy concerning the safety of my precious person. It might have the most deplorable repercussions if I managed to break my neck.... Who could tell what the reactions of the French authorities might be? ... So he sent off his best friend Selmou in search of me, with his principal *hartani*, Moukhtar.

Their calls rounded up the hunters. One had broken the wing of his bustard; the other had lodged a bullet in the gazelle's shoulder. The two animals were far away, but honour was saved.

But their hunting exploits were soon forgotten in their desire to appease the wrath of Ould-Deïd, who was waiting for us with his stick raised and his eyes blazing, and who abused Armeddou and M'Hammed back to their most remote ancestors.

For my part I remarked with some vehemence that if I could not at any rate have one of my men with me all the time, I could easily find others.

"You're quite right, and so is the Emir," said Armeddou. "It is not nice, M'Hammed he leaves you all alone to run after bustard.

... Bendir same thing, worth nothing, Ach!" Of his own defection he said nothing. M'Hammed, more subtle, gracefully asked forgiveness.

When the tea was being drunk at the midday camp, Bendir at last appeared. After a third reprimand I was surrounded by smiling faces and willing hands.

The journey to the *Mahssar*, perhaps continued to the *salines* of the Dahar, was already something considerable, but the three of them knew that after that there was to be a journey to the Sudan, which would mean many days of pay, considerable presents with which we were to reward their valour, and the glory and profit of being included in the fêtes which would be held in our honour all along the route. That was worth making a few efforts for, at any rate at the start. Later on, far from the Emir and all French posts, there would be time enough to take liberties. Each in his heart of hearts hoped to oust the other two, becoming exclusively our guide or sharing the work with some chosen relative. And they slipped into dreams of grandeur, magnificent dreams and quite impossible. They saw themselves returning to their camps clothed in *boubous* embroidered from head to foot, knotting huge packets of five-franc notes in the loose ends of their *aoulis*, and driving before them camels laden with Sudanese cotton stuffs, calabashes, loaves of sugar and glass beads.

They dreamt also of the power and generosity of their Christian employers. If any sordid reality came to destroy their dreams, they would make others. In relating any enterprise, even of the most modest kind, they would always manage to embellish it, just as when they thought of the camps of Sidi or the Emir they were easily able to transform a group of shabby tents into a sumptuous capital. After all, the Sahara, even the western part of it, is really Oriental in character.

The journey now went smoothly. We rode fast in short stages.

We rode sometimes south, sometimes west or northwest, this indirect route being taken so that the Emir could visit a number of camps, like a country landlord going the round of his tenants. At each camp a long halt was necessary and astute inquiries with a view to determining how many young camels, and asses, calves, lambs and kids had been born since his last visit. What had become of the tired camels which the Zenagui were to turn out into the pastures? What had the gum harvest been like? How many animals had been requisitioned for convoys, and how many men for enforced labour on the roads?

No, it was by no means easy to find it all out. The chief of the camp would start off by prevaricating, but in the end he would tell all, so as to be rid of this company of hungry men who consumed his sheep and millet.

The days passed slowly, all alike, empty but without boredom, as in the old song composed by a nomad poet which M'Hammed was so fond of singing:

> *Time flies and the poet is not astonished.*
> *Mm ... emmmmmh! ... mmm ... mmmmmmh!*
> *Without respite, indefatigable,*
> *The days and nights make nature old. . . .*

The rides and the halts, the hard bottoms of the valleys and the soft sandy summits of the dunes, the five daily prayers, the beat of the tom-toms, the pounding of the millet, the greetings and benedictions of meetings and farewells—day after day they succeeded each other with a monotony that got hold of one like a rhythm, and gave a charm and even a stability to this wandering life.

And it gave one a certain feeling of security to live in this round of traditions, habits, and customs which had descended from time immemorial, ever since the Eternal Father had taught them to Abraham. It gave one a sense of immutability.

We went to camps of Zénagui, *marabouts*, slaves and Tiabs. These last were despised by my companions in spite of their wealth and independence. The Tiabs were a warrior tribe who had renounced arms and allied themselves to the *marabouts*, without, however, winning the esteem of anybody.

At the midday camp we would drink sour milk mixed with water called *n'sri*. In the evening, however, when the herds had just been brought in, we often had quite fresh milk, and the slave attached to my tent would sometimes wake me up late in the night to offer me the last calabash.

Moukhtar, the Emir's chief *hartani*, would come to see me before each meal. With all his master's keys hanging round his neck he looked a very imposing major-domo as he inquired what I would like to eat. It was a courteous attention, but I wonder what sort of face he would have made, under his huge negro turban *à la Ballet Russe*, if I had had the caprice to ask for anything other than tea, *méchoui*, millet, or milk!

Four times a day the Emir and I would exchange formal visits, which, however, became daily more cordial. He was amused by my taste for nomad life, and by my *camaraderie* with the women and playfulness with their babies. He would laugh silently, his hand before his mouth, when he heard me painfully trying to pronounce a few words in his language, or when his companions joked about the white *siroual* I was wearing. A strange custom, peculiar to the Trarza, had determined that this garment was a sign of royalty. These native trousers might almost be called the Emir's crown, for he wore no other. Ordinary mortals contented themselves with *sirouals* made of *chandorah*, probably from a discarded *aouli*. Only the Emir had the right to wear a white *siroual*, and if one of his warriors had attempted to share this privilege, his life would have been in grave danger.

The sixth morning after we had set out, the little white cock that had slept beside me, perched on a saddle, at the camp of Tigbarren, woke me up with his crowing. Outside, the camels were already assembled while the men were just filling the teapot.

The evening before, Ould-Deïd had gone off in front to get things ready for my arrival. He wanted to organize a magnificent reception in my honour. Half his men had been left behind to accompany me, and Moukhtar to see that all my wants were attended to during this last day. Ould-Deïd and his party had ridden off at a fast trot, frightening the doves, raising a cloud of sand, and with their loose tunics and scarves floating out behind them.

Directly after the prayer of dawn we set out shivering in the keen wind which blew through our cotton clothing. We were to reach the *Mahssar* before the sun was high.

We had just climbed up the dune which sheltered Tigbarren

from the west wind when we heard a dull rumbling. They asked me if I heard it, and told me that the Emir was having his big war-drum beaten for the fête.

From dune to dune this great heavy sound got louder and louder. As we got close its rhythm became mingled with the chanting of slaves. Then a volley was fired on the other side of the last valley and two horsemen galloped down the opposite slope and rode towards us.

The Saracens of the days of chivalry and romance came back to me as I watched those riders. I could see the glitter of their eyes through the openings of their blue turbans, which looked like helmets. Their open tunics, knotted behind them, revealed brown muscular bodies. They brandished their rifles above their heads. Skins were spread over the saddles and fell over the flanks of their white steeds. Suddenly the small, nervous horses reared in a whirlwind of sand as their bits were tugged at cruelly. Their tails, dyed red with henna, looked as though they had trailed through the blood of a battle.

Having joined us, the horsemen rode round us in circles as we went forward, simulating pursuits, charges, and the triumph and ecstasy of victory. The shots of rifles made a chorus with their barbaric cries, the neighing of their horses and the roaring of our camels. Then they rode off at a gallop once more, and our camels, by this time thoroughly excited, followed at full speed, their pace never slackening till we were at the top of the hill where the great tom-tom of the *Mahssar* thundered before the brown tent which was to be mine.

The fête took place in the midst of a throng of wildly excited people. There were noble parades of warriors, obscene mimicry of slaves, half-clothed in grotesque tatters, while among the dancers horses plunged and pranced, spattering those around them with blood-flecked foam. There were many shots fired, a lot of cries, laughter and dust. Sure hands brandished sticks and rifles and threw them in the air.

The great tom-tom was fine—but to describe the many tom-toms of Mauretania would make a monotonous recital. . . .

I sat near the Emir, who gravely presided, sitting between his *griots* and his two youngest sons. When passing before us in their dance the slaves struck their private parts with their fists and made the gesture of lifting their legs like dogs. Or again they would hurl menaces, pointing at me the drivers' sticks which they held between their thighs. Strange as it may seem these performances had no other object than to do honour to their master and his guest.

"So this is the famous *Mahssar*," I thought as I entered my tent devoid of any furniture; and I could not but admire the power of illusion which could transform the camp into a place replete with every luxury and bliss. But this time I had been wise enough to expect nothing, so I did not suffer any disillusionment, and I felt capable of enjoying whatever hospitality the Beïdane could offer. Not least I enjoyed their naively generous way of offering their penury as if it were of unmatched excellence.

Of the fifty tents which were scattered here and there among the acacias and the *adress* bushes, mine was the finest, notwithstanding its holes through which the sun threw darts of fire such as would have forced me to wear a sun-helmet had I had the habit of wearing one. The sumptuousness of this 'capital' consisted in effect of a carpet of manure outside my tent, where the herds were kept at night, and a carpet inside it composed of a *faro* folded under a Moroccan rug.

A monstrous creature flopped down beside me. It was Toutou, the daughter of Ould-Deïd, a wretched child of ten, stuffed full of milk and stupefied with fat. She could hardly cross her short thick legs in the Arab manner under her swollen belly.

The smith had carefully shaved large circles on the sides of her head where the bare skin showed white between the tufts of hair stuck with butter. The largest tuft on the top was adorned with glass ornaments. One could hardly say it was becoming, but it was certainly informative, as one knew at once her caste, her tribe, and her eligibility for marriage.

Toutou sat there, formless, without looking at anything or saying anything; a toothpick of *adress* wood in her half-open mouth—just sitting there for men to covet and women to envy.

Sid-Ahmed, *griot* to the Emir, and the Emir of *griots*, sang the genealogy and glory of his protector:

> *Men accustomed to praises*
> *From their childhood*
> *Are Ould-Deïd and Selmou. . . .*

The glory of Ould-Deïd consisted of course of his feats of arms, directed against his family, his enemies of the north, and the French.

The minstrel also sang his own praises. For he, Sid-Ahmed, feared no rival, not even that other Sid-Ahmed, *griot* of the Adrar, whose throat he would tear with his wolf's teeth if Moulana, the All-just, would grant them to meet one day face to face.

And Sid-Ahmed, at this exciting thought, started to howl the war song with all the grimaces and snarls of hate, the song which formerly the *griots* would sing between advancing armies as a prelude to the ensuing battle.

> *The camels, the night and the desert*
> *Know me well;*
> *The sword, the lance, paper and the pen*
> *Are equally familiar to me.*

I cordially detested this man with his ferocious face and aggressive cries, but without question his singing gave the Beïdane the most intense aesthetic joy.

Sid-Ahmed redoubled his efforts in honour of two stout women who entered. They were elegant women, their *chandorah*s having a dark brilliance like blue carbon paper. The younger of the two was Lalia, daughter of the former Emir, Brahim-Saloum, and the wife of Ould-Deïd. Astride on her hip she carried a little naked girl whose face was covered with milk and snot.

The other was the widow of Lalia's father, though she was not her mother. Her two sons were the legitimate heirs to the Emir's throne, but they were living in exile to avoid any possible complications.

The Emir and his Family

The two women sat down beside me and smothered me with caresses, smiles and compliments.

Bouerika, Lalia's little daughter, was frightened by the light colour of my skin and began to scream. Her mother, who kept her mouth decently covered by her veil, produced from beneath her *malahfa* an enormous breast which hung down on her knees and on which Bouerika pounced greedily.

Ould-Deïd and Lalia presented a rare example of conjugal fidelity, in fact a model of diplomatic marriages.

It had been a ticklish matter to arrange. Under the anxious eye of the Commandant of the Trarza, Ould-Deïd and Brahim-Saloum had met, rifle in hand. The rifles were theirs, but not the hands which held them. They were held by their *haratine* who stood just behind them. In this posture Ould-Deïd solicited the hand of Lalia and Brahim-Saloum gave his consent. But only the slightest movement would have been necessary for shots to have been fired at point-blank range. Though prudence is necessary, it would, however, have been ill-bred for men of quality to show anxiety. Thus the two warriors were themselves unarmed, sitting peaceably face to face with their eyes cast down while the barrel of a rifle projected over each man's shoulder. Between them the Commandant trembled inwardly for the issue of the negotiations, which were to put an end to the internecine struggles of his district.

Agreement was reached, the dowry fixed, and Ould-Deïd's succession to the ageing Emir was assured.

As soon as the marriage had taken place, the parties involved in the agreement went, with the Commandant at their head, to the Government at Saint Louis, solemnly to confirm the arrangement by which there would be henceforth 'peace and nothing but peace' in the Trarza. That meant a long journey with an imposing caravan of chiefs, dignitaries, native troops and slaves, all mounted on fine camels.

Everything was going well. Everyone returned thanks to God. And at Saint Louis a sumptuous reception was being prepared.

The second day, when halting amongst the millet fields on the border of Senegal, expecting to reach Saint Louis in time for the festivities on the following evening, Ould-Deïd came to the

Commandant. He said he was his son, his humble *zenega*, that he confided his benefactor to the care of God, etc.—and that he was going back to the *Mahssar*. He wanted to visit 'his tent' and swore he would rejoin the caravan before it got to Saint Louis. And sustained by his memories of the marriage night he rode back the whole way at full speed, changing camels on the way, to pass a few moments with the beautiful Lalia that were not in the least concerned with diplomacy.

The next day, before Saint Louis, he caught up the caravan to the immense relief of the Commandant, who had been divided between trying to pacify the furious Brahim-Saloum and to prepare a suitable way of announcing Ould-Deïd's defection to *Monsieur le Gouverneur de la Mauritanie*.

My days at the *Mahssar* passed as days always pass when consecrated to official receptions in the camps of great chiefs. Ceremonial visits were constantly being exchanged with all their greetings and benedictions. There were more dances, and a shooting match which the Emir won with my revolver.

Lalia made me a present of a *tassoufra* of which I was greatly in need, and Ould-Deïd gave me a large comfortable saddle, stuffed with sheepskin, with a girth of giraffe's leather fastened with a carved brass buckle.

To satisfy my curiosity two relatives of the Emir beat the great war-drum which had been specially hung before my tent on a forked stake. With a heavy drum-stick covered in white leather they struck the two lugubrious notes which could call men to arms within a radius of fifty kilometres.

We drank masses of tea, and several sheep and goats died in honour of my visit.

I learnt a new recipe of Moorish cookery:

Take a good stout slave and a tough sheep. Get the slave to cut the latter's throat, skin it, and eviscerate it, which he will do with a small broken knife such as will serve equally well to trim a moustache or shave a child's head. He should then cut a piece of the large intestine twice as long as his hand, and laying it on his knee squeeze out as much of the contents as possible. This piece of the gut should then be filled with bits of meat and fat, tied at the two ends with thongs of leather, and plunged into the boiling water in which the millet is cooking. Add a handful of rancid butter and season with the magnesian salt of the Dahar.

At the same time the slave will make some *meghloub*, which consists of bits of the small intestine stuffed with fat and then grilled over the fire.

The results of his labours will then be put in a calabash which serves for carrying embers, milking the cows, washing faces and also the hands and feet of European visitors. But before using it for the food in question he will be careful to wipe it with the tail of his tunic.

If the odour of this dish does not repulse you, murmur *Bismillah*, to ward off evil spirits, and eat until you come upon a bit of sheep dung which has been overlooked. That is what happened to me at the third mouthful, and enabled me to win the hearts of the Emir's two small boys who gave me considerable help in finishing it.

For these boys my visit was an occasion for great joy, for they got their first *boubous* . These consisted of a width of white cotton stuff, folded over, and a slit cut for the head to go through. The corners were knotted at the level of the knee. What made these particular *boubous* so beautiful were the trade marks, stamped in blue on the chest. Baba, aged seven, got a British lion, while his younger brother, Ahmed-Saloum, got a highly decorative fish, surrounded by Japanese characters.

These first *boubous* were exceptional favours caused by my presence. For as a rule the little Moors, even those of royal blood, go about naked until they are circumcised, which misfortune only comes to them about the age of ten. Baba and Ahmed-Saloum were very proud of theirs, though a little embarrassed, and they generally wore them rolled up across their stomachs.

They were very pretty boys. An artless boldness combined with precocious gravity gave them an irresistible charm. The hard lines of their father's face relaxed with tenderness when he saw them. All Moors love little children.

Baba and Ahmed-Saloum made great friends with the foreigner who would let them play with her empty revolver, fountain pen, great sheets of white paper, and so many other marvellous things that they had never seen before.

In fact we were such friends that when Ahmed-Saloum heard his father tell off a man to accompany me on the morrow, he stoutly declared that he would himself escort me to the post of Mederdra. I should have liked nothing better, but it could not be denied that the old *hartani*, Meïmoun, was capable of rendering more service than a little page aged five.

The first shadows of the evening would find me feeling rather sick as a result of the strange food, devoured by vermin, stunned by all the deafening music I had listened to, and my legs stiff from the long hours of squatting. The hour of prayer brought me a moment's peace and I took advantage of it to go out around the camp, hoping to find a little silence and coolness. It was the hour when in France the angelus would be ringing across the quiet countryside, when smoke would be rising slowly from farmhouse or cottage, and sparrows quarrelling in the tall trees. In other words it was the moment when a wanderer's thoughts turn to his own country....

Across the great silence in which the dunes were sleeping the voice of the *marabout* came clearly to my ears: *Allah ou akbar! Allah ou akbar!* Close at hand a negro was breaking branches for the fires. Pots boiled in front of the tents. At regular intervals a woman sent up a long cry, which was the name of her little girl. And all these noises seemed to me only to emphasize the great background of silence, without really disturbing it.

Space too seemed immense, and in the middle of it this little camp so fragile and ephemeral; all trace of it would before very long be obliterated by the winds.

In front of one of the tents the Emir's wife, her sister-in-law, and Toutou beckoned to me to come and sit beside them on the sand.

Here at least there was no ceremony to be gone through. Out of the Emir's presence they could give full rein to their curiosity. With their sticky little hands they fingered my clothes, my arms and my hair, pouring out a stream of questions which Bendir, who had sat down behind me, translated.

"Lalia asks if French woman never put black on their eyes and henna on their hands? ... Why do you not make the beautiful *coiffure* with butter and beads? ... Why have you come? ... She asks if you are pleased for the Trab-el-Beïdane? ... Is it true in France women give money to get married? ... Where is your husband? ..."

It was an unheard-of thing for them that a woman of my age had not already got five or six husbands! It would in fact have been impolite to suppose it. When told of my unmarried state they were at first struck dumb with astonishment, then they burst into a fit of laughter, drawing their veils across their mouths.

"They say perhaps you are too small (by which was meant too thin). You have seen Toutou, she is big, fat, *mon vieux, c'est belle femme complete, ach!* To marry with her, one give more than fifty camels, and lots of presents too to everybody."

Out of politeness I paid what compliments I could to the girl. "Pretty, very pretty! *Zeïne, zeïne ate!*"

Thereupon, without more ado, Lalia stripped the veils from her daughter and showed with pride the rolls of fat on her body, and the shoulders and flanks where the distended skin was covered with fine pink cracks.

But figures will give a better idea of her dimensions than any description: she must have weighed twelve stone though she was of the height of a child of ten to eleven years old. A man—no doubt some rich old chief—could well be proud to marry her, for the obesity of his wife is the sign of a man's fortune.

I had to inspect and prod her and express my admiration while Toutou, impassive, made no protest. She well knew the ordeals young girls have to go through as a penalty for their beauty. I was soon to know it too!

The round moon told me it was after midnight. Under my tent my three men and a few others snored peacefully. Their rifles served as bolsters and their cartridge pouches as pillows. Half a dozen *sirouals* were hanging from the two crossed poles which held up the tent. I listened to the monotonous chewing of the cud by a cow that was lying against the tent. Lambs were sleeping at my feet. All was calm and customary.

My thoughts wandered to the anomalies of existence and the

undeniable originality of my situation, resting under a canopy of dirty pants between men I hardly knew and beasts. Suddenly I was startled from my reverie by a cry of pain.

The scolding voice of a man alternated with that of a child who stammered out a few words between her tears. The cries got louder, half strangled, pleading. Amongst the words spoken by the man one recurred continually: '*Charbi*,' which means 'You drink!'

Stirred by curiosity I slipped out of my tent as softly as I could so as not to wake the sleepers, who might have put a stop to my investigations.

A short distance away a feeble light oscillated at the entrance of a small tent. It was from this tent that the noise was coming. Avoiding the animals, the dying embers of the fire, the tent cords and other impedimenta, I reached a bush through the branches of which I could watch the scene without myself being seen.

And what I saw filled me with horror.

Held by an old woman servant, the unhappy Toutou was struggling on the disarranged *faro*.

I could not at first make out what the man was doing, kneeling at her feet, but creeping closer to the tent I saw that he was pressing the toes of the wretched girl between two camel sticks. It must have been a cruel torture. Every time that his victim opened her mouth to protest he dropped the sticks, snatched up a calabash of milk and made her drink. She dribbled, she cried, she set her teeth; then her torturer began to beat her and to squeeze her hands and feet.

To my astonishment, as he turned towards his old accomplice, I recognized Meïmoun. I could hardly believe it, but Meïmoun it was, Meïmoun, the most trusted servant of the Emir, the *nounou* of his children. "Ah," I thought, "if only Lalia were to see her precious daughter of whom she is so proud being bullied by this brute!"

But what could I do? Call Ould-Deïd? I would not even have been able to find his tent in the dark. . . . Call for help? The wretches would have made off before anyone was awake. . . . The best, I thought, would simply be to show my presence so that at any rate the martyrdom should cease.

But when he saw me step into the circle of the light, Meïmoun, far from being disconcerted, smiled broadly like a man surprised in the fulfilment of his duty.

Toutou, delivered for a moment, readjusted her clothes, and murmured *Alik essalam!* The old *hartania* confided to me in despairing tones that Toutou was really not a good girl; that Meïmoun and she had already fattened many young ladies for marriage, but that none had ever given them so much trouble as Toutou had. She was beginning to be beautiful, and a result so satisfying, which showed the favourable intentions of Moulana, should encourage her to drink her milk.

Then she turned to her charge:

"Toutou, my joy, the apple of my eye, drink to be beautiful, beautiful as the moon. Drink, my dove; do not dishonour your old nurse."

Intimidated by my presence the 'dove' started to empty the calabash, spilling a good deal. The vessel must have held two to three litres of milk. Before she had finished, however, she had received a further five or six blows with the stick, a few compliments and many supplications. Then she lay down painfully and went to sleep, while the negress went off to draw a further supply of milk from the best cows to provide the next ration.

Meïmoun held up the five fingers of his right hand, giving me to understand that between evening and morning Toutou had to drink five calabashes of milk, the produce of half a dozen cows. She made so much fuss over it all that her parents could not keep her in their tent and so it was he, Meïmoun, who had all the trouble.

It was also his job to do her hair and shave her 'everywhere,' rid her of vermin and put on her veils and her jewels. And it was Meïmoun who had helped the *mallem* to extract her canines to enable her front teeth to separate agreeably. This had been done when she was still a little girl, naked and happy, and slim as a young gazelle. And it would be Meïmoun who would before long be rigging up the white nuptial tent where Toutou, conducted by the *griote*, would rejoin her husband every night. For a year she would have to return to her parents' tent before daybreak.

Meïmoun loved Toutou as his own daughter, but it was a lot of worry for a man of his age, and he was certainly not displeased to be leaving the camp with me the next day, to be for a time out of reach of the exacting Lalia and the capricious Toutou.

There was now no question of my calling for help, and I returned quietly to my tent, where a slave was just bringing me some sheep's milk which filled me with horror. Finally, I went off to sleep thinking of all the rich young girls who were, like Toutou, being fattened for the marriage market, who suffer to be beautiful, and even sometimes die in the attempt.

One never sleeps very long in Mauretania. All the same, after a disturbed night, Moulana might have spared me the virulent reveille with which Sid-Ahmed the *griot* woke me at the peep of day.

My dormitory mates were already up. A servant was lighting a fire. Very carefully M'Hammed poured me out some frothy milk from a particularly dirty calabash, blowing hard as he did so to drive away the hairs and other foreign bodies that floated on the surface. The others drank out of the calabash, but M'Hammed had a double reason for pouring my portion out into a separate receptacle. Firstly, he was demonstrating his zeal on my behalf. Secondly, to preserve the dirty rim of the calabash from the impure contact of a Christian's lips.

Preceded by a slave bearing tea and sugar-loaves, the Emir appeared, flanked by Selmou and Moukhtar. Ould-Deïd expressed his regrets that this day which might otherwise have been so beautiful should be marred by my departure. Like his brother, he too would have liked to keep me always in his camp, which I was henceforward to regard as my own. But as I was bent on going he prayed Moulana to bless my footsteps. The fine *azouzel* which I had ridden from Boutilimit would remain at my disposal as long as I wished. And Meitmoun had orders to obey me as his own master and to demand all that I needed in the camps through which we passed.

At this point Moukhtar put the sugar-loaves beside me and a little bag of tea for the journey.

Then Ould-Deïd, his eyes half-closed, assumed the mien of someone who is just coming to the culminating point of a conversation.

It was like this: he had done all in his power to give me a good reception; he hoped I was satisfied, and that I should say as much to the District Commandant....

Frowning, he let the sand run through his fingers with a casual gesture. A fine aristocratic hand, long and nervous, the hand of a chief whose enemies were of no more account than this flowing sand.

... Yes, the Christian woman would of course speak as her heart dictated and in accordance with the will of God, but she should perhaps know that Ould-Deïd had no need of camels or sheep or money, and that he only wished she would write nice things about him in the French newspapers.

The Press, it seems, is a power even in the Sahara!

Then he went on to say something more, which was certainly not confidential and must have been important; for he had brought me from Boutilimit for some purpose and had waited eight days to play his card at the right moment.

"The French are stronger than we are, but we are stronger than either the R'Gueïbat or the Spanish. Nevertheless, the French forbid us to go into Rio de Oro to collect the tribute which the R'Gueïbat owe us. Why should they forbid it? The R'Gueïbat are enemies of the French as much as they are ours.... The Trarza tribesmen alone, under my command, could without difficulty conquer the R'Gueïbat.... Well do I know the route to Smara...."

His tone became reminiscent. On the sand he marked the Trarza with the imprint of his fist and Smara with a piece of camel dung, and between the two his finger traced the long track he had followed with Colonel Mouret.

"What does it matter," he went on, "if the Rio belongs to Spain since it is we who would go. The Beïdane belong everywhere where there is sand and wells. You understand? We would take the camels which the R'Gueibat owe us and share them with the French. And then the French would also get the tax on our share. It is to their interest that we should be rich."

With his open hands, palms upwards, he signalled his good faith and the advantages of his proposition.

"Yes, it is only the fear of the French courts, which would confiscate our spoils, which prevents our going.... At one time I hoped. It was after the Moutounsi affair. I rode off with four hundred warriors, and I knew the spot where was the *razzia* of Mohammed-el-Mamoun. But then the Governor forbade me to pursue him, and he went and raided the flocks of the Brakna, while we came back to Trarza with empty hands, without having been given a chance to fight the dogs. . . . What we want are arms, ammunition, and a free hand. Then the French would have peace in the north. ... A long time ago the R'Gueïbat came and made submission at Saint Louis, but having got arms and presents they went off to Seguiet-el-Hamra. And even today, do you think the arms of the people of the north are all Spanish? Not at all—their agents buy secretly even as far away as Senegal. Ach! And for us, nothing!"

Having said his say Ould-Deïd was silent, thinking no doubt of the fine camels of the R'Gueïbat peacefully grazing in the pastures of Rio.

He crushed a leaf of tobacco in the palm of his left hand, and filled his iron pipe, lighting it at my cigarette. He took a long puff and then handed it to Meïmoun, who afterwards passed it to Moukhtar, who handed it back to his master.

La illah ill Allah! But the will of God was not easy to accept when it manifested itself through those of Frenchmen.

The Emir rose, shook the sand from the folds of his tunic and left me to get ready for my departure.

The diplomatic role which he had assigned to me was obviously flattering, but I had no time to feel pleased or to wonder how much substance his words had contained.

I mercilessly settled up accounts with the sad Armeddou. I jumped into the saddle and restraining my impatient camel I called out once more my gratitude to the Emir and his family who, on their side, recommended me to the care of God.

A few months later Ould-Deïd was to learn that the French had surer means than his for establishing peace in the north, and a peace which was not quite the same as that of the Moors.

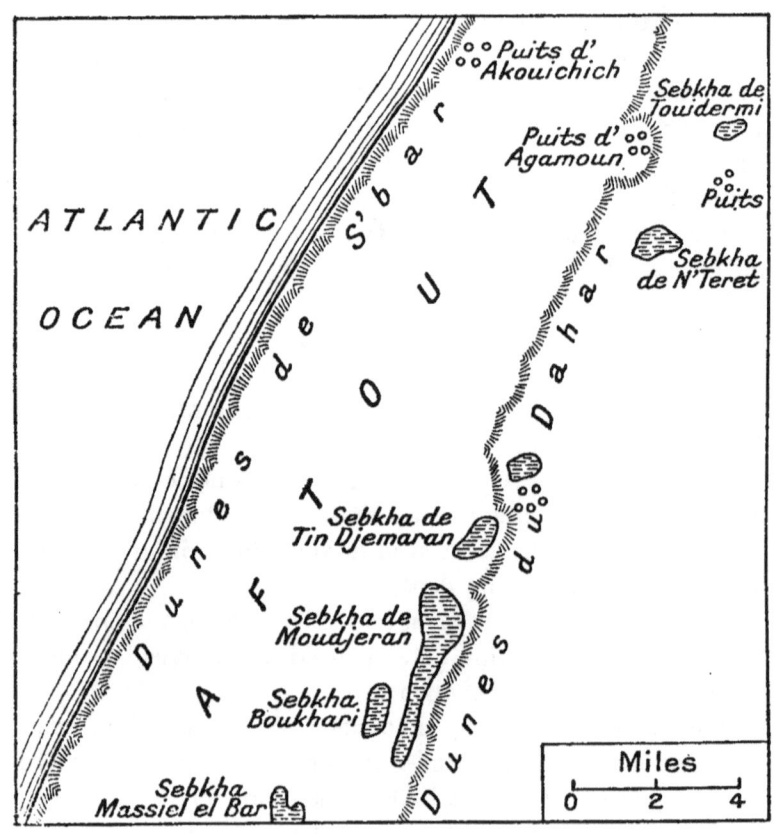

The Salines of the Dahar

Chapter V

The Salines *of the Dahar*

WE were riding towards Mederdra. I certainly wanted to see the salt-workings of the Dahar, but that was not my immediate object. I wanted first to have news of Marion and to inform her of my new project, and we were going round by Mederdra so that I could telephone to her from there. In Mauretania distance as well as time is reckoned on a different scale to ours, and it did not seem at all extraordinary to ride eighty kilometres to reach the nearest telephone.

I thought Marion might easily be anxious about me, for according to the Commandant's estimate of the length of my trip I ought already to have been back at Boutilimit. So I urged on my camel, leaving it to my escort to keep up with me as best they could, they being less well mounted than I was.

Meïmoun particularly had his work cut out not to be left behind. The Emir had provided him with a lame camel advising him to change it en route. At first he trotted behind us. Each time I turned his silhouette was further behind. I could just make out his smooth shiny head like a ball of polished mahogany, and could see him unremittingly beating the flanks of the wretched beast. Then he disappeared altogether, and I only saw him at brief intervals throughout the day. Each time he would be on a different camel requisitioned on the way, in spite of the protests of their owners. At one time he appeared with the camel's owner, a shepherd, riding pillion behind him. The shepherd was calling Moulana to witness that the camel was already requisitioned by the authorities, or that it belonged to some powerful chief and that the affair would land him in prison. But it was of no avail: the *hartani* of the Emir was not to be imposed upon, and Meïmoun rode on with his reluctant passenger.

Camels that one does not know what to do with are abandoned to the care of God, and they generally manage to find their way back to their camps, unless on the way they are borrowed by other travellers, in which case they may be taken far afield.

And then one day—it may be the next moon or the next year—moved by a desire to get away from his tribe for a while, to listen to and tell stories, taste new foods and look at other women than those of his tent, the owner of the camel may take it into his head to set off in search of it. He will go by easy stages, seeking news and glasses of tea, welcoming every meeting and ready for any detour. He will journey without haste or anxiety. Time does not matter. And even if it is at the other end of the country he will always end by recovering the stray animal, whose neck is branded with his mark.

It is in this way that news is carried round the country, that the blood of tribes is mixed, and the social life of the Trab-el-Beïdane is maintained.

By midday I had got to the wells of Inierk. I had just finished my meal of boiled millet and sour milk when an old *marabout* entered my tent and greeted me. He sat down opposite and stared at me for some time before he spoke.

"I thank Moulana for having led you to my camp," he said. "I did not hope to see you as I knew you had already got to Boutilimit. Where is your sister?"

Mohamden-ould-Soufi, without having left this isolated spot, knew the whole of our itinerary from Port Étienne onwards, the names of all our various travelling companions and those of the nomads in whose camps we had stayed. He too had wanted to receive us and was anxious at Marion's absence!

Another old man came in and squatted beside us.

"This man," said the *marabout*, introducing him, "has come over from his camp because he heard of your arrival."

He then produced an old leather case from which he took out a bundle of papers tied up with a leather thong. He held out two letters for me to look at. One of them, a small sheet yellow with years, read as follows:

> Mohamden-ould-Soufi, a member of the Djemmâa *[assembly of the notables of his tribe]* of the Ouled-Daiman tribe is

authorized to travel from Mederdra to Saint Louis.
6 January 1904.   Coppolani.
*Le secretaire général en mission,
délégue du gouverneur
général en pays maures.*

While I read it Mohamden threw back his fine patriarch's head as his mind went back to the proud times of his youth. After thirty years, the memory of Coppolani, the great hero of the pacification, lived on in this quiet forceful handwriting on a bit of squared paper torn out of a notebook. This commonplace order had been reverently preserved along with letters from Cheikh-Sidia and copies of miraculous prayers.

The other sheet was larger and quite new. I read with astonishment that "Mohamden-ould-Soufi, chief of the Idag-Bahani group of the Ouled-Daïman tribe, had paid 100 francs for himself and 150 francs for his group as voluntary contributions towards the funding of the short term debt."

I could not understand what such financial matters could have to do with the old priest.

"Why did you pay that?" I asked.

"I wanted to please the *agent spécial*," he answered.

The *agent spécial* is the much dreaded person who at each of the posts is authorized to collect the taxes.

As we got further south trees became more plentiful. On the trunks of the flowering gum trees the great beads of gum were oozing which the slaves collected with a little sickle mounted on the end of a long stick. They worked five days for their masters and two for themselves.

Formerly the gum had been a valuable article of trade, being bartered on board European ships on the Senegal River for glass beads and cotton stuffs, and in more recent times being sold. But the use of gum had been greatly affected by the introduction of dextrine. The production in the south of Mauretania was still some 3000 tons a year, but the price had fallen from six francs a kilo in 1927 to as little as one franc in 1934.

Gum trees that had died from old age or from the rough treatment they received were never replaced. Such trees belonged to God, to whom alone it belonged to cause them to grow or not, as he thought fit. To plant a palm or gum tree would have been an audacious, and even impious act. This superstition was the more respected because it accorded perfectly with the laziness and improvidence of the natives.

The prairie and the bushes were already dried up. Between the thickets the passage of herds had traced hollow tracks. Towards the evening we got on to the French road which joins Mederdra to Nouakchott. The workmen requisitioned for the maintenance of the roads were filling up the ruts with the hard straw of the *markeba* so that lorries could pass. They saluted us as we passed and pointed out to M'Hammed the nearest camp, that of Boudafia, which was some way off the road, well hidden behind gum trees.

I thought it would be as well to sleep there, as there was no question of getting to Mederdra that night.

It was a camp of *marabouts*, and my three companions showed a great veneration for the old Moukhtar who received us.

Women and slaves charmed my sleep with the sound of a tom-tom very different from those I had heard in the warriors' camps.

A woman chanted the verses of a song which she accompanied with a drum, while two choruses of women came in alternately at the refrain. The voice of the principal singer was grave and beautiful; those of the choruses of an indescribable savage sadness. The songs were pious hymns, stories of the prophets, or some long recital of an exodus. Around the kneeling singers, other women danced religious dances, lifting their black veils against the blue night sky with slow silent movements.

I never came across any other music and dancing of this style. No others ever expressed religious fervour like these singers and dancers. In their performance I felt more keenly than ever the immense fatalism of these people and their capacity for complete self-abandonment in prayer.

Next day we followed a narrow white path which wound in and out between the thickets and the prairie. The latter with its tall dry grasses resembled fields of ripe corn. As the morning drew on we approached Mederdra, and by eleven o'clock we were in the courtyard of the post.

There were four or five houses of yellow *pisé*, beds of flowers, tennis courts, small forts, and pigeons flying about. There was also the native village of tents and huts. Below was a large valley of grey clay running south-west towards the Kachim.

The commanding officer was absent at the moment, and it was the *agent spécial* who received me.

In spite of previous experiences I had not yet got used to colonial hospitality and felt rather shy. But this visit was to lead to permanent friendship.

The *agent spécial* seemed rather astonished at my appearance — a Beïdane who was nevertheless a Frenchwoman. He asked me where I had come from, and I told him I was travelling from the *Mahssar*.

He offered me refreshments, but I answered rather formally that he was not to bother. I was only stopping for a moment—just long enough to telephone to Boutilimit—and then I should be off again for the *salines*.

At this he laughed and explained that in Mauretania if one rides eighty kilometres for a telephone call, the latter could not be done so perfunctorily as if one was just stepping into a Paris post-office. He took me into his house. I dare say he was influenced by my appearance and thought that both I and my clothes could do with a good wash.

An hour later I was washed and sitting in a borrowed blouse and *siroual* at a delicious *déjeuner*. I had already telephoned to Marion.

In this unaccustomed comfort I relaxed and began to realize how tired I was. And after the hard riding we had done the camels too were in need of rest. So it was not till the morning two days later that I set out again with my little escort, taking the route to the Dahar. In the meantime the commanding officer had returned, and I had been entertained by him and his wife, and had secured from the local merchants supplies of tea, sugar, and tobacco.

At the same time another caravan was travelling in the opposite direction. It was that of a Polish vet. who was going round the wells vaccinating the herds. Incidentally the Moors have for ages practised a kind of primitive vaccination, making an incision in the muzzles of the calves.

When I saw it I realized, not without some confusion, the kind of caravan a European ought to have if he has any self-respect. A whole band of attendants were strapping boxes and baggage of all kinds on to the backs of pack-camels. There was a camp bed, blankets, folding table and chair, canteens, a portable stove and a large stock of tinned foods.

The whole array was certainly impressive, but I could not help wondering how many orders had to be given each day for the proper utilization of all these things, and I thought with horror of the complications which all this comfort must involve.

***

I had by this time got accustomed to camels. I could mount easily, and could surrender myself to being rocked by their supple, swinging step. The fine *azouzel* I was now riding was responsive to the least murmur or to the slightest pressure of my bare foot against its warm woolly shoulder. I liked this *entente* between man and beast. But it must be confessed that I had not yet learnt to spare my mount, nor to look after its food and rest.

At every stop I would seek the shelter of a tent and share a meal with nomads. Our hobbled camels would wander off by little steps in search of pasture —thorny bushes or dry grasses—but I took no further interest in their welfare.

My escort was well disposed and surrounded me with attentions. They carefully filtered the water through their tunics before giving it me to drink, and scraped away the sand and cinders from the surface of the meat before offering me the choicest bits. My *tassoufra* had less secrets for M'Hammed than it had for me. At the bottom of it my revolver slept permanently, rolled up in a bit of stuff. It had greatly amused the Moors, while the Europeans had smiled at it, saying that in case of trouble it could at any rate serve to give me a decent suicide. But as from my point of view a living slave is better than a free woman dead, I put it aside without regret.

Yes, this life was good, under the invariable blue sky. I had now been living it for five weeks, but it seemed to me that I had never lived any other— nor did I desire to.

Every evening, surrounded by the naive admiration of *marabouts*, the praises of Me'imoun, and the flattery of my two warriors, I abandoned myself with all simplicity of heart to the pleasure of being a queen!

I could imagine no end to this marvellous trip. I did not yet know the exhaustion, the hunger and thirst, the storms, and the instability of the Moors, the illness which one drags from camp to camp under a sun that gets more scorching every day, the great solitudes of the north where vast sterile tracts of land are unpeopled because the wells have dried up, and all the other ordeals which the future had in store for Marion and me.

The evening of the second day, between the dunes which concealed the horizon to the west, we could see a hollow which, as we approached, gradually took on the proportions of an immense amphitheatre.

The high dunes of Charim, red with the setting sun, encircled a strange sort of lake, shining and unruffled. On the beach of white sand which edged it, dark green samphires were growing, twisted by the wind, like those of the Breton salt-marshes. On the sides of the dunes I could see the thin spurge bushes and titarek.

We were getting into the country of the Dahar, and before us was the salt-marsh or *sebkha* of Touidermi. Beyond Charim was a long narrow plain, beyond that the dunes of Sbar, and then the Atlantic. A cold wind brought us the smell and noise of the sea.

We went up to the *sebkha*, which was composed of hard grey mud with holes dug here and there where the salt was being extracted. At the edge of the *sebkha* sacks and bars of salt were waiting to be removed by a caravan.

The slaves of the *Cadi* of Mederdra, who dug out the salt, had finished their day's work. They ran up to us and entertained us to the best of their ability in their humble tents.

I left them early the next morning, and rode on to the great *sebkha* of N'Térert, the most important of the whole littoral. This one too was encircled by an austere circle of dunes, the dunes of Terouma, but it was much larger still than Touidermi covering an area of some forty-four acres.

When I arrived the salt-workings were in full activity. In every hole were black slaves up to the knees in the wet salt mud which they were bailing out with calabashes, tins and spoon-shaped shovels. Where they had been splashed by it their bodies were covered by a glistening crust of salt.

At the edge of the *sebkhas* a troop of donkeys were trotting along. Each carried two large slabs of salt some five inches thick and together weighing a good hundred kilos. They were carrying them to Rosso. Other similar slabs, white and hard as marble, were lying about the place. They looked rather like tombstones, and with the holes dug in the ground and the general desolation of the scene, the effect was very funereal.

At N'Térert, as at Touidermi, the salt lay in regular compact layers under the covering of mud. When the latter was removed the slaves cut out the salt with axes. There were four layers of salt separated by thin layers of mud. When the upper layer of salt was removed, the water of the saturated mud beneath would invade the working and would have to be bailed out before the next layer could be got at. The second layer was not of such good quality as the first, but the best layer of all was the bottom one, which was nearly ten inches thick.

Not counting the efflorescences of salt and that which lay outside the central part where the workings were concentrated, it has been estimated that N'Térert contains not much less than two hundred thousand tons of salt.

When the rains come in winter they dissolve the splinters of salt in the workings, but this crystallizes out again by evaporation.

N'Térert, Touidermi, and a few other *sebkhas* to the south of no great importance constitute the *Salines* of the Dahar. There are also the *Salines* of the Aftout near the sea which produce salt in coarse granulated form in unlimited quantity. Here the *sebkhas* get flooded by the winter rains. Later as they dry, the salt that has been dissolved is deposited in crystals over the whole surface. The most important of these *sebkhas*, Tin-Djemaran, could produce over a hundred and fifty thousand tons of salt a year from its hundred and fifty acres, if properly exploited. But the Moors only get four or five thousand tons a year from the workings of the Dahar and the Aftout together.

The salt is bought from the slaves at five to seven francs the hundred kilos by native merchants who transport it by caravans and boats to Senegal or the Sudan.

Before the French occupation the salt trade, like the gum trade, was relatively free. Anybody could come to buy salt from the negro village of Keur-Massen on the Senegal River, and it was there that the Moors bartered their salt for millet, cotton and spices. There was a tax paid to the Emir of the Trarza. He had a representative at Keur-Massen who collected a tenth of the value of the salt sold or exchanged. And the caravans going to the Sudan were taxed before leaving the *sebkhas*. This tax was equivalent to fifty centimes for an ass's load, twice that for a bull's and three times for a camel's.

The French gabelle, called the *n'koubel*, amounting to ten francs on every hundred kilos extracted, soon ruined the market of Keur-Massen and the negroes of Dara and Tigmaten for whom the salt trade was the principal source of livelihood. The tribes too in the west of the Trarza, who also took part in this trade, got discouraged. For it was not only the gabelle itself that mattered, there was also the *zekkat*, the annual tax of six francs per head on all camels, a further tax of sixty francs a year on every camel employed to carry goods, and various other trading dues. If one considers, moreover, that a pack-camel could only be kept at this arduous work for six months in the year, it is easy to understand that most of the old traders preferred to sleep in their tents rather than undertake the long journey to sell salt on the Senegal River. It is also understandable that smuggling was not infrequent.

The French had already reduced the salt-tax, but, defrauded by the native collectors, they found it in the end preferable to hand over their rights to the Emir in exchange for a fixed rent. Those engaged in the trade could only rejoice to find themselves once more under their old master. For, however grasping he might be, he had at least the sense not to kill the goose that laid the golden eggs.

With a little literary skill it would not be difficult to paint a hellish picture, or at least a purgatorial one, of these mournful *sebkhas*, with the slaves floundering in the salt mud. In fact the salty crust on their bodies could easily pass for some hideous leprosy. One would not need to add that the said leprosy dissolves every evening in the fresh water from the wells of Benaman, from which the slaves return to their camps with skins shining, wearing turbans and fresh *chandorah*.

All the same the *sebkhas* are by no means a paradise.

They are simply workings—places where men bend before necessity and earn their bread by the sweat of their brows. Incidentally they earn it amply, that is if I can trust the word of M'Hammed, who assured me, not without an envious look, that 'the slaves of the salt, it is too rich.'

These slaves sell direct to the traders. Afterwards they share with their masters, keeping part for themselves. The reckoning is left very much in their hands, for the masters are much too grand to come paddling around in the mud of the *sebkhas*. At N'Térert the masters were either Ould-Deïd himself or tribes that were vassals of his. At Touidermi it was the *Cadi* of Mederdra.

In four hours two men can cut out of the top layer four slabs weighing fifty kilos each. As a rule it is only the top layer that is worked. If they only get six francs for two slabs, it must be remembered that in the Trarza that is the common price for a sheep. Thus the slaves working in the *sebkhas*, like those collecting gum, are rich enough to have flocks of their own, and their wives can wear jewels. I saw one with such heavy rings around her ankles that she could hardly walk. They wear great lumps of amber attached to their hair and falling over their foreheads, which are their patrimony, even a kind of savings bank, for they will never sell them but will exchange them for bigger ones whenever they have the means.

There is a Moorish proverb which says: If you meet a slave bedecked with jewels, you may be sure she owes them only to God and to herself.

There are many ways of 'only owing one's jewels to oneself.' If the slave, having one night pleased her master, increases in girth as well as in the possession of pearls, she experiences neither shame nor remorse. On the contrary, her son will become a freed slave.

And if she has twins she will herself become a *hartania*, living honoured in her master's camp, and exempt from all heavy labour.

The workers of N'Térert included every sort and condition of slave. Among those who ran towards me, driven by curiosity from the holes in which they were working, were rich and poor, negroes and half-castes. Some were proud of the fact that their families had belonged to the same warriors for many generations; others, bought quite young, had served several masters. Some owed their present situation to war indemnities or commercial exchanges. Those whose fate had been settled in the neighbourhood of a French post had not been bought, but had been hired for ninety years.

There were also *haratine* that had been liberated for various reasons: birth, exceptional service, friendship of their masters—or they might have bought their freedom. One of them who had been ill-treated had availed himself of an old custom to get a new master. He chose someone he would like to serve and managed to catch him asleep, then making a slight cut in his ear. By this act he himself became the 'price of blood' which his old master, responsible for the acts of his slave, must pay to the victim.

These slaves had a chief for themselves, a slave too. He was a very decorative person, an immense brute, extremely proud, but kindly almost to the point of weakness. He was dressed in a short dark blue tunic and wore one of those magnificent turbans of which slaves have the secret. A glittering knife was stuck in his belt, and he was never to be seen without a great knotty stick which he carried as the insignia of his dignity. It was this man who conducted business with the caravans and settled accounts with the Emir and the *Cadi*.

It was plainly visible that all these slaves were really happy, living in the peaceful condition of humble people heart to heart with nature, with neither ambition, nor hate, nor useless complications of existence, whose only care is their daily task.

M'Hammed and Bendir, when they did not happen to know their names, would call them *lhamm*, which is the word for meat. But they did so without malice or scorn, simply because it was the customary appellation. The slaves on their side were not shy. They and my escort joked together with hearty laughter and sound slaps on the shoulder.

There was no question of any more work being done on a day marked by so flattering a visit, which made a pretext for games and dances. The whole band with their chief at their head escorted me to a dune where the negresses with their floating veils had rigged an extempore tent to save me the trouble of going over to their camp. Three girls, who had taken part in the fête given in my honour the night before at Touidermi, were climbing up the side of the dune beating tom-toms as they went.

T'barek Allah. Praise be to God. The stranger is come among us.

It was at N'Térert that Bendir lost any chances he ever had of going on the *grand voyage* he had set his heart on.

I was counting on making a trip to the shore during the afternoon. I was possessed by an irresistible longing to see the sea again. But as soon as we had drunk our tea, Bendir informed me that he was going over to a camp near by where there were *marabouts* who would lend him camels. He assured me he would not be long, and I watched him ride off without any misgiving about his return. Riding with him was Sidi, a boy belonging to one of the warrior tribes, whose camel Meïmoun had seized *en route*. It was quite a good camel which the boy was taking to its new owner at Rosso. The boy, after many vain protests, resigned himself, like the others whose camels we had taken, to making a tour with us as a pillion rider. But this afternoon he had a camel to himself, so that only left us with two: my own *azouzel* and an old beast that was on its last legs.

The sun slipped little by little down into the west, and we had to give up all hope of getting to the sea, for Bendir did not reappear, and we could not go, the three of us, M'Hammed, Meïmoun and myself, on one camel.

After the siesta, slaves and their wives claimed my attention with songs and mimes, a heritage of ancient Sudanese traditions.

A young woman placed a calabash on the ground upside down. The chorus began singing: *Look at the little crocodile! Look, look at the crocodile*. And they continued the song interminably, clapping their hands and holding them out towards the crocodile. Meanwhile, a dancer approached slowly, cautiously, a knife in her hand. In mime

Bird Dance; on the left the Dancer is imitating the Marabou

she portrayed the search of the hunter, the discovery, and then fear. ... And all the time the song went on: *Look, look at the crocodile*. And the chorus seemed to press the dancer forward to her quarry. With priest-like dignity of movement she came forward again. In her trembling hands the knife glittered before her face. Her whole body was trembling and bent, weighed down, with anguish. She leaped into the air with starts of fear and dashes of courage. ... And in the end she killed the little calabash-crocodile to the accompaniment of triumphant *you-yous* and a wild thundering of the drum.

A strange bird was squatting, all hunched up, by the drum. It was the dancer again. She was now covered entirely by dark blue veils. She was imitating a bird, the marabou, the stork with long beak and pointed head. To imitate the latter the dancer held her hands above her head and held a stick in them, all this too being covered by her veil. The chorus started singing:

Adanaï, Adanaï, n'goup abakh! Black bird, marabou, eat your millet.

The bird approached the drum, held up its head, hesitated, bent its neck, leant over the drum and began with little pecks to eat its millet. At first the pecking on the drum was timid, then bolder and quicker, the beak rapping out a sonorous rhythm on the stretched sheepskin of which the drum was made. The light hands of the women around beat like wings. The stuff which covered the dancer was brilliant like plumage.

Adanaï, Adanaï, eat jour millet.

But now the chorus changed. The women were now peasants and their tone was menacing. With *you-yous* and the clapping of hands they chased the bird away from their fields.

Then they in turn were pursued by men who held sticks against their bellies and ran after the women with erotic menaces. Of their faces all that could be seen were their great rolling eyes, black and white, which showed through the opening on their enormous *aouli*s. The men surrounded the women dancing wildly. Shouts and laughter mingled in confusion. Bronze arms with frenzied hands were held up above the whirlwind of veils and sand. A dull beat was hammered on the drum.

The men had gone. The chorus of women had formed again in a circle. A piercing cry called:

Bouissa! Bouissa!

Obedient to the call of her companions a girl lay down on the sand. Hannah, the dancer, advanced slowly towards her, to the song of the chorus which was set in a minor key:

I am happy. God be praised! Bouissa is sleeping.

The dancer had thrown open her *malahfa* showing her proud breasts. She danced with her necklaces jangling. *Bouissa, Bouissa!* Her steps got quicker and quicker; her flying shawl prolonged her supple gestures.

Bouissa is sleeping. Bouissa, Bouissa! The song became more tender under the evening sky. The drum beat gently in the shadow. . . . Hannah leant over the sleeping figure, barely stroking it with her trembling hands—trembling with desire. For an instant she lay on the recumbent form—it was the merest symbol—then she slipped, ecstatic, on to the sand, and then again sprang up to throw herself into a dance of voluptuous triumph.

Thus every day songs of primitive joy, simple and graceful, went up from the solitudes of the scrub in honour of the wanderer who passed.

T'barek Allah! Elhamdou lillahi! The Christian woman has come to visit us.

In front of my tent squatted a woman dressed in rags. She was faded, but must have been beautiful in her day. She seemed indifferent to the joy of the others. Beside her stood a good-looking child, whose skin, however, was too light in colour. Neither did he take any share in the general gaiety.

My curiosity was aroused and I questioned my companions. It was explained to me that the woman was of noble caste, a Ma-el-Aïnin of the Trarza who had 'got little one with a European.' Her tribe had cast her out and she had taken refuge with the slaves. For the folly of a night she was to be henceforward a beggar, a *meskin*, and her child a pariah.

She stared at me intently. But when I dropped in her lap a present for the child of my race, she did not thank me, and I was forced to turn my head away from the flash of hatred that lit up her dark eyes.

Night was now falling over the *sebkhas*, but still Bendir had not returned. The sea wind blew across the Aftout in icy gusts which swept under the upturned edges of the tent, exposed as the latter was on the summit of a dune.

Obviously we should have to sleep there, and I tried to convince M'Hammed and Meïmoun to arrange the tent so that we could get some shelter. My notions of comfort, however, passed the imagination of the slaves, while my own two attendants were too concerned with their dignity to do any work in front of servile people. Accordingly they assured me that it was impossible to lower the edges of the tent to the ground.

Not having been born in the desert myself, I was not prevented by dignity from displaying a little energy. But when the others saw me starting to move the tent pegs and the cords and bank up the sand against the draught, they rushed forward, bursting with laughter. The sight of a European woman working was so comic that to help me now became a game.

The tent was made almost comfortable, and rolling myself in an old sheepskin I warmed myself with scalding tea. Meanwhile, Meïmoun started on a panegyric interspersed by wild cries to express his naive enthusiasm.

"Yes, yes, I know what I say. You are little but your heart is big, big. Moulana wished you to be strong. You come into the scrub with no European, no family, no sharpshooters, no fiance, ach! You have no helmet, no luggage, and you are not tired. . . . And now you know how to arrange a tent better than we do! *Ouallahi!* . . ."

Meïmoun had a way of hiding a gentle soul beneath a furious countenance. It was really very funny to watch this grandiloquent old man with his flashing, angry-looking eyes, waving his long thin arms above the lamp, while his distorted shadow above him on the tent seemed to imitate and mock him. With his fist he struck his hairless head.

"Ah! *Ouallahi!* you are great. You have thought all that in your head. Soon you will be going back to your own country. Meïmoun will never see you again, and you will forget the poor Meïmoun."

I made a suggestion: "Perhaps, if I asked him, Ould-Deïd would give me Meïmoun, and I could take him to France."

But this proposal terrified him. Holding towards me the palms of his hands he implored my pity. No, no, he wanted to go back to the *Mahssar*, see Toutou married, and teach the Emir's sons to ride a camel. . . . Yes, really, his heart was there in the Emir's camp. . . . And then he wanted to send away his old Mabrouka to marry a young slave he had seen at Touidermi. With vehemence he assured me that a white cotton *boubou*, bought at Mederdra would suffice to perpetuate my memory—still more if I gave him a new *aouli* too. . . .

"No, no, by the Prophet (and may his name be blessed), you must say nothing to Ould-Deïd. For if he has given you his best camel, how could he refuse you a poor old *hartani?* "

Suddenly Meïmoun and his shadow stopped dead as Bendir and Sidi made their appearance. They started to explain, but a triple volley of abuse cut them short. All the same, Bendir finally got in a few words: After a whole day of negotiations they had secured two good camels; they had worked for the good of everybody, and now God could witness their shame and our ingratitude! With an air of disgust they retired to a corner of the tent to dream of the pretty slaves who had made them forget the passage of time.

Some slaves brought in a calabash of milk and made a big fire whose flames lit up the disdainful profiles of the two camels who, with their knees tied, were peacefully ruminating, careless of their destiny and indifferent to the quarrels of men.

***

Although we had left N'Térert at dawn, it was night before I reached the great tent of Mahamedzen-ould Mohammed-Fall, the *Cadi*, whose camp was near Mederdra. I could hardly walk, I was so tired.

It was a very fine tent indeed, enclosing a space about twenty metres long and five wide. It was made of thick stuff, and when rolled up it was so big and heavy that it required a string of twelve pairs of asses to carry it. It was lined with a Sudanese cotton stuff made of narrow strips sewn together. Its whiteness was almost dazzling. The posts were of hard yellow *aguilal* wood. The pegs were ornamented with poker-work. From the wooden spine of the tent hung long fringes of white, beige and black wool mixed with coloured cotton. Fine matting with a satin-like surface covered the sand.

This tent was the centre of a very large camp. For besides his family, his pupils and his slaves, Maham-edzen, a powerful and venerated *marabout*, gave protection to a multitude of poor people who rigged up their ragged tents all round.

All this I saw next morning. All I saw on my arrival was this lovely white-lined tent, so marvellously clean.

We had ridden fifty kilometres, only resting a short while at midday. (The Moors believe that at midday the sun itself stops still in the sky.) We rode late in the darkness in spite of the difficulty of avoiding the thorny bushes. We had not come across any camp the whole day.

I was quite exhausted. My drooping eyelids hardly allowed me to see the face of my host, a handsome old man who was sitting opposite me. Paternally he said:

"My slaves are not putting up the stranger's tent for you. You will stay in my own tent, as my daughter or my sister."

We were surrounded by young people, silent and thoughtful. Mahamedzen's wife retired with her servants to one end of the tent. At the other end some leather cushions had been placed for me against chests containing books.

I can just remember a little wild-cat which was playing with the loose end of Mahamedzen's turban and one of those enormous tame sheep which are kept by the rich and which come into the tents to get their share of tea, milk and *méchoui*. Then sinking on to the cushions I fell into a dreamless sleep.

To wake up and find a woman leaning over you with a greasy black face and holding in one hand an enormous knife, in the other a little naked baby, might well make you doubt your sanity. Astonished, I rubbed my eyes, but the strange being wished me good-morning in the most friendly manner and called her step-son.

A young man dressed in white came forward and gracefully presented himself, followed by a slave bringing tea. This was the

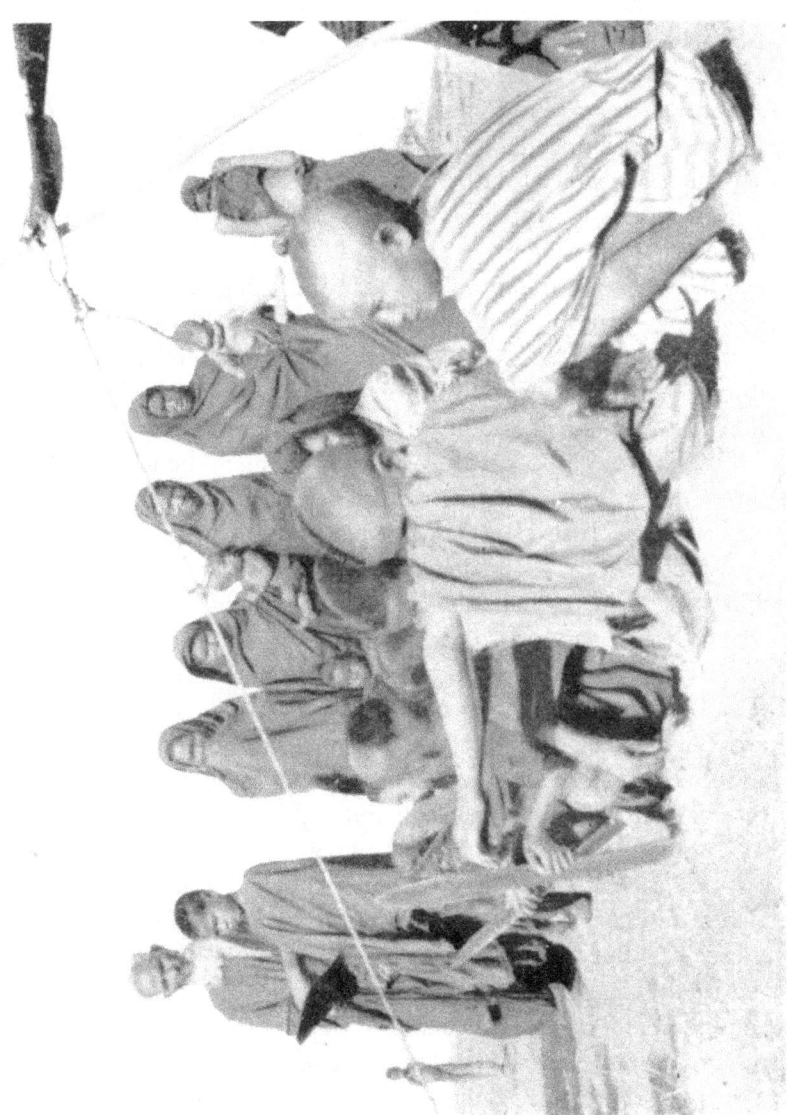
A native School

eldest son of Mahamedzen, whom he was destined one day to succeed at the court of Mederdra. He had just finished his studies at Saint Louis, where he had done brilliantly. He spoke excellent French, called me *madame*, and unlike the others addressed me in the second person plural. He asked a lot of questions about France, speaking very intelligently. And he told me how pleased he was that the absence of his father, who had been called to Mederdra, enabled him to talk to me in the tent in spite of the presence of his step-mother.

Attachment to traditions is a beautiful thing, but I could not help being somewhat taken aback when this intelligent, educated young man explained to me without the slightest embarrassment why his stepmother, who had recently had a baby, was obliged to cover her face with a thick coating of soot and butter.

"This custom is observed by Moorish women," he told me, "to frighten away evil spirits that threaten a new-born baby for the first forty days. It also has another object: to discourage a husband from approaching a woman who was still unclean.... And the big knife which you saw in her hand—she will not put it down, either, during these forty days. It is a symbolic weapon against Iblis, the chief of demons.... When the child is born the warriors fire their rifles, but we *marabouts* say prayers. Giving the child a name is postponed till the seventh day, so that the evil spirits shall be kept in ignorance of its existence as long as possible. That day is a great feast day: animals are sacrificed, and the humblest beggars, the 'poor of God,' receive their share. And slaves celebrate the occasion with music and dancing. Those of the tribe who can write compose poems extolling the child's ancestors and the qualities of its family, and wishing him a happy life agreeable to God."

I listened to the young man versed in science and letters, both Arabic and French, and I looked at his step-mother, Selima, covered with greasy soot. They belonged to the same family. They were rooted in the same race; a race composed of men of faith and of credulity, who in the face of an arid hostile nature forget their destitution in dreams of an imaginary world, peopled by good and evil spirits; men who, possessing nothing, adore a God from whom nothing is asked and whose sacred will must be obeyed without murmur.

Chapter VI

Men and Camels

IN the courtyard of the post of Boutilimit, near the eastern gate, M'Hammed and his nephew, Mokhtar-Saloum, were trying to squeeze on to the saddles of four camels a quantity of baggage which, during the journey from Memrhar to the Trarza, had been carried by a minimum of six. Their efforts were accompanied by invocations to Moulana, to the Prophet, and to the latter's family, as well as by maledictions, sighs and blows. During the last two hours several skeins of the cord made of baobab fibre and many straps had been used up, but there were still several items to be tied on: a large *faro* of black lambs' skin, two tin cans, a kettle, a camera, and a wild-cat cub that mewed behind the bars of its box.

In spite of the difficulties with which they were contending, these two young men had to keep their brows serene and their *aouli*s at the right angle. They had to watch the gracefulness of their movements, and see that their new tunics fell in the proper folds. For they were working under the eyes of a crowd that regarded them with mixed feelings: those of derision, admiration, envy, and pity.

In the front rank of the crowd were all the Europeans of the place: recent arrivals who would much enjoy a journey through the scrub and old *habitués* who were laughing in their sleeves and whispering to one another: "A lot of fuss for nothing: The caravan will not get far."

On the right was the Emir and his suite; on the left Abdallahi with his. Then there were the chief interpreter, his assistant, the schoolmaster, Abdo Galilar, and the merchants and other notables of the village. Behind, were some native sharpshooters, the water-carrier with his asses, and the prisoners who, to see better, climbed up on to the pile of *banco* bricks with which they were building a house. The rest of the courtyard was filled with a mixed population of servants, smiths, herdsmen, prostitutes, concubines, slaves and children—hordes of children, all the children of Boutilimit, Moors, blacks and half castes. A line of children formed a frieze along the top of the wall.

The air was full of predictions and comments; for everybody had travelled further than his neighbour and knew better than anyone else how to choose a camel, load it, and look after it during a long and difficult journey. Envious looks were cast on the 'boys' who, on the most slender pretext, would push their way past the others and fuss round the camel looking as important as they could.

The departure of a European caravan is always an important event. Still more important was this one on Friday, March 2nd. For not only were two Frenchwomen setting off alone with Moors, but the journey was to be a very long one. Those among the crowd who were well informed described our route to their more ignorant neighbours: Aleg, Kaédi M'Bout, Kiffa, Tidjikja, Moudjéria. How many moons would wax and wane before our return? How could these unarmed infidels escape the clutches of jinn, marauders, lions, elephants and horned vipers? To say nothing of the negroes of those parts, who grew more dangerous every day as they forgot their former masters, the Arabs!

The most optimistic approved of our departure when the moon was full, and on a Friday, a day propitious for undertaking a journey. And they calculated that we would still have two months— the Second-month-after-the-Breaking-of-the-Fast and the Month-of-the-Feast-of-the-Sacrifice—before the dreaded month of Achour (coinciding this year with the month of May), which was famous for the overpowering heat and drought which heralded the season of storms in the eastern districts.

Yes, there were a lot of people there. Only one was missing and he unfortunately was the District Commandant, who had gone off on a tour the day before. Unfortunately: for he was the only one that could have told us the truth about the soundness of our camels, the excess of our baggage, and the general incapacity of the two young men on whom fell the responsibility for our security and provisioning, in fact, the whole success of the journey.

It is true that M'Hammed did say with a long sigh that we really were taking too much. But was it too much for the camels or too much trouble for him? . . . We consulted the authorities around us, who, not wanting the bother of hurriedly finding us pack-camels, answered that everything was all right as it was, and that a camel could easily trot with a load of three hundred kilos on its back....

For the moment M'Hammed and Mokhtar-Saloum were away shopping in the village, buying salt for their family with whom we should be camping in two days' time at the wells of Dekhone. The camels ruminated under their loads. The Moors, knowing well how long it took to bargain over a lump of salt and say goodbye to some pretty little cousins, sat down where they were in patient groups. While carrying on with our compatriots the sort of conversation that usually takes place on railway platforms, we saw the sun sink slowly down behind the buildings. For two weeks we had been waiting for this departure: what difference could an hour or two extra make!

It had all come about in this way. On my return from Mederdra the Commandant was away from Boutilimit. The interpreter told us that we were not to bother about either camels or outfit, Abdallahi making himself personally responsible for everything. To start with, he sent us a very beautiful *tassoufra* and a leather case containing a letter of introduction to the *marabout*ic tribes we should come to on the way. He would see to the rest as soon as the Commandant had returned.

No date was mentioned for our departure, but we had no other course than to thank him and wait patiently for the fulfilment of his promises. After his handsome offer we should have given him great offence had we taken any steps to buy or hire camels. Nor would it have been easy to do, and the price would have been ruinous.

Then one day Ould-Deïd arrived. He too had written a cordial letter of introduction for the warlike tribes. He would also like to provide a camel, but like Abdallahi he would wait for the return of the Commandant.

The reader may perhaps wonder why I had not kept the fine *azouzel* I had been riding. Simply because, when I got to Mederdra from the *Salines* I found the Emir's chief *hartani* waiting for me. He had been sent from the *Mahssar* to recover Meïmoun and the camel.

Each day's delay brought the hot season nearer. Great efforts were made by a number of people to secure appointment to our escort. Men would come to us and proclaim their devotion, punctuated by heavy thumps on their chests. Intrigues were set on foot; alliances were concluded—and betrayed; long-cherished hopes were disappointed, to be supplanted by others or by resignation. And all this for the sake of honour and five francs a day.

In the end M'Hammed got us to engage his 'little brother,' who was really a nephew or a cousin—we never found out quite what relation he was—a young man of modest demeanour and the profile of a Persian prince. M'Hammed assured us that Mokhtar-Saloum would obey him implicitly and that we should only have to give our orders to him and he would see that our wishes were carried out. These two seemed to be bound by ties of tender affection. They would walk about the place linked by their little fingers, which I found very touching in young men in their twenties.

The ninth day the Commandant's car appeared in the court of honour.

Camels were produced. The Emir's contribution was an awful hack with a bleeding sore on its nose and a wounded leg. Abdallahi's was a young *azouzel* which looked good, and which he had bought for a hundred and fifty francs, from M'Hammed, with a she-camel and her foal. M'Hammed had assured Abdallahi that it was the very mount I had been wanting. Needless to say, I had never seen the beast, which, when I tried it, revealed a character that can only be described as fantastic, and a trot brutal enough to unhook one's soul.

I complained to Abdallahi, and the deal was cancelled. M'Hammed when accused of lying, broke out into an innocent laugh and suggested that we could quite well change it *en route*, but I had already seen enough of that method of procuring camels. Then after endless hunting, bargaining, and complications of all sorts, one of the men I had refused as escort revenged himself by providing a camel at a stiff price. It was a big animal and its good looks spurred the Emir to rivalry, and at the last minute he replaced the one he had given.

Both Ould-Deïd and Abdallahi were greatly distressed by the fact that there had not been time (only twelve days!) to bring us some really splendid camels from their pastures.

But if our caravan only inspired us with a modicum of confidence, at any rate it was ready at last.

We had intended to set off after the siesta, but it was twilight before we were actually riding through the village. It was very late, but the essential thing had been done: we had started. The first stage would be done by moonlight.

***

It was the first time we had ridden a stage by night, the first time we saw what the Sahara was like when brilliantly lit up by the moon. It was a revelation. The camels noiselessly trod down the silver grasses as we rode through the translucid country. Luminous dunes rose out of shadowy hollows. There was no breath of wind, not a murmur of any sound, no sensation of heat or cold: nothing but the exciting though rather awe-inspiring impression of floating through a phosphorescent and enchanted world.

After riding for an hour, Marion suddenly felt her camel give way beneath her. It was the one Ould-Deïd had given. It knelt down without any previous warning, which was very disquieting. M'Hammed's shouts got it on its feet again, but in its effort to rise a cord broke with a snap releasing a *tassoufra* and the kettle.

Our saddles were dragged this way and that with weight of our equipment, and of course we swayed too. The third time Marion's camel stopped I took advantage of the delay to re-set my saddle, which had now swung over to an angle of forty-five degrees. Next, the rebellious camel began to make efforts to lighten his burden by rubbing it against those of the other camels, so that something would fall off, or by passing under the low branches of the acacias. Then he stopped once more and this time refused absolutely to go a step further. In the end, however, with M'Hammed holding the bridle and Mokhtar-Saloum belabouring the creature from behind, we managed somehow to get to the wells of Tiniark.

This camel lacked courage and training, but was not deficient in good sense. But what would happen if camels were to start giving their opinions on the undertakings of men? Anyhow, our affairs seemed to have begun very badly. It was useless to try to go on as we were, so Mokhtar-Saloum was sent back to Boutilimit with Marion's camel, and a letter of explanation.

It happened that at Tiniark we found a man who was delighted to put his bony camel and his own ill-fed person at our disposal to carry some of our things as far as the camp of the Ouled-Daman who, according to M'Hammed, possessed wonderful herds.

The next day was drawing to a close when Mokhtar-Saloum rejoined us with a short, thick-set *azouzel* that answered to the name of Boudaïl. A letter from the interpreter explained that Ould-Deïd had been mistaken in the first camel, and that he had not hesitated to pay even the exorbitant price of six hundred francs to provide us with a better one.

Our things were now distributed more reasonably on the five camels. I rode Boudaïl, leaving Marion to ride Abdallahi's camel, called Boukhzeïma, who pouted like an old hag but was nevertheless good-natured. Four camels to ride, two attendants, a pack-camel and a man to look after it: that was what our caravan now consisted of, in addition to ourselves. It was a modest caravan for two Europeans, but we considered it satisfactory, and with some variations we kept it like that all the way to Kiffa.

We had all been depressed by our bad start, but our spirits now rose. Songs were sung. Then some gazelles were sighted as they sped madly through the thorny bushes. This excited our young warriors, who immediately saw useful employment for the twenty-five cartridges they had got at Boutilimit.

In all the countries of the world special clothes are worn for war and hunting. For the latter the Beïdane puts on the 'green *boubou*.' This is a short tunic, the stuff soft from long use, the colour a mixture of browns and verdigris, derived from dirt, sand and *chandorah* dye. The black hair is hidden by a cotton cap which has acquired the same colours by the same means.

These clothes in themselves are nothing: it is the way in which they are worn that counts. There are three things that obey the

Moor: fire, camels, and stuffs. No one but he could transform into the tunic of Artemis this dirty and ragged article of clothing. It is drawn in at the waist by the long strip of stuff that normally makes the *aouli*, and it is so arranged as to leave the shoulders bare and the outer sides of the thighs. No one but he could look like an Assyrian archer under the homely nightcap of our great-grandfathers.

At the sight of the herd of gazelles M'Hammed stopped us near a clump of bushes. The two young men jumped off their camels leaving us to look after them and ran off in pursuit. They ran with small rapid steps hardly bending their knees at all. They kept this up for quite a long time until their figures gradually got confused with the grey-green of the bushes that they used as cover. They imitated the sound made by gazelles; they watched, darted here and there in zig-zags, and looked very cunning. Sometimes they separated to surround their quarry. Then we could no longer distinguish them at all, but suddenly two shots rang out almost simultaneously. It was a good idea to fire together, so that if anything was hit they could both claim the honour.

This time, however, there was no such result, though of course a number of gazelles were honourably wounded, though not sufficiently, it seemed, to affect the speed of their flight. The Beïdane really knows nothing of firing at a moving target. For him hunting is a sport of endurance and cunning—this patient cunning which is the genius of his race, and which takes the place of real intelligence and competence. But give him a whole day to stalk his quarry and he will not come home empty-handed. Even after he has exhausted it he will take aim for a long while before firing. This is how he has managed to acquire the reputation of being a good shot, but nobody will be impressed by it who knows the cartridges, time and trouble that are expended.

All the same, the morning of our arrival at Dekhone, M'Hammed and Mokhtar-Saloum brought in a fine gazelle which they had both shot and then cut its throat before its last breath in accordance with ritual. They cut it open and disembowelled it with their dirty little pocket-knives, and detached the bones of the feet, which they put away carefully in their cartridge pouches. With these they would later make pipes, after having first sucked the raw marrow. They then tied the boneless feet together and hung the animal from one of the saddles. Next they found the paunch among the entrails, opened it, and washed their hands with the thick green contents, drying them afterwards with a handful of sand. In times of drought and thirst the contents of the paunch would be strained through a rag, and the nauseating liquid thus obtained would be regarded as a precious drink.

They then put on their *sirouals* that had been removed for hunting.

"Why do you take off your *siroual* to hunt gazelles?" I asked M'Hammed.

"To run quicker, and not to get caught in thorns and *initi*," he answered

"But you run quickly enough for bustards and other animals, and there are just as many thorns, yet you keep them on."

Driven into a corner he could no longer be evasive, and he proceeded gravely to explain: "The *siroual*, there is piss and the dirty in it, and that not good for killing the *dami*." Then he politely changed the subject.

This is probably an observance so ancient that whatever reason it is based on has long been forgotten. And the Moors murmur *Bismillah* in taking off their dirty *sirouals* without pausing to wonder why one should have to be as pure for killing a *dami* as for saying a prayer.

The Ouled-Daman had been warned of our coming by Mokhtar-Saloum, who had ridden on ahead, and they had made thorough preparations to receive us. Volleys of rifle shots greeted us as we approached, and the warriors rode out to meet us. They conducted us to a pretty little tent which was very clean, and where the tea was already waiting for us. On three sides the tent was hung with bright-coloured striped Algerian blankets. These had reached Mauretania via Paris, having been bought at the Colonial Exhibition by M'Hammed.

Before long a slave brought in the roast gazelle. We were very comfortable and everybody was gay.

M'Hammed was married and was the father of a little boy. His wife and child were in a neighbouring tent from which we could hear the sound of jokes and laughter. M'Hammed was not the eldest of his family. He had an uncle and two older brothers in the company. He sat beside us during the meal, and it was not until it was over that he rose furtively and went off to greet his wife. We could see other women leave the tent discreetly, the last one drawing a white curtain which shut the opening of the tent.

It is difficult to imagine the perpetual constraint imposed on the Moors by their family customs. Tent life offers very little privacy. M'Hammed was only home for a few hours after a long absence, yet his wife could never be with him in public. The short times they had together seemed rather like clandestine meetings. If they caught sight of each other outside the tent, they would turn their heads quickly away. When we finally rode off M'Hammed said goodbye ceremoniously to all his other relations, but his wife sat to one side with her servants, and he did not so much as give her a glance. And if M'Hammed was playing with his son, and his uncle or one of his elder brothers appeared, somebody would immediately take the child away.

In front of his family M'Hammed showed off a good deal, making the most childish display of his familiarity with European things. He took photographs, pointing the camera the wrong way. He borrowed a pocket mirror and scissors to trim his moustache, took a dose of aspirin and then some quinine, and put some iodine on a scratch.

The others were duly impressed, and they too asked for medicines. The Moors adore medicines. Then a slave came to us, sent by a woman whose daughter was suffering from a strange illness.

She was a pretty little thing, three or four years old. On one of her buttocks was a plaster of gum arabic, encrusted with sand and camel dung. With a great deal of difficulty Marion managed to get them to boil some water, and while the poor child screamed in her mother's lap, she carefully bathed the swollen buttock which looked like a rotten apple. She succeeded in removing the crust on the surface, and then suddenly a mass of puss spurted out over the mother's *malahfa*, which latter was perfunctorily dried with a handful or two of sand.

We had already seen a good many of the Moor's medical practices. We had seen tobacco leaves used as a dressing for cuts, and cauterizations made on the head and temples of a child with incandescent camel dung as a remedy for ophthalmia; we had heard of horns used for cupping, and severe bleeding being used as a remedy for migraine, as well as all the amulets used against illnesses and accidents. But we had never imagined that anybody could be capable of shutting in an abscess with a coating of gum arabic.

A ragged old sorcerer, the doctor of the camp, looked on at the proceedings with a furious expression, muttering maledictions. But he probably reflected that, as we would be off again on the morrow, the field would soon be his again, and his manner changed to one of smiling obsequiousness. It was, after all, more profitable to cadge tobacco than to curse us. The lowly condition of doctors in Moorish society allows them to beg like the minstrels and the smiths.

Yes, as I have said before, there is great work to be done by European doctors and the Red Cross in the poor tents of the Sahara. And there could be no better way of securing the friendship of the nomads; for they have complete confidence and welcome any treatment offered them.

The only woman who had the right to go about the camp as she pleased and enter any tent without considering the age of the occupants was the old Mariam, M'Hammed's mother. She was older than any of these men, who trembled before her like little boys.

In the evening she came and sat in the middle of our tent, casting a reproving eye on Gatt', the little wild-cat, who was gnawing a gazelle bone with the growling proper to a wild beast. Imperiously she demanded tobacco, which she crushed to powder in the hollow of her hand. She then inhaled the powder, sniffed, spat, blew her nose into her fingers, spat again authoritatively, and then sat quite still, her lower lip hanging down like an old camel's.

The men of the tribe sat silent round the queen-mother. Now that all the usual politenesses had been exchanged, it was time to get on to serious business. The hiring of the pack-camel which M'Hammed had promised us had to be discussed.

Unfortunately, M'Hammed himself could not supply one, as his herd had just gone off to graze further afield. But his elder brother who had one might perhaps come with us.

The first three days of the trip had made us alive to the danger of having an escort composed of men bound by those family ties which are so important to the Beïdane. We feared we had already been imprudent, and were determined not to make matters any worse by engaging a third Ouled-Daman.

"We have no need for another guide," answered Marion gently but firmly, "but only for an extra camel for our things. You can quite well lead it by the bridle, and if it has nobody to carry it can take an additional bag."

"No way to take camel without a fellow to look after it," said M'Hammed.

"Has your brother no confidence in you?"

"Oh yes . . . but perhaps he has no camel."

"M'Hammed, come here. *Taala Ha!*" Marion rapped out in a dry voice.

M'Hammed got up at once and joined his brothers.

This action divided us visibly into two opposing camps. On the one hand were half a dozen men sitting in a semi-circle round Mariam who held forth making the gestures of a prophetess. She had once been a beautiful girl swollen with milk; now she was a disagreeable thin old woman whose clothes hung limply on her bony body.

In the other camp were two Europeans who waited to learn their fate, feeling as helpless and resigned as if they had been slaves for sale in the market place.

It is true our liberty was not at stake, but something very nearly as important, the success or failure of this journey we had so rashly undertaken. It was clear that we could not reach our destination with our overladen camels, and should not be able to replace whichever camel succumbed to fatigue. Modest as our equipment was for two people a pack-camel was absolutely indispensable, considering we should be travelling for several weeks.

The situation was like this: in the scrub there were camels, but we had absolutely no authority to requisition them. In the French posts, which were as a rule far from any pastures, there was plenty of authority to fall back on, but no camels. Ner, the man with the camel whom we had enrolled at Tiniark, did not want to go any further with us. M'Hammed and Mokhtar-Saloum did not want to have five camels to harness, load and unload; in fact, they would have preferred the deal to fall through, although hiring out camels was good business, rather than have the extra work to do. The elder brother would have been glad to let us have his camel on condition that we accepted a third retainer, which for us meant so much extra trouble. And the old Mariam, furious with me for having upset the business between M'Hammed and Abdallahi, wanted, through her sons, to get her own back with interest.

According to official statistics, Mauretania possesses sixty-five thousand camels. But it so happens that this animal is an article at once the most useful and the most difficult to purchase or to hire.

The conference dragged on to a late hour without any agreement being reached. In the end Ner, who perhaps felt some pity for us, consented to come with us as far as Aleg.

The next morning we started out again, taking leave of the Ouled-Daman. M'Hammed and his *'petit frère'* Mokhtar-Saloum were riding superb camels, in which Marion placed all her hopes.

Once more the scrub was ours, silent and deserted. The long regular stride of our camels carried us through the white valleys, the thickets full of nests, and the dunes of fine sand whose sides were deeply scored by the last rains. At our approach, many birds flew up: metallic-looking blackbirds, red and black sparrows that have been nicknamed *chasseurs d'Afrique*, weaver birds, birds of prey, white, grey, or reddish, and plaintive doves. An Abyssinian passerine passed in a flash of turquoise and malachite. The plumage of this bird is so brilliant that the Moors call it 'the bird who has sold his father'—to buy himself the most beautiful clothes. The gazelles were more numerous, and at night the hyenas and jackals made more noise than ever. Water was not far.

Here and there we saw isolated little woods that looked like abandoned orchards. The trees were covered with pale yellow blossom. If we came across tropical bindweed we had to stop, even if we were late or in the scorching midday heat, so that the camels could eat it, as it has particular health-giving properties. One evening we saw the great fires which proclaimed a *Cadi*'s camp, and the next morning heard the monotonous sound of an elementary school. It was one of the three hundred nomad schools in which children learn to spell the Koran, writing on wooden slates.

But what impressed us most was the sight which greeted us when we entered the province of Brakna. Beyond a rust-coloured plain, half covered with bright green verdure, was an immense expanse of blue and grey extending right to the horizon. It was the Lake of Aleg, the centre of the life of the province.

After the burning sands the sight of water is good, both to man and beast. Hundreds of goats, sheep and zebus jostled each other as they ran down the slopes and galloped across the plain to the water's edge. There were also she-camels with their young and a few small grey horses. They walked knee-deep in the water and drank deeply, one might even say religiously, for drinking is a serious business for all that lives in the Sahara. Shepherds went in too fill their waterbottles. On the banks were nomad families resting in the shade of the bushes with all their scanty possessions scattered around them in disorder. Thousands of birds were looking for food in the water or among the weeds on the bottom-a few were standing on one leg, their heads under the wings, dreaming of the sun. There were ducks with shiny green-black plumage, white and grey wading birds of which the bigger sorts held aloof from the smaller, majestic cranes, and a whole assembly of marabous looking solemn and ridiculous. White bulls jumped on the backs of the cows. Vultures and ravens watched for opportunities from the top of the acacias, where they had built their aeries. Suddenly a flock of birds rose in the air and flew round and round in great circles with piercing cries, though there was no apparent reason for their excitement.

When our camels had done drinking, we followed the paths which innumerable feet had trod between the fields of millet which stretched as far as the eye could see. Little holes were dug in the ground, and in each hole a young plant was already shooting out its shiny leaves. My camel, Bouda'il, began to limp. One of its right legs was swollen right up to the top.

M'Hammed in a casual way remarked that perhaps it had too much blood in that leg. Mokhtar-Saloum was equally unmoved.

"Camel of me, very good," was all that he vouchsafed.

***

After many days of wandering and solitude in the desert, a European traveller cannot fail to be moved by the sight of one of the French military posts. The more so as these are usually built on some denuded summit, which gives them an air of grandeur and of pride.

Aleg seemed to us perhaps the most striking of them all. It looked like a mediaeval fortress with its turrets and crenelated terraces. Its high walls were made of the same brown clay as the ground we trod.

We were made welcome by the young *administrateur* and his wife. The latter was a thorough colonial, energetic and sporting.

The evening of our arrival there was a fête on the upper terrace of the post. Around the little group of Europeans there was a crowd of Moors and negroes who had come to listen to the concert given by a celebrated family of *griots*.

The mother, the eldest daughter and her fiance played a prelude on an *ardin* and *tidinits*. Then Menina appeared, a dark blue silhouette against the evening sky. She was entirely enveloped in her *malahfa*. It was wound closely round her head, which was heavy with tresses and with jewels, closely round her opulent body, and fell in folds over her bare feet. She stood with her knees slightly bent. Only her hands moved, her supple hands dyed with henna: they flew like palpitating wings, they vibrated now like an appeal, now like a refusal. Her fingers opened and closed in ritual gestures which spoke of unknown things. A painful tremor passed over her small face with its blackened lips and quivering nostrils, a tremor which expressed the whole sensuous soul— cruel, refined, inaccessible—of the people of the desert.

In the end we had more than enough of Menina, Aya and their

Menina Dancing

mother. The whole of the next day they were telephoning their songs to the students at Boutilimit, to Ould-Deïd, to the future Emir of the Adrar, and to the interpreters of Tidjikja and Moudjeria. ... It seemed as though all Mauretania wanted to hear them. And as each of their auditors had sent fifty francs by telegraph the singers were only too willing to perform. Unfortunately the telephone was next door to the *case de passage* in which we were lodged, and Moorish music at the telephone, stripped of its gestures and its atmosphere, is apt to lack charm to European ears.

Moreover, they were surrounded by an admiring audience while they telephoned, and when the admirers had had enough they came without ceremony and sat down in our room. I have never occupied a *case de passage* whose doors could be shut from inside. They open outwards, and the only way to shut them is to put a large stone against them outside. The one at Aleg had no windows, but to make up for that deficiency it had two doors: one opening on the terrace for the bats, and the other opening on to the courtyard for the Beïdane. Between the two one had to sleep, clean oneself, wash one's clothes, and write letters in the darkness, all in the company of termites and *margouillats*.

Marion had a horror of bats. For my part I was terrified by the *margouillats*, the grey lizards which turn orange and violet when they breed. We were each of us very critical of the other's pet aversion and the panics it occasioned. As a matter of fact these animals which swarm in the south of Mauretania are really quite inoffensive, but they were the cause of many little dramas in which our friendship came near to being wrecked! If one is upset by such things one ought perhaps not to travel in the Sahara!

Always after a stay near civilization I returned with the greatest pleasure to the tents, where one did not need to wash oneself, and where there was always plenty of air and light.

Walks provided a pleasant diversion. We visited the *adabaïe* or negro village. It was different to others we had seen, as the dwellings consisted each of two separate round huts, joined together by a thatched roof. In the space between, the pestles resounded as the millet was crushed.

The *administrateur* showed us his garden. Great trees were reflected in the unruffled surface of a small dark lake. The melancholy charm of the picture reminded one of Lamartine's *Lac des Cygnes*, but the poet's Lucie was now a black woman who carried on her head a basket of tomatoes. Tomatoes are the treasures of these gardens. In the absence of fruit they are elevated far above their usual status of vegetables.

The Commandant of the Chemama came to Aleg on an unexpected visit. He invited us to his 'capital,' Boghé, and ran us over in his car.

We drove seventy-five kilometres on a real road, through country that became more and more wooded as we approached the river. Boghé was a charming little Franco-Toucouleur town whose straw huts of pinkish hue were shaded by mango trees and tamarinds. It was situated between a large lake and the Senegal River.

We saw our first hibiscus trees, a tame lioness and a negro market, which after the barrenness of the Sahara seemed to us a marvellous profusion of good things. An old merchant was selling Phoenician pearls worn down by centuries of use, great lumps of amber, calcedonies, real and imitation, and heaps of cowries, formerly used as money. Three or four thousand of them used to buy a cow, and half that number, a slave.

There were also vegetable marrows, and little round tomatoes like cherries which were sold at twenty-five centimes a large calabash. There were slices of crocodile's tail, strange cakes made with pimento, raw and tanned skins, cola-nuts, cotton stuffs, perfumes, amulets of fantastic shape, herbs of magic properties, vegetable butter, seeds of the baobab covered with their white flour, which are sold for flavouring milk.

A crowd of negresses bargained interminably, gossiped and showed themselves off with airs of great self-satisfaction. Had not each of them the finest loin-cloth draped under the handsome bust? Had not each of them the finest hair-net over the finest head of hair? Had not each of them the finest ornaments of pure gold, and the best baby slung over her back?

Every colonial official takes pride in the celebrities of his district. At Aleg we had been introduced to a very old chief who had with great difficulty undertaken the journey to Aleg some years previously. He had come as a voluntary hostage to the creditors of his sons. But when finally the debts were paid the old man had no longer sufficient strength to mount a camel, so he was unable to return to his camp. We had also been shown a Moor who might have had a brilliant career in a department of criminal investigation. He had just recognized a bandit, having seen his tracks in the sand on the scene of the crime four or five years before.

The *administrateur* of Boghé brought a Toucouleur prince to see us. This was Bailea Biran Wan, who had formerly been interpreter to Captain Psichari. He was now honorary interpreter. During the 'Great War of the Whites' he had enlisted as a common sharpshooter, but had returned wearing a lieutenant's uniform and the Cross of the Legion of Honour. Then, as if it were the most natural thing in the world, he changed his uniform for his long white toga and resumed his life of millet and bananas. When he danced a fantasia on his foaming little horse, with his extraordinary conical hat of sparterie, his lance stuck out, his knees stuck out, and also his feet in the heavy iron stirrups covered with spurs, he looked like some barbaric but aristocratic *samurai*.

He wanted his son to have a French education and sent him to the *lycée* in Saint Louis. But, when he heard that he had been put into the conventional schoolboy clothes, he took the first boat down the river, and with his own hands undressed his son and put on him the embroidered tunic of his tribe, one that had been worn by his father and grandfathers before him. He then returned, but not before threatening to take his son back to Boghé if he ever again forgot that he was a son of the Kings of the River.

Another hero, though more humble, was Zanzibar, who acted as porter to our host. He had formerly been a trumpeter in the spahis and had won a medal for distinguished service, having saved Colonel Gouraud's column at Tizegui on May 15th, 1909. His action is thus described in General Gouraud's book, *La Pacification de la Mauritanie*: "thanks to his exceptional activity, to his ingenuity, and to his intense work by day and night, six hundred men and eight hundred animals were enabled to get water." Having seen so much water, Zanzibar had lost all taste for it, and showed, on the other hand, a distinct partiality for wine. All the same he was one of those who made me glad to have visited Mauretania in time to meet some of those who still remained of the heroic period.

We only spent the day at Boghé. When we got back to Aleg we found M'Hammed in a bad temper. The camels were starving, the temperature was rising every day, and if were to stay longer we should catch the hot season in the Assaba. He grumbled too because the administrateur had persuaded us to go round by Guimi to see a certain Lobbat, chief of the Ouled-Normache, who was a candidate for the Emir's throne. That would mean an extra two hundred kilometres. . . . But Lobbat had fine camels. . . .

Among the curiosities for the entertainment of the tourist, each district likes to have its Emir.

***

On Sunday, March 11th, we left the hospitable fortress of Aleg, leaving two bags of clothes behind us to reduce our load. Ner had left us, but we had engaged another in his place, a very jolly fellow whose name even seemed a joke: Aroya-ould-Fil, which might be translated 'Little-camp-son-of-the Elephant.'

He told endless stories which from now onwards absorbed the attention of our two guides from the Trarza. Besides, Aleg marked the limit of the zone where they were known and could be more or less supervised. Now they were free and could put an end to a zeal that had become fatiguing. They could show the people of the Brakna, the Gorgol and the other provinces we were to pass through, that the warriors of the Ouled-Daman tribe, if they stooped to accompany women, at any rate did not sink so low as to obey them.

So we had tea when our companions wanted it; we slept when they were tired of relating their deeds of prowess; and we started off again next morning when they had had sufficient sleep. Our questions remained without answer, our orders without result, our reproaches without effect. If anything was done for us, it was done by slaves we came across on the way.

M'Hammed's *'petit frère'* assumed languid airs under the indulgent eye of his uncle. And we discovered little by little that their relationship was of the sort in which the youngest pays with his most intimate favours for the protection of his elder.

Boudaïl went on limping. At the first camp we came to, Aroya and M'Hammed resorted to drastic measures. They cut three crosses in the leg, at the shoulder, above the knee, and at the fetlock. It was a feast for the flies! When the blood had run sufficiently they stuffed the wounds with a mixture of grease and charcoal and they were then dried with sand.

In exchange for the lame Boudaïl, Mokhtar-Saloum lent me his fine camel, Boulilima, taking the opportunity to get me to appreciate its gentleness and strength.

"Camels of me, very good," he said once more.

We were to some extent reconciled to our own disgrace by the fact that after all it was the camels who in the last resort were the real masters of the caravan. They obliged us to make detours and halts to procure the water and food they needed. The halts before bushes or trees were not agreeable, but one forgot the fiery weight which struck down on one's shoulders when one saw the eagerness with which the animals devoured the leaves.

It is quite right to have called the camel the ship of the desert. You ride on its back with all your worldly possessions tied on around you. Its force is your security, its weakness your doom. Man and beast sink or swim together: if the camel goes under, very likely so will the man. This breeds a certain solidarity between them. The man has all the time to be ready to sacrifice rest or pleasure to tend to his precious charge. And in doing so he will in an obscure way come to love it.

In spite of discomforts and vexations there were moments of peace and contentment—for instance, when we stopped at Kreïmi, between Aleg and Guimi.

The sun was beating down on a landscape of almond green. We were resting under the thick shade of some large *iguinins*, letting the time slip by without bothering about anything. We lived in the moment: to sleep, hunt one's vermin, mend one's clothes, smoke, drink tea . . . we asked for nothing better. This was the peace of Africa, biblical and simple. We were neither hungry, nor thirsty, nor too hot; and that in its humble way was bliss. Our guides slept near us. Gatt', a little ball of wild silk, purred on Marion's shoulder. In the sunshine we could see flame-coloured butterflies that were excited by the smell of the acacias. Further off the camels were contentedly chewing thorns as long as one's finger. Every creature was happy in its own way.

"Time flies and the poet is not astonished. . . ." I recalled the words of M'Hammed's song. It was now sunset and the men were bowing themselves down in prayer.

The kettle was simmering on the embers. Mokhtar-Saloum got the teapot out of a *tassoufra*, and the goatskin full of green tea, and the sugar-loaf in its wrapping of blue paper.

Suddenly two men appeared in the deserted pasture, a *marabout* and his slave. They came up to us and, invoking Moulana, squatted down beside us. It was often like this, and I sometimes thought there was no corner of the desert that could not produce somebody to share one's tea.

Ismaïl seemed to be an important *marabout*, for M'Hammed touched his hand and then reverently passed his own over his face. The *marabout* asked for nothing; neither did his slave, who sat behind him. They just sat and waited. Life in the desert is largely composed of waiting.

The tea was begun in silence. The only noises came from the Moors sipping their tea, the ruminating animals, and the faint rattle of beads as they were turned over in Ismaïl's fingers.

Night fell, a night without a murmur, a night of Arab tales. The sky was full of stars, and, during the pause between the second and third glasses of tea, Ismaïl raised his bare arm to the Milky Way.

"That," he said, "is the track of El Bourak, Mahomet's horse. Before him, before Aissa, there was the father of Sidi-Brahim, the Prophet Saleh who refused to adore Moulana. Then Moulana, wishing to convert him, struck a stone and out of it came the first she-camel. Her milk could nourish all the children of men, and all animals that suckle, and all plants whose sap is white, as well as Bentou-machen, her own offspring. Moulana also created an inexhaustible well whose water belonged one day to men and one day to Naga Saleh the beautiful white she-camel. But men are unworthy of the gift of God. A *mechbour*, or raiding band, swooped down from the north and cut Naga Saleh's throat, while her young escaped into the sky. You see those four bright stars," and he pointed to the Great Bear. "Moulana seized the chief of the *mechbour*, and all can see the stars of his feet, of his head, the three stars of his belt and the star of his right hand, eternally red with the camel's blood." Ismaïl was now pointing to Orion.

From now onwards even the sky was for us the sky of Islam.

Thin, delicate music now rose into the night. It came from a pastoral pipe and was in a minor key, very melancholy. The slave, Souilem, had got out his flute, which he had made himself from a branch and which was his only companion during many hours of his solitary shepherd's life. Souilem wanted to thank the strangers who had given him tea, and he gave what he had to give: his song.

M'Hammed explained to us the meaning of the song Souilem played. It was about a little cow, *petit-le-vache*. Its refrain was a prayer, *La illah ill Allah*. All joy of the Musulmans is freely mixed with devotion.

This was M'Hammed's rendering:

> Gottara, *petit-le-vache*, it is lost, him.
> Gottara, Gottara, where are you?
> The lion has found *petit-le-vache*!
> Why did you leave the *marabout*'s camp?
> Gottara, Gottara, the lion will eat you.
> *La illah ill Allah!*
>
> The *marabout* make run to save his cow.
> Sbâ, ô sbâ, you leave my cow.
> *La illah ill Allah!* ill Allah. . . . Ah!
>
> Gottara, Gottara, where are you?
> The lion has got eaten him!
> *La illah ill Allah! La illah ill Allah!*

It went on a long time, Souilem praying to Moulana, calling *petit-le-vache*, and roaring into his flute the lion's answers. It went on so long that we were half asleep before it ended in a plaintive murmur.

Ismaïl and Souilem set off at dawn next day towards Aleg. The *marabout* was chanting at his beads, while the notes from Souilem's flute mingled with the cooing of doves. It was a lovely morning, fresh and gay, a morning such as we could imagine in this same month of March on the coast of Brittany or in the meadows of Anjou. A fresh breeze brought us renewed vigour. Our track was straight and easy, being well trodden by the caravans which brought provisions from the river to Moudjeria, Tidjikja and Atar. The camels, feeling well fed, trotted willingly, even Boudaïl whose scars were now healing.

Marion was riding gaily along on Boukhzeïma, rocked by the camel's sure and rhythmic stride, her native optimism quite recovered. Between her lips was a *messouak*, the little stick with which the Moors rub their teeth.

"It is, all the same, incredible, the ground one covers doing thirty to forty kilometres a day."

"Incredible!" I answered. "Certainly if one does not count the days...."

But Marion went on imperturbably: "After all, these camels are really excellent, and if we look after them well..."

This was the moment M'Hammed chose to let fall three little words:

"Boukhzeïma is tired."

Three little words said almost casually; but their effect was like a stone thrown into the smoothest of mill ponds, or like the rap over the knuckles which a schoolboy gets when he stares out of the window at the passing swallows, or like the signal of a stage-manager for a change of scene.

Marion turned round shocked and incredulous.

What clown could be so tactless as to speak of fatigue? Who could be tired on this exquisite morning, especially as it was after a day of rest?

Boukhzeïma's stride was steady and Marion, in the saddle, could hold to her illusions. But I looked at the camel, and suddenly I saw it as it really was with its flat flanks and shrunken belly, and its spine sticking up like an old cow's. We knew well what the word fatigue meant in the mouth of a Beïdane when he spoke of camels.

"Yes," continued M'Hammed, "he is tired *forcément*. Since the last rains he has been carrying mails from Boutilimit to Rosso and Nouakchott."

That made five months and a half. For a respectable camel the year was divided into two equal parts: six months' work and six months' rest.

"Never mind," we answered. "We shall leave Boukhzeïma at Guimi until we return, and Lobbat will surely sell us another to take his place."

"Perhaps," said M'Hammed in an off-hand way.

"*Inch' Allah!*" added Aroya in echo.

And Mokhtar-Saloum, with his head full of schemes, turned the subject to his own camel: "It is good camel, Boulilima."

And indeed Guimi proved a disillusionment.

Admittedly the warriors who rode out to welcome us wasted a lot of good gunpowder in the air, and the dances performed in our honour provided us with a new spectacle. The dancers were women, entirely enveloped in veils which were drawn tightly in at the neck by a scarf or by a string of beads. They advanced slowly, two by two, their feet treading on the edges of their clothes which hung down well on to the ground. They moved with slow, heavy movements and looked like a procession of sepulchral figures.

Admittedly the *méchoui* was abundant, the tea flowed freely and the slaves did not stint the rancid butter on the great flat millet cakes. We had a fine tent with an article of furniture that was new to us: a *techgal*—that is, a bed made of plaited branches and bamboos. In it one slept off the ground, and were thus removed from scorpions and other sorts of vermin, and from dampness in the rainy season.

In the middle of the night a slave woke us up, bringing presents from his master, as though Lobbat wanted to prove that he thought of our welfare even in his dreams.

Perhaps we had begun to get tired of the official receptions of the Trab-el-Beïdane. Perhaps we wanted rather less festivity and rather more rest.

Perhaps also Lobbat was a man not altogether to our taste. He was a quiet, soft-spoken little man without much personality. He spoke French pretentiously, using the second person plural which sounds so strangely false in an African tent. He was just the man, we thought, who would be a candidate for the rank of Emir.

He expatiated on the greatness of his family and on its claims. He, the chief of the Ouled-Normache, was descended from Barkani, who had taken the Tagant and given his name to the Brakna, while his brother Terrouz had taken the Trarza. This was in the sixteenth century. These two branches of the family had later become rivals and enemies like the descendants of the two brothers Oudeï and Delim.

Lobbat, son of the ancient Emirs of the Tagant, was as noble and as rich as Ould-Deïd, whose position filled him with bitter envy. His cousins of the Trarza were shown every favour by the French, while the disinherited people of the Brakna got neither subventions, arms, nor Emir. Not even an Emir! Above all, that was unjust. Moreover it was incomprehensible, for there he was, Lobbat, all ready to be given honours and revenue.

He may have been right, but it was not for us to meddle in business of that sort. If we had wanted to, we could have done nothing for him, and his camels interested us far more than his ambitions.

Undoubtedly some evil spirit had passed by, taking off all the fine camels that we had so sincerely admired that very morning. Lobbat had none, neither to sell nor to let on hire. Nobody in the camp had any. Besides why should we even speak of buying? If Lobbat had had a camel, only a single one, that was worthy of us, he would have given it gladly to the travellers who had so honoured him by their visit. The *marabouts* with whom we should lodge at Mal were more fortunate than he was for they would surely have some to offer. For their chief, Cheikh-el-Nagi, was a saintly man and Moulana would always bless his herds.

No, certainly Guimi had not been worth the addition of two hundred kilometres to our journey.

It was a day and a half's ride from Guimi to Mal. We should

have liked to push on quickly to make up for lost time, but the ground was not suitable for hard riding.

On the second day of the journey, the first camp we came to was that of some poor vassals. We stayed with them for our midday rest. There were no men in the camp, only women, children and lambs. All they could offer us was some milk and a tiny little gazelle. The latter was being suckled by a young woman, side by side with her own baby. We left the poor little thing to its wet-nurse, and started out again for the camp of Cheikh-el-Nagi, riding over beautiful undulations of pinkish sand and through wooded valleys.

Cheikh-el-Nagi was away. His brother had a large tent rigged for us, removed from the camp and its noisy herds. There we would be able to sleep in peace. It looked out on to a stretch of bare ground where some thin yellow dogs were eating a dead ass.

But our stay was not so peaceful as we expected. Firstly, we found again the three *griots* we had listened to in Aleg, who were touring the country. Their performance attracted the whole tribe to our tent. Our meeting these musicians again had unexpected results and led to our getting rid of Aroya.

It was soon evident that Mokhtar-Saloum was keen on Aya, and that at Aleg, M'Hammed had become tenderly attached to Menina. Between these four people Aroya acted as a go-between.

Tea succeeded the *méchoui* and finally the company dispersed. The musicians went with the rest, followed by Mokhtar-Saloum. Of the two protectors left us, Aroya soon sneaked off on a confidential mission.

M'Hammed remained, looking sombre and absorbed, and got the tent ready for the night. He agreed to our suggestion that we should be off at dawn, put out the candle between his finger and thumb, murmuring *'smillah* as he did so, and lay down in his usual place with his head on his rifle.

Outside the jackals had chased off the dogs and were disputing the ass between them.

Late in the night Aroya came back and whispered something in M'Hammed's ear. The two then slipped stealthily out and made off. We were now left alone with no arms and with no help within call.

A sinister raucous cry came out of the bushes near by, then

another closer. It was two large hyenas coming to claim the ass. By the time they reached the carcass the jackals had already beaten a retreat, whining plaintively. In the night life of the scrub the hyena's supremacy is uncontested.

At dawn our three attendants crept in furtively and lay down beneath their rugs.

Then we had a good row. I was furious. I called them all the names I could think of, cursing them all, and their common ancestor the first dog. A fortnight's bottled-up rage suddenly found vent. In the situation we were in we could not think of dismissing them all three, but Aroya was sacrificed as an example to the others. We would see about replacing the other two at Kaédi.

The head *marabout* now made his appearance. We had asked him for camels, but we were not astonished to hear amongst his expressions of devotion the phrases that were beginning to sound conventional:

"I do not possess any camels, but at the next camp, if it is Moulana's will..."

But Moulana's will was not so favourable. At the next camp all we could find was a guide to replace Aroya, and his camel, a thin, small, bad-tempered beast. However we engaged them, and the camel carried part of our baggage as far as Kaédi. We also found at this camp a *marabout*, dark and sad as a crow, who with two scarcely more lively disciples was going to beg for alms in the Chemama. They said it would be a great pleasure to accompany us—us and our tea.

And the saddened Aroya took the road back to Aleg in spite of his fervent supplications.

The retribution meted out to Aroya made the other two reflect a bit, much to our peace and comfort. From Mal to Kaédi we were all at once surrounded by every care and attention. At the great lake of Mal, crowded like that of Aleg with animals and birds, they filled our waterbottles carefully with the cleanest water, instead of dipping them in between the legs of the camels. This was the last water we should come to before the Chemama, which we were to reach the evening of the next day.

Along the way an attentive *tebbou* would constantly be raised to hold aside the long thorny branches while we passed. And in the evening when we stopped, our things were put, and not thrown, on the ground. Not that it was any particular use: all fragile articles had long since been broken. Fresh straw was laid out for us; tea was got ready with alacrity. And as we had no cigarettes left, our cavaliers offered us little pipes of iron and some of their acrid tobacco, rendered a little milder by the addition of *mocouaressa*, a grey lichen with a perfume of incense.

At dawn the camels were ready as if by magic, and we got the full benefit of the early morning coolness, all the cooler for the great trees which now shaded our route. At Dielouar the track widened and the trees on each side formed a splendid avenue, at the end of which one could easily have imagined the gates of a *château*. We had never yet seen so much shade in the western Sahara.

Sometimes we would come across a negro collecting gum. He would walk quickly, his amulets rattling as he went. Passing us he would only speak the name of Moulana. Behind him the silence would fall once more, broken only by an occasional hare dashing past or by the flight of a guinea-fowl.

Suddenly we left all shade behind us and rode out into the implacable midday sun. It was a vast clearing in the woodlands, and the track across it wound in and out amongst the giant nests of termites and the deep pits in the ground. We had reached the wells of Mousouden.

Slaves seemed to be waiting for us, to water our camels, sell us a sheep, and wash our ragged clothing. A silk-cotton tree, a twisted mass of aerial roots and tropical bindweed, offered shade enough to shelter a whole tribe. And we found a supreme luxury, a hollow tree-trunk in which we could wash.

Thus, clothed in clean tunics and attended by a respectful escort, we were able to accept with serenity the unexpected homage which was to be paid us by these slaves, who grow millet, rice and *sorgho* to the south of the Gorgol.

It was in the evening, in a tent that had been put up for us by the *haratine* of some Brakna *marabouts* near their camp. After the tea and the boiled millet they stayed with us silent, for a weighty question was worrying their simple souls. The eldest of them especially stared at us hard, his chin resting on his knees, his forehead puckered with thought. He muttered to himself, shaking his bald head. Finally he spoke, not in Hassani but in the ancient Zénega language which is still used by old peasants. M'Hammed translated.

"The slave there, Malek, says he look after the camels of Coppolani in the Brakna and the Tagant. Very, very long time ago, but Malek always keep Coppolani in his head, because Coppolani very strong and good altogether. . . . Malek says too: 'The two women-the-Europeans, it is daughters of Coppolani, who come to see their father's country.'"

Every time M'Hammed pronounced the name of Coppolani, Malek carried his hand to his breast, grunting approval. The others listened with eager eyes to the strange words which gave expression to their anxious thoughts. In vain M'Hammed assured them they were mistaken. They would not abandon their illusion and looked in our faces for Coppolani's likeness. When M'Hammed stopped speaking, Malek bent forward quickly towards us, saying: "Quite right! Daughters of Coppolani, *Ate! Menti Coppolani, Menti Coppolani*" He took our hands between his own, which he then passed passionately over his face. Then he jumped up and ran off.

We had been riding since the early morning. Our camels advanced only under the stimulus of cries and blows. We ourselves were overcome with thirst and heat. All at once we heard cries behind us which roused us from our torpor: some slaves were running after us. To our great surprise we recognized old Malek. He was quite out of breath and made us a sign to stop and wait for him. He had during the night been round all the neighbouring camps, calling on brothers, relations and friends—all who had been with him tending Coppolani's camels—telling them of the presence of the latter's daughters. Bringing them all with him, he had followed our tracks all day with no thought of heat or fatigue. Now they were rewarded. They came forward one by one, resting for a moment their sweating foreheads on our hands while they murmured:

"*Essalam alik, ment-Coppolani!*"

We were touched by their faith and had not the heart to undeceive them. What use would it have been to destroy the illusion they cherished, the illusion that in us they recovered something of their long-lost and venerated master? His daughters! What did it matter whether it was Marion and myself or any others? The important thing was their joy, and that was real enough.

We distributed tobacco, tea and a sugar-loaf. He would have done the same, surely! Then they stood motionless and watched us disappear like the last reflections of their distant youth.

In the peace and quiet of the evening our thoughts turned on the man who had given to the Trab-el-Beïdane its French name of Mauretania, the man who loved this country, who had trusted its nomads with a confidence that had in the end cost him his life.

What efforts had been made, what sacrifices? ... to the end that all should be so peaceful this evening thirty years later.

In the subdued splendour of the dawn the Ouolom-Néré appeared, rising up against the rose-coloured sky. How shall I describe it? One could not call it a peak, because its summit is truncated, and however massive and imposing it appears in contrast to the immense flat stretch of country around, the word 'mountain' would be an exaggeration. The Moors have settled the question poetically in their language full of imagery. They call a source *aïn*, which means 'an eye,' and for such as Ouolom-Néré their word is *guelb*, meaning ' heart.' Ouolom-Néré and the other lesser *guelb*s that mount guard round it are more like gigantic rocky tumuli than anything else. Only Ouolom-Néré is sacred.

From the track we could see the gaping mouths of caverns among the broken stones that covered its surface.

At Kaédi the Toucouleur interpreter, Mahmadou-Ahmadou Bâ, explained to us why the mound was sacred. Sixty years before, a great *marabout*, Hidjaj, knowing his end to be near, told his disciples that, as soon as he was dead, his body was to be placed on the back of a bull, which was then to be allowed to wander where it would. Wherever it finally stopped his grave was to be dug. The bull walked for six kilometres along the Chemama, and then started to climb the Ouolom-Néré, which was really miraculous considering that the mound rises abruptly from the plain, like the frustrum of a cone stood on a tin tray.

But a bull carrying a saint on its back can do things of which ordinary animals would be incapable; and it carried its holy burden right to the top, where Hidjaj was duly buried. After that several other *marabouts* claimed the honour of sharing his last resting-place, amongst others Toumadec, who enjoyed a very great reputation. All this was a boon to miscreants; for popular superstition decided that anyone had the right of asylum on the sacred *guelb*. Moreover, one could not even recover the spoils they had taken with them. It accordingly seems quite possible to be a saint during one's lifetime and a receiver of stolen property after one's death!

After Ouolom-Néré the argillaceous plain was uninterrupted once more, except for its yellow villages of straw huts and its great blue river. The track had now become a real road. On it we met many negro peasants in long tunics, dark blue or white. Some were riding zebus, others grey asses stronger than horses, while still others were on little horses that trotted like asses. Women followed them on foot. Their chests were bare. Their walk was stately, due chiefly to the piles of calabashes they balanced on their heads.

The landscape was not beautiful, but it had a graver defect than that. It was absolutely destitute of all verdure that could serve as fodder. There was not one thorny bush to nourish a camel. We began to wonder what would happen to our animals during our stay at Kaédi. They had already been fasting since the previous day.

I was again riding Boudaïl, who was now going well. But Boukhzeïma, thin and tired, could only be induced to keep up by Mokhtar-Saloum's *tebbou*. It was Marion's turn to appreciate the qualities of the fine Boulilima, which the *'petit frère'* had lent her. The pack-camel dawdled along in rear, showing every sign of fatigue and ill temper, quite out of proportion to its nominal load.

The row we had had at Mal began to be forgotten. The new attentiveness of our escort began to weaken our resolve to look for others. As for them, they affected a gay confidence and were very careful not to touch in any way on the dangerous subject.

The Moors have three proverbs which enjoin this sort of prudence: Leave your lice alone if you're not itching. Don't go out in the sun if your hair is dressed with butter. Don't start a fight if you have a bone in your stomach.

In any case, if they were at all worried, it was not for long. Half an hour after we had halted in front of the *case de passage* in Kaédi, we were informed by an official that we should not find either men or camels in the place. M'Hammed and Mokhtar-Saloum had no doubt found it out still sooner from the natives who gathered round at our arrival.

Our camels were unloaded and unharnessed and given to a herdsman. When the pack-camel was relieved of our baggage it turned out that it had also been carrying a hundred kilos of salt concealed underneath. Then M'Hammed and Mokhtar-Saloum strolled off to the large Toucouleur village whose sordid little lanes surrounded the military post and the French villas.

***

Compared to the other French posts in Mauretania, Kaédi, centre of the Gorgol district, is regarded as a big town. It has an imposing civil residence (a horrid barrack-like building though it is), good European houses shaded by trees, important commercial concerns, and a very large native village of straw huts stretching right down to the banks of the Gorgol and Senegal rivers. Rivers always bring wealth.

We were of course made a fuss of by the little French settlement. The assistant *administrateur* was very kind to us. So was his young wife, an enthusiast on all questions of Toucouleur ethnography. But the lack of pasture-land in the neighbourhood forbade our staying long, and we had to go speedily about our pressing business, the purchase of a pack-camel and the engaging of a camel-driver to look after it.

Rare as camels were at Kaédi, M'Hammed and Mokhtar-Saloum were not long in finding one which Moulana seemed to have provided expressly to fit in with their plans.

After the siesta M'Hammed came to us with his hand on his

heart and his face all smiles. He discoursed at length, and the upshot of it was that Boukhzeïma was going to die, and that after Kaédi we should not have another chance to replace it.

"And what do you do without camel in the scrub?" he asked, throwing out his two arms to indicate the immensity of the disaster.

He and Mokhtar-Saloum, sure of their own mounts and satisfied with their pay, had nothing to worry about on their own account, but they did not wish to see their 'friends' in trouble during the journey.

They had met a cousin in the place and had persuaded him to sell them his she-camel. Mokhtar-Saloum, out of devotion to Marion, was ready to let her have Boulilima, the beautiful, the gentle, the indefatigable Boulilima.

"You give only two hundred francs and Boukhzeïma," he explained, "and after that everything is all right till you get back to Boutilimit. Boukhzeïma return to Trarza with my cousin ... or perhaps he die on the way.... *Inch' Allah!*"

M'Hammed made it clear that he was taking a great risk to do us a service. But we must decide quickly, say yes, and give the money at once, as the cousin was anxious to start.

"And what will Abdallahi say if we sell the camel he has provided?"

"Abdallahi nothing to say. He give Boukhzeïma for you. You do what you like, and if when you get back you give Boulilima to Abdallahi, he only too much pleased."

"Very well. Go and fetch your cousin. We will buy his camel ourselves and Mokhtar-Saloum can keep his Boulilima."

"No way to do that. Camel not trained, not nice. Only good for Beïdane to ride.... No. You buy Boulilima quick. Cousin of me, no way for him to wait."

So much insistence, such great haste and so many protestations of friendship, were enough to put us on our guard. And this story of a cousin who could not wait—as if a Moor was ever in a hurry! In spite of her hankering after Boulilima, Marion thought it best to proceed warily.

"Arrange with your cousin as you like," she said. "I will only give my answer this evening when you come and bring the camels to our hut."

That at least would give us a little time to think it over.

At eight o'clock in the evening we were all in the courtyard—Frenchmen, Moors, an interpreter and many others besides ourselves. For an hour we had been attempting to thrash the matter out, while the camels that all the fuss was about ruminated disdainfully.

The opinion of our advisers was definite; Boukhzeïma was an excellent camel, rather tired for the moment, perhaps, but nevertheless capable of doing long marches. If left to graze for a while he would soon be in superb condition again. This camel and two hundred francs made an exorbitant price for Boulilima.

Marion and I cudgelled our brains for a solution. To be taken in was certainly humiliating. But to go with an unsound camel was dangerous. Kiffa, Tidjikja, Moudjeria, Boutilimit—it was a long circuit. Storms were due in two months' time; we should have to be in a position to ride fast. We had heard so many stories of exhausted camels going down without any warning and never rising again.... To buy a camel at a camp on the way was a possibility we no longer believed in. ...

What were we to do? Certainly we had to mistrust the Moors, but also to mistrust the European's mistrust of them, which was often exaggerated. It seemed we had to mistrust everything and everybody. Boukhzeïma seemed to our eyes a fine camel, Boulilima too. Only one thing was clear: our own incompetence.

At her wit's end, Marion decided:

"If I am to make a mistake, better make it in buying a camel I really like. I should like to have Boulilima. So I will take him."

Our advisers shrugged their shoulders. The Toucouleur interpreter congratulated all the parties, and Mokhtar-Saloum gave way to lamentations on the evil chance that had thus deprived him of his cherished mount. But the sparkle in his false eyes told a different story.

The morning we set off there was no longer any question of the mysterious camel the cousin was to have provided. Boukhzeïma was saddled as usual, but for Mokhtar-Saloum.

We had another guide, Amar, a *hartani*, who rode a funny little black horse who trotted like a mechanical toy, was incapable of carrying any of our equipment, and demanded his daily ration of millet and of water.

The baker at Kaédi consented to let us have a miserable pack-camel together with a young slave who was making his debut as a camel-driver.

In this company we set out on the track which led from Kaédi to M'Bout.

Chapter VII

The Country of Mistrust

WE had now passed out of the country of brown tents spread out in the sun amongst the pale bushes, the country of hospitality where you are received like one of the family, the country of huge dunes, solitary valleys, and vast horizons.

We were now entering the black country, a troubled zone touching Mauretania, Senegal, and the Sudan, and in which the men, fauna, and flora of these three countries meet and mingle.

Among the population were Sarakollés, Toucouleurs, Peulhs, some Berbers and a few Arabs. There were both nomad and sedentary peoples, the oppressors and oppressed of former times, living in these dried-up marshes. In spite of their different origins they had one trait in common, a deeply-rooted mistrust. The pillage of bygone days had left its heritage in the form of a cruel avarice. They would refuse to let us have a sheep even at the double of its price. If we had managed to buy some milk and a few platefuls of boiled millet, and if our innocent curiosity tempted us to approach the miserable dwelling, we would be chased away with oaths and threats.

For the first time since we had been in Africa we actually bought water. We paid fifty centimes for a small calabash of water so filthy that in France I would not have dared to wash my hands in it. Even Amar and the young slave could not manage to melt their compatriots.

To cut down our baggage we had brought with us as little provisions as possible. We had only brought tea, sugar, a few biscuits and some monkey-nuts. More than once we had to tighten our belts in lieu of dinner.

The fact that we had an Arab escort did not help matters. Indeed, we learnt what it was like to travel in the Gorgol and the Guidimaka with descendants of the old slave-raiders, the hereditary enemies of all the river peoples of Senegal.

Between Kaédi and M'Bout the people we met most often were Peulhs, a mahogany-coloured race. They are also called Foulhs, Foulbes, Foulhas and Felletas. Although nomads and great herdsmen they are connected with the Toucouleurs, a sedentary agricultural people, just as the Sarakollés are related to the Gangari of the mountains.

One must not judge the Peulhs by the colour of their skin but by their features. Their faces are oval, their lips thin, and their noses often aquiline. Their language is still more indicative of their origin. According to Homburger it is the language of the Egyptians of the Twelfth Dynasty. Their name means 'the separated,' like that of the Bafours, who are perhaps Peulhs themselves. They are supposed to have come from Syria, Egypt or Ethiopia at the dawn of the Christian era in one of those Trans-saharan migrations, those slow-moving human waves which, in obedience to some inexorable law, carries men from east to west across the deserts.

From the Kanem to the Senegal we met these Peulhs, sometimes nomad, sometimes temporarily of fixed abode. They are indefatigable walkers, driving before them their white or reddish sheep, bigger than the sheep of the Beïdane, and their white zebus with long horns. The latter are often incurved, looking like a lyre. Further east, in the Niger, their sheep walk from Agades to Bilma across the waterless desert of Tenere, while the goats of the Touaregs have to be carried on the backs of camels. In the English colony of Nigeria they have black zebus with white horns.

Once when we halted under the banyan trees by the pools of Kow there were several hundred magnificent zebus which had been brought there for water. They seemed so quiet and harmless that in my ignorance I came nearer to look more closely at them, picking out the most decorative to photograph. As luck would have it their herdsman was quite close, filling up his waterbottle. Later I learnt that the Peulh zebus are only tame to their own herdsman, whom they will follow like dogs, the herd being led by the favourite bull or cow. If the herdsman goes away, the whole herd becomes wild, and will readily attack any passing stranger.

The Peulhs look after their animals very carefully. They live on milk, and only the men (or sometimes childless women) are allowed to milk the cows. If an animal is slaughtered on the occasion of a great festival, religious custom forbids them to drink milk that day.

Sometimes we would follow a track trodden by the zebus to see what it led to, and would come upon a round low hut made of branches which was difficult to distinguish from the bushes around, like the nest of a water-fowl. It was a Peulh hut.

Women carrying little children on their haunches and young girls would come out, attracted by the noise of our caravan. The Musulman women wore a strange headdress, a network of silver coins, over their plaited hair. Amongst these coins we saw the old French five-franc piece, thalers of Maria Teresa, and Spanish money. But the majority of Peulhs were fetishists, and these women had their hair done up in a cock's comb except for two plaits which curved down over the cheeks. Several rows of white china beads ran along each side of the crest of black hair. The Peulh women were slender and strong. The movement of the muscles at the least gesture played with the lights and shadows on the silky skin. All were naked down to the waist. The rest of the body was clothed, clearly showing, however, the perfect line of their hips. All were beautiful, and all were hostile. Mistrust glittered clearly in their jet-black almond-shaped eyes. The most prized concubines of the Songhaï kings of Timbuktu and Gao belonged to this race of Peulh women, famous alike for their beauty, their shrewdness and their noble carriage.

They handed us large calabashes of milk. When we had drunk our fill they threw away the rest disdainfully. The men were away looking after their herds in distant pastures.

We were later on to see Peulhs very different from this race of simple herdsmen. At Kayes, for instance, we saw two young chiefs, strangely effeminate, covered with jewels and amulets, walking with great dignity through the rowdy strident Sudanese crowd. Their faces were painted with ochre and antimony. Their hair was plaited and adorned with shells, beads and silver coins, just like the women's. At Dakar, on the other hand, we saw a Peulh tax-collector who seemed perfectly Europeanized, with hair as brilliantined as Josephine Baker's. But he confided to us that each Peulh tribe venerated a totem which punished severely the least offence.

"And the totem of my family is the snake," he told us. "We have to take great care not to touch a snake, nor even walk unwittingly

Peulh Women

where it has passed, or immediately our hands and feet would become covered with scales."

Certainly it would be a very awkward thing to happen to an elegant young tax-collector.

Our progress became more and more governed by the question of pasture for our animals. Two factors were present to complicate matters: lions and heat. We could no longer leave the camels to graze as they pleased during the night on account of prowling lions. On the other hand, in the middle of the day the heat was such that they had no appetite.

The camel takes more time to eat than most other animals. It nibbles a bit here, and a bit there fifty paces further on, and needs several hours to eat its fill. And eating is not all: it has then to chew the cud.

The solution of the problem was simple, if not very agreeable. We rode right through the night, put the camels to graze morning and evening, and tried to sleep during the heat of the day while the animals ruminated their scanty morning meal.

Things were still further complicated by Amar's horrid little horse, for we had endless bother to get his daily water and millet from the Peulhs.

Looking back on our journey through the Trarza— what fine times we had had! We were now riding through magnificent scenery; but, hungry, sleeping badly, and worn out by fatigue, we were too dispirited to enjoy the beauties of nature.

It was Sunday, March 25th, at a place called Silliwol. I was sitting patiently on Boudaïl's back in front of a gum tree waiting for him to finish his *déjeuner*. Suddenly, for no apparent reason, he took fright and dashed off into the bushes. A dead branch lay across our path, a branch just like a thousand others, with its little hooked thorns disposed in groups of three. After tearing my tunic the thorns scratched my right hand and some of them remained hooked in the skin.

This was a very ordinary occurrence; in fact, in Mauretania one is hardly ever without a thorn somewhere in one's hands or feet. I myself attached no importance to it. I had worries enough without that, both on account of the scarcity of food and of a *cro-cro* which I had had for a week on one of my toes. A *cro-cro* is a sore caused by a microbe, which is very common in tropical Africa.

I managed to pull out the largest thorns with my teeth, and at our next halt M'Hammed extracted others with his *moungache*, this being a little instrument consisting of tweezers and stiletto which a Moor always carries hung round his neck. One thorn, however, remained in the fleshy part of my thumb, too small or too deeply embedded for us to find it. If one was to make a fuss over a thorn, Mauretania would be quite uninhabitable, and I continued the journey without the least suspicion that a tiny foreign body under my skin was later to put a stop to our travels.

The journey went on as before with the same worries, the same privations, the same halts at the same hours and under the same sort of trees, the same arguments with the Moors, whose periods of attentiveness followed periods of ill-will in the same invariable cycle.

They would slip gradually into laziness and insolence. Then one day there would be a row and straightway they would be charming and considerate. Softened by their newly recovered zeal, we would perhaps so far forget ourselves as to give some present. This would be regarded as a tribute due, and a sign of then: importance or, alternatively, as a sign of our weakness.... Besides, what need was there now to make an effort when the prize was already in the hand: the fine new *draa* or *aouli*, or the beads for one's wife's hair? Then fresh sulkiness or indifference, fresh row, fresh zeal, etc. ... It was a perfect circle, and would never come to an end.

M'Hammed and his '*petit frère*,' far from having been replaced at Kaédi, had not only kept their jobs, but had done a good bit of business into the bargain. They accordingly felt secure. And they made us feel it.

I know very well that my story is monotonous.

But how could a nomad's journal be otherwise? Monotony is part and parcel of his life.

M'Hammed and Mokhtar-Saloum wanted to get to M'Bout by the longest route. Amar wanted to go the shortest way and we were of the same mind, being impatient to get somewhere where fresh water was available as well as milk, mutton and millet. M'Bout we thought of as a paradise where bananas grew and green lemons.

The two Moors, however, traded on their knowledge of camels, and managed to get their way. They made out that the shortest track was in some places covered with loose stones which would lame the camels. The unfortunate beasts were to encounter plenty later in the Assaba . . . but on such a matter as this we could not argue with our guides.

The detour did in fact have one advantage. We got an excellent reception from the Tadjakant *haratine*, whose huts we found on the last slope of the rocky ridge, the Oua-Oua near Kow. When we arrived they had just slaughtered sheep in the Aid-el-Kebir, the great religious festival in which, from one end of Islam to the other, the sacrifice of Abraham is repeated. It is for this festival that so many pilgrims go to Mecca.

At last we had a good feed of *méchoui* again. And once again we listened to the women beating the tom-toms and watched the dancers in their blue tunics, dancing until the day was done.

***

At M'Bout we did not find much to raise our spirits. It was a melancholy place and looked abandoned. We were lodged in a large dilapidated house, where one of the guards told us haughtily that everything was ready for our reception. All we could find on looking round was a jar of water, containing perhaps ten litres, which was supposed to do for six thirsty and filthy people. However, we managed to hire some frayed matting and to buy a goat and some milk.

The District Commandant of the Gorgol had arrived the same day from Kaédi, but he did not deign to receive us. The next day we met him walking with his colleagues of the Guidimaka and the Assaba, and this time he saluted us in the distance. One can hardly imagine how ridiculous it looks for five French people to bow to each other ceremoniously in the heart of the wilds of Africa just exactly as they might if they passed each other on the Place de la Concorde.

The Commandant's two companions, however, understood it perfectly, so much so that they made a point of calling on us at the first opportunity.

It was from these visitors that we first learnt of the existence of the guinea-worm, *Filaria medinensis,* a horrible parasite, the young of which bore their way into the bodies of the tiny crustacean, Cyclops. The latter are then drunk in the water taken from lakes, and the parasite thus enters the human body, then finding its way into the subcutaneous connective tissues. If it is a female it may grow to a metre or more in length, though the male is only a few centimetres long. The female is viviparous, and one day will find its way to the surface to discharge its young by the thousand, at the same time causing an abscess on the body of its host. This is the moment for the host to try to get rid of it. The end of the worm must be taken and delicately wound round a match. The winding must be done with the utmost patience— only three or four turns in twenty-four hours. For if the worm breaks there is nothing further to be done but to wait for the next abscess to form and begin the whole business over again. The parasite is generally located in the arms or legs, but she may, when she comes to give birth, take it into her head to come to the surface at an eyelid or on the nose of her host.

"It is very common," one of our visitors told us, "in the neighbourhood of M'Bout." (And I thought of the buckets of lovely fresh water I had drunk since our arrival the evening before.) "But it also exists in the south of the Brakna, throughout the Gorgol and the Assaba, and occasionally in the north. To prevent one's getting it, all one has to do is to filter all the water one drinks through fine cotton stuff. One can see the animal quite well with the naked eye. ... I suppose," he added, "you always filter your water?"

Alas! A long time had passed since we demanded such services from our attendants ... or, for that matter, from ourselves. We had been drinking the dirty water just as it came from the well or from the muddy edges of a lake where animals were drinking. Our only care had been to drink all we could at a single gulp so as not to see what we were drinking nor have time to notice its strange and complex taste made up of mud, old cheese, and mouldy leather.

"And how long is it," we asked our informant, "before one can tell whether one has got the guinea-worm or not?"

"That all depends.... But in any case by the end of a year you can feel sure!"

But I must make haste to reassure my anxious reader: up to the present neither Marion nor I have made the acquaintance of *Filaria medinensis.... El hamdou lillahi*!

After that we discussed other dangers we ran: wearing no sun-helmet, nor wearing any boots as protection against the horned vipers. But we had heard so much about the vipers! And as the danger never materialized we had come, perhaps wrongly, to doubt its existence. On the other hand, we knew all about the yellow scorpions and the little grey lizards which we would find every morning under the bags and saddle-mats which we used as pillows. M'Hammed called the lizards the 'evil-as-fire,' *les michants-comme-le-feu*.

As a matter of fact, in the Sahara dangers of all kinds abound, most of them invisible. In the end the traveller does not bother about them, not so much by reason of any courage, but rather from a feeling of impotence, which makes one wise as an Arab, abandoning oneself like him to the laws of chance and to the Will of God.

After all, our lack of prudence began and culminated in the fact that we were inexperienced women. But what were we to do about that?

The next day we left without regret this place of poor welcome. The Commandant of the Guidimaka was taking us in his car to his own headquarters at Sélibaby. He even managed to stuff all our things in his car so that our camels could rejoin us without fatigue.

Each of the French posts in Mauretania had its own particular physiognomy. The character of Sélibaby was decidedly Sudanese.

Its buildings were of reddish and white *pisé* with lozenge-shaped openings, the architecture being at the same time massive and complicated. They keep relatively cool under their thatched roofs, civilization not having yet brought its benefits in the shape of corrugated iron. The Residence and the other French private houses showed rustic facades over the walls of their gardens. Little birds, the 'millet-eaters,' boldly made their nests in the joists of the verandahs. The centre of animation was, of course, the market place, shaded by fine trees thick with foliage.

The negro peasants included Toucouleurs, Bambaras, Khasonkes, Ouoloffs and, most numerous of all, Sarakollés, who were the real masters of the country. The peasants grew millet, *sorgho*, monkey-nuts, pistachio-nuts, rice, indigo and cotton. The last they themselves spun and wove in their leisure time during the dry season. There were also some Berbers of the Tadjakant and Idouaich tribes whose dark tunics of *chandorah* were in striking contrast to the white, pale blue, and brilliant coloured clothes of the negroes. But in spite of their presence we had very definitely the feeling that we were in negro territory. If it was technically Mauretania from the official point of view, it was certainly not the Trab-el-Beïdane, and the character of that nomad's country was no longer to be felt, that complex character made up of dreaminess, haughtiness and noble fatalism. Here was boisterous vulgarity and childish vanity. We found the feverishness of the negroes rather disconcerting, just as we had found their wooded country disconcerting after the wide horizons of the north, though it should perhaps be added that the negroes did not possess the majesty of their trees.

The Sarakollés claim descent from Dinga, an amphibious king, who one day left the waters of the Senegal River at the bottom of which he had been living without even his clothes getting wet. Fifteen generations have passed since Dinga took to the land.

Historians, on the other hand, give them other origins, making them come from the North Sudan where, allied to the Oualatten, they had founded the camp of Birou and the powerful city of Oualatta. From this country they were progressively driven southwards by the invasion of the Berbers under Boubakar in the eleventh century and that of the Hassan Arabs in the seventeenth, after which they finally settled round the lakes and streams of the Assaba.

During the daytime Sélibaby is a small, simple but colourful village of negro peasants, buzzing with the sound of looms. At night a prey to tom-toms, sorcery and ruffians, it shows quite another face: angry, mistrustful, cruel, and of almost bestial sensuality. If you are too curious of its nocturnal habits you can easily have an unpleasant encounter with some docker from one of the ports along the coast, or some fireman from train or steamship out of work or on leave, who has a cap pulled down over one eye and an insult on his lips.

There are three secret powers in Sélibaby: the sorcerers, the *griots*, and the League of the Rights of Man.

The sorcerer's power is based on poisons. The country furnishes these in abundance, and they make abundant use of them in their magic philtres and their alarming pharmacopoeia. They are familiar with the properties of the *tidinouar*, a sort of aloes. A decoction of this is mixed with goats' urine and poured over the wounds of a dead animal. The latter is then left to be devoured by wild beasts, who are poisoned almost instantly. Another plant they use is *Hademium Honghel*, which the Beïdane call the lion's baobab. In February and March this pretty bush is covered with pink flowers whose perfume is produced by a violent hydrocyanic poison which is put to many uses.

For wild beasts are not the only creatures whose dispatch may be desired by an honest Sarakollé!

The *griots'* power, on the other hand, is based on the tom-tom, whose insistent and potent rhythm breaks out on the least pretext.

The Sarakollé *griot* has a drum shaped like an hourglass, which he holds under his left arm. In his right hand he holds a drum-stick curved like a crozier. With this he can go on indefinitely beating two notes as sinister as a tocsin. The notes can be made higher or lower as the drummer varies the pressure with which he squeezes the strings which stretch the sheepskins. His drumming is answered by the *ardin*s, and the sound of these when the instruments are placed on water in a large calabash is heartbreaking in its sadness.

While we were there there was a fête to celebrate the marriage of the *Cadi*'s daughter to a Peulh chief. The Peulh tom-toms joined with those of the Sarakollés, and various Moorish tom-toms, moved by a spirit of emulation, joined in too. The combined efforts of drums, calabashes, empty pots and flutes made a most deafening din, the confusion being completed by an incredible tumult of epileptic and obscene dancers. The real object of all this noise was to cover the supposed cries of the bride. The next morning the crowd was shown a loin-cloth on which a matron had splashed some chicken's blood. After this the young bride, covered with thick veils, retired to the home of her parents for a week's retreat. When this was over, her final assumption of conjugal life would be celebrated by another outburst of drums and shouts.

It was after we were rejoined by our escort and our camels that we had the honour of being brought to the notice of the League of the Rights of Man, an organization some of whose members were as picturesque as they were unexpected.

One evening as the sun was setting our men at last arrived from M'Bout. M'Hammed and Mokhtar-Saloum seemed in excellent form, but the animals showed surprising signs of fatigue for unladen animals doing only twenty-five kilometres a day.

There were various weak points in their story, and in the end we discovered that a certain merchant called Tidjani was giving up his business in M'Bout to start another in Sélibaby, and that hearing of our free camels he had arranged for them to transport all his belongings and his good wife as well. M'Hammed and Mokhtar-Saloum, who of course had not lent our camels for nothing, had taken the precaution of unloading the animals two kilometres outside Sélibaby. Naturally they were ready to deny everything, including their little hunting parties by the way and the detours they had made to pass through various villages that Tidjanï's presence rendered hospitable. We now had to postpone our departure for a few days more, so as to rest the camels, purge them with salt, and rub their feet with suet.

When it was time for us to be drinking tea Tidjani appeared, bland and smiling, to pay his compliments. He was greeted with a storm of reproaches. Far from appearing penitent, he assumed an air of indignation and complained of our ingratitude to one who had so devotedly given his services to act as guide to our caravan, travelling as it was over an unknown route. It was a well-marked route, I may add, as straight as could be, that any child, a stranger to the country, could follow without any risk of getting lost.

And why, pursued Tidjani, should he have pinched our camels, when he had finer and stronger ones of his own? He had done us a service, and then had had the politeness to come and visit us in spite of his fatigue after a journey on a bad camel, and this was how we received him, standing in the sun, without even asking him to sit down!

At this Marion lost patience and told him to go to the devil. That put the final spark to his indignation. He told us we were merely women and very badly brought up into the bargain, that he, Tidjani, occupied a high position in Saint Louis where he was on the roll of electors, and finally that he was in correspondence with the League of the Rights of Man, which would immediately be informed of our insolence to a coloured gentleman.

And with this Tidjani went off full of righteous anger, dragging his canary-yellow slippers, to the hut where his four wives, his concubines and his slaves awaited this defender of the rights and liberties of humanity.

***

At dawn on April 4th we set off from Sélibaby in the Commandant's car. There were five of us in the party: the Commandant, Moussa Koro, the Commandant's chauffeur, Marion and myself. Moussa Koro was a ravishing half-caste woman whose mother was a Beïdane and whose father was a Mossi. She was always quick to throw a shawl over her hair, plaited like wicker-work, when any outing was proposed. We were somewhat cramped by the piles of luggage in the car, but we were in excellent humour at the prospect of seeing at last the mountains of the Assaba towards which we had ridden for so long. In his box, our mascot, Gatt', protested against this mechanical means of locomotion.

M'Hammed, the '*petit frère*' and the camels had started off the day before, and were to wait for us at Beida, a Sarakollé village near the Tak-Tak pass. From now onwards Boukhzeïma was to accompany us as a tourist, unburdened by any load, led by the bridle by one of the Beïdane. Mokhtar-Saloum had a new mount, a great muscular umbrageous creature bought at Sélibaby. He was very proud of it, although he continued to bewail the loss of his dear Boulilima, the finest camel in all Mauretania.

The landscape rolled past us, flat scrub, dried up by the sun, but which would soon be green again after the coming rains. Above the tall yellow grasses the baobabs stretched out piteously their mutilated arms. The natives pick the leaves, which they eat like spinach, and the fruit, the *pains de singe*, which hang on a thin stalk like presents hung on a Christmas tree. To save themselves trouble they hack down branches so that they can pick the leaves and fruit on the ground. Around the damaged trees lay also branches of thorny bushes, thrown there so that the sheep could browse on their scanty foliage.

On the other side of the plain reddish peaks rose abruptly one behind the other. They were formed of an earthy Devonian rock from which formerly the negroes extracted iron.

The Commandant pointed to the north-west where a sort of long grey wall ran along the horizon. He turned round towards us, calling out:

"The Assaba."

As we advanced the ground became more and more uneven, being cut into ravines. At the same time the trees got bigger and disposed in clumps. The road wound round huge marshes whose surfaces were dried and cracked by the long dry season. At the noise of our motor, guinea-fowls and partridges flew off into the woods. Parakeets interrupted their quarrels to fly to the highest branches, where they continued their irritable screeching. Red baboons, prudent but fearless, ran in front of the car. They ran in formation, young adults in front, females in the centre with their young on their backs, large powerful males in rear, looking at us out of the corners of their eyes. They thus escorted us up to the foothills of the Assaba, which they then proceeded to climb in easy, supple bounds.

We were now quite close to a mountain which stretched its long tabular profile before us, a profile characteristic of the mountains of the Sahara. It was bare and forbidding, a massive rectangular block that looked as though it was defending itself against any intruder. It was only one of the long Devonian chain which runs up from the Sudan through the Adrar and the Tagant right up to Rio de Oro.

The Assaba hardly exceeds a hundred metres altitude. Several transverse valleys, cut sharply into the plateaux, serve as passes: Tak-Tak, Sou Galoula, Goussas, Faram. Then comes the Tagant. Sources rise in its foothills. The limpid waters of tarns or *gueltas*, lying in deep hollows, are peopled with crocodiles and cat-fish. Here water was no longer a problem. Even when the little watercourse were dried up there were always these enormous natural reservoirs, to say nothing of the *marigots* or lakes of the plain which were never dry.

The most southerly pass, as well as the most frequented, was the Tak-Tak, and it also provided the best means of getting to Kiffa. But we had be advised by the Commandants of the Guidimaka and the Assaba to keep to the western slopes of the range where we would be able to see some curious rock-inscriptions, and also visit some little-known *gueltas*. Accordingly we kept right on, passing the Tak-Tak, the Soufa and the Galoula, intending finally to take the Goussas pass which led to Bil-Haratek. This pass was quite difficult but very beautiful.

The car stopped under a baobab tree at the entrance of the Tak-Tak pass. On the left the sculptured mountain thrust forth a hostile snout. On the right were volcanic peaks looking Japanese, whose bases spread wide on to the plain. Rocky bastions flanked by towers and terraces guarded the pass.

But a hundred metres from this severe landscape was a limpid mountain stream coming out of the rock, widening out into a *guelta*, and then disappearing once more. Through the water we could see the white sandy bottom. It was surrounded by reeds and here and there the water was hardly visible beneath its covering tufts of plants. On the wet banks all the diurnal and nocturnal drinkers of the animal world had left their imprints. Tracks of lions and hyenas and many others mingled with those of birds, and again with those of men and their camels. There were also the huge round footprints of elephants, a herd of which roamed about the Guidimaka.

We crossed the stream by a ford. On the other side of it was a wood of palm trees. It was still early and we had time to walk over to the wood before our *déjeuner*.

A mixed crowd of animals were drinking: bulls, goats, sheep and asses. The herdsmen, a Moor and two negroes, dressed in a few rags, were making tea near the water's edge. As soon as he saw the Commandant in our party, the Moor jumped to his feet and darted off to hide in the tall grasses.

Moussa Koro called out a name. The Commandant put his rifle to his shoulder, shouting out:

"Stop or I shoot."

What good was a knife against a loaded rifle? The fugitive resigned himself to his fate and came towards us with his head down. His hand, however, still gripped his dagger.

It was an old bandit of the mountains. His trade consisted in catching isolated travellers. A stab in the back or a push over a precipice was all that was necessary, and the camels and their baggage were his. He had already been arrested but had succeeded in escaping from the prison at Sélibaby only a fortnight before. This he had done with the assistance of accomplices who had not been found. But now by a stroke of luck the Commandant had captured all three, the criminal and his two slaves. Their arms were tied behind their backs, and they were then taken to Be'ida, where there would be no lack of volunteers to take them back to Sélibaby, for there were many who had at one time or another been robbed of cattle or sheep. Fatalistically the three marched off with good grace, even laughing at the derisive abuse poured on their heads by Moussa Koro, who was proud of having spotted them and teasingly struck them with a palm switch.

Considering the cruel features of the Moor and the two fearful anthropoids that belonged to him, we thanked our stars we had met them in the way we did. If this trip by car had not, luckily, been arranged we might easily, with our camels and things, have provided a tempting prize for the brigands, and been easy victims in these lonely places.

About four o'clock, in front of the straw hut which had sheltered us, and in which M'Hammed and Mokhtar-Saloum had shown what they could do in the presence of an official, the Commandant said goodbye and started back to Sélibaby. Before leaving, however, he reminded us that the brigands of the Assaba had not all been captured, and advised our men to leave lions and apes alone. They would never attack us without provocation, but if wounded or even frightened would be implacable.

Moussa Koro begged us not to go into the mountains at all, as they were the haunt of the most baneful of evil spirits. It was enemies of this sort that our two warriors also dreaded more than anything else.

As for us, our chief terror at the moment was our new guide!

We had looked all over the place for one, and we thought we were saved when a woman told us that her Ali would be delighted to show us the way. A little later, however, we received a shock when Ali appeared, a leper on a mangy camel. What made things worse was that the wretched man was animated by a zeal that was quite extraordinary, and touched us in spite of its being so misplaced. He would finger our belongings, and be for ever handing us things. Worse still, he was prepared to drink tea out of any glass, quite forgetting that we were no more than impure Christians. We had never before realized quite what an advantage it was to be untouchables amongst the pious Musulmans of the Sahara.

Through the holes of his ragged tunic we could see the scabs and sores.... But Ali dug his heel into the flanks of his miserable mount and proudly rode at the head of the little troop of which he had the honour to be the guide.

Chapter VIII

Our Luck Turns

N'DIO was a small place consisting of some fifty huts of pink *pisé* roofed with thatch. It was situated between a muddy *marigot* and hot, earthy mountains. On our map it was just where the 16th parallel north of the Equator cuts the 12th meridian east of Greenwich. The country round was desolate in the extreme, this being the most torrid and the most austere part of all Mauretania.

Hunted for centuries of misery both by Berbers and Arabs, various peoples had finally found asylum in the caverns and steep gorges of the Assaba. There were Toucouleurs from Senegal, Bambaras from the Niger, and a small Sudanese people, the Gangaris. The peace brought by the French delivered them in 1905, and they timidly left their hiding-places and came down into the plain to build huts like other people, breed cattle and sheep, and grow cotton, rice, and *sorgho*. They are thoroughgoing settlers, hardworking, and of gentle manners. They are often confused with the Sarakollés, although they are very different both in physical appearance and in character. They themselves do not like the idea, and will admit no more than that they are very distantly related.

The only strangers they had ever seen were a few French officers making tours of inspection, or now and again a negro trader from the river come to barter tea, sugar, and beads for sheep and cotton stuff. This time, to their great surprise, they were confronted by Frenchwomen.

The hut which formerly had been set aside for travellers had for long been in use as a stable. But a young woman came forward from the curious crowd that had gathered round us, and beckoned us to follow her. She led us to her hut, the best in the whole village.

Above her deep blue loin-cloth Khoukhou displayed an admirable bust and the arms of a goddess. Her strangely plaited hair formed a sort of crest on the top of her head and fell in a fringe of fine plaits and beads around her thin well-carved face. There was something about her which I felt to be Egyptian. The attitudes she assumed had a priestly nobility; she had broad shoulders and a long slender neck, and a mass of ornaments of unrefined gold, chased silver, amazonite and amber, which she wore in her hair, round her neck, and on her arms and ankles.

Khoukhou stopped before her hut, drew back a large wooden bolt, and made a sign for us to enter. The gesture was eloquent, indicating that all she had was ours.

Her 'all,' however, consisted of a sort of cell destitute of furniture. Its walls were decorated with large geometrical designs in pink, grey, black and white, somewhat like those which our wallpaper manufacturers have inherited from the Colonial Exhibition. Interwoven laths and palm branches formed a ceiling in which purple lizards ran about. Palm matting covered the dry earth which was both floor and bed. This humble dwelling was in fact something between a jar and a basket. A second door opened on to a little courtyard, where presently two girls appeared with calabashes and pitchers of water. These they carried on their heads with one bare arm held up to steady them.

Seïdi Naïgé, the village chief and husband of Khoukhou, was away with his herds, so that it was on her that devolved the duties of hospitality. She boiled millet, killed a tough little white cock and dispatched some boys to fish for cat-fish in the neighbouring marigot. We watched their slim, shining black bodies in the distance as they dashed after the fish, brandishing their two triangular nets which looked like blond wings.

In front of one of the huts was a group of women carding and spinning, making a buzzing sound like bees. Snowy-white heaps of cotton were scattered about them, which they took by handfuls. Some would card it between two boards covered with iron spikes; others would spin it on light spindles ornamented with black and white lines. Their stools and their calabashes were naively sculptured; for primitive people like to embellish the most humble objects of daily use.

Weaving was done only by the men. The cotton was woven into narrow strips no broader than a man's hand. These strips would then be returned to the women, who would sew them together

At N'Dio, women spinning

into loin-cloths and tunics. These they would dye with indigo, leaving patterns in white. Other bands of stuff, still narrower, striped with imported cotton, red, green and yellow, had been used to trim the clothes of the spinners. I call them clothes, but that is rather a pretentious word for the little aprons hanging from the waist, one in front, one behind, secured at the waist by a rope of white beads.

These white beads were very much in fashion with the Gangaris. With them they made necklaces and diadems, and interwove them with their plaits. To obtain them they would give the traders large quantities of soft cotton stuff.

Amongst the spinners were some little girls who would have liked to drop their work and gather round us. But they worked under the watchful eye of a 'supervisor' who held a bamboo ready in her hand.

Our friend Khoukhou persuaded her brother, Dumbo, to take us up into the mountains in search of Gangara archaeology.

It was hardly a pleasure trip for the good-natured Dumbo, nor, for that matter, for us either. Mountain climbing at a temperature of over 110° Fahrenheit is not in the least agreeable, particularly if one has to walk barefoot over slippery and burning stones.

For the younger generation, however, it was quite otherwise, and we were accompanied by seven enthusiastic little boys. Some carried our sandals, some our sticks; one was assistant photographer; but proudest of all were the oldest, *boubou* and Malek, who took charge of our provisions. I have never met creatures more trustful, tender, and gracious than these little savages.

As for M'Hammed and Mokhtar-Saloum, they did not attempt to hide their anxiety and disapproval. For them mountains were nothing else than the haunts of jinn, and, as everybody knew, jinn were highly susceptible beings who did not like to be disturbed. Anyhow, if the jinn of N'Dio were to punish the intruders it should not be by reason of any lack of propitiatory prayers. *Bismillahi* and *La illah ill Allah* were muttered continually.

At first sight the mountain seemed to be a solid unbroken mass, absolutely inaccessible. But Dumbo, walking ahead with his springy step, led us by narrow crevices in the rock-face, crevices in which the heat of a thousand years seemed to have accumulated. They got wider as we climbed, but more and more like ovens. Higher up we got on to narrow terraces covered with thorny bushes and tall dry grasses. We now put on our sandals to protect our feet from the thorns with which the ground was covered, but we had hardly done so when one of the children removed them again, so that we should not slip on the slippery rocks whose surfaces had been polished by wind and sand and by the rushing of water during the rainy season. Sometimes we would stand on some overhanging ledge, the heat of which so scorched our feet that we had no time to think of giddiness. Whenever the climb got difficult, Dumbo, always smiling and attentive, would make us mount by his knee and shoulder.

When we were about half-way up, the narrow ravine we were ascending in single file suddenly opened on to the platform of some ancient fortifications on which now a few palm trees were growing. The ruins of foundations showed where circular walls had formerly been. Scattered about were stones and broken pottery. In one place was a ring of tall flat stones that had enclosed the village. Behind these stones Dumbo knelt down and, stretching an imaginary bow, showed how his ancestors had defended the place against attack.

Then we sat under the trees and listened while Dumbo told the story of the Gangaris and their chief, Ganne, who, having come to Ouaghadou by the Hodh and the Tagant, had vanquished the King Maka, calling the country Guidémaka, which means the Mountain of Maka. It was in the grottos and labyrinths of these mountains of the Tagant and the Assaba that they were able to escape extermination at the hands of successive invaders who drove each other into this wild country.

All at once a terrified voice in the distance brought us to our feet.

"*La Utah ill Allah! La illah . . . ah!*" The prayer was called out quickly in a single note.

"It is Mokhtar-Saloum," cried M'Hammed, and he rushed off,

rifle in hand.

What could it be? ... A lion? ... A bandit? ... Or even perhaps a horned viper? ...

In face of his peril we forgot all prudence and all rancour, and ran to the rescue after M'Hammed.

An enemy with feet (or even without) would have been nothing to what Mokhtar-Saloum had found behind the spur of rock that enclosed the platform on which we were. No, he would have been daunted by nothing into which he could have stuck a knife or fired a bullet!

We found him petrified, trembling, and praying in front of a rock in which were long, narrow, horizontal openings. In one of these fissures we vaguely perceived some round white objects. These were the enemy. ...

They were nine human skulls, and with them were a number of other bones. They were certainly nasty things to come upon when one's head was already bursting with tales of ghosts and devils!

The fissure, a sort of flattened cave, was so shallow that it seemed impossible that any human beings could crawl hi to die inside. Perhaps besieged Gangaris, having no earth or other place to bury their dead, had pushed them in here. Nobody could tell us anything about these remains (or possibly they did not want to), except that the old men of the tribe knew that the men of bygone times were very big and very strong, and that there were many ossuaries in the mountains.

This one formed the advance post of a mysterious domain: titanic blocks made a colossal portico at the entrance of a passage which ran right into the heart of the mountain. This portico, as well as the neighbouring caverns, were decorated with strange designs. For the most part these were rectangular, and were painted in red ochre on the reddish or blackish earthy rock. Sometimes they were painted high up on the walls of the caves, sometimes in very low galleries, and one could not help wondering what giants and dwarfs the people must have included. On the subject of these drawings our companions were as uncommunicative as they were about the skulls.

"*marabouts* do that very, very long time ago, because of the jinn," said M'Hammed.

'*marabouts*' in the broken French spoken by the Moors may mean pious men or priests of any religion, not necessarily Mohammedan. We could well believe that the drawings were of religious significance, for we could easily imagine primitive people taking refuge there, terrified both by their worldly enemies and those of the world of spirits, and tracing on the walls of their shelter magic signs to appease the jinn or solicit the help of benevolent gods.

Dumbo was hardly more at ease than the two Beïdane, and urged us to return to the village. Besides, the sun would soon be sinking. So we started to retrace our steps, looking back on the barbaric Acropolis whose grandeur was exaggerated by the evening light.

If one lives in close contact with simple people, leading the same manner of life as they do, one is easily infected by their primitive philosophy. Alongside these simple men, imbued with supernatural fear, we walked in silence and under the weight of some oppression back to the village, where the evening fires, more comforting than usual, were just being lit.

The humble streets of the village were crowded with animals, for the flocks and herds had now been brought in. Our camels, hobbled at the knees, were ruminating near our hut. Our leprous guide was sleeping peacefully on the matting inside, but in spite of his presence we found it good to be 'home' again, and with Khoukhou. She had been waiting for us at the door, a perfect statue of polished mahogany.

She handed us a calabash of milk, and then called the other women to entertain us while we drank our tea. This they did by singing very barbaric and monotonous music in voices astonishingly shrill and out of tune.

Quiet descended on the village, fires died down, and the animals took possession of the night. Then another concert started, whose echoes reached us from the mountains: the roaring of lions, and the cries of hyenas and jackals, to be answered near at hand by the furious barking of dogs and the plaintive sounds of frightened cattle.

We found the hut intolerably stuffy, and, wrapped in our burnouses, we went outside, where a sand-laden wind was blowing.

In vain we tried not to notice the clouds of dust, and the animals that wandered about us. We found it impossible to sleep. Even the wild kitten on Marion's shoulder made it a point of honour to growl angrily in response to the barkings and roarings in the air.

The nights at N'Dio were all like that. But the inhabitants slept soundly at the thresholds of their huts.

At dawn the animals grew quiet, and the wind, as if by magic, suddenly dropped. We might then have got a little sleep, but it was time to get ready to go off to the mountain again to resume our explorations before the sun was too high.

It was an exhausting day with its chances and mischances. The first event of importance was the departure of the leper.

Dumbo had taken such a liking to us that he offered to take Ali's place and guide us to a camp of Tadjakants who were camel-breeders. He could take our things on his ass and the unwanted Ali could return home. The jinn, to start with, seemed to regard us with favour!

In our joy at being rid of the poor leper, we shook with great cordiality the diseased hand he innocently held out. On his side, he thanked us warmly for all our kindness!

Degrees of temperature are one thing, and heat is quite another. Even at Kayes in the middle of May, just before the rains began, with the thermometer showing over 120° Fahrenheit, in the 'cooled' rooms of the military sick-quarters (and Kayes shares with Djibouti and Chandernagor the reputation of being the hottest place in the world), I did not suffer from the heat as I did that Sunday, April 8th, at N'Dio, though it must be admitted that my occupation was then very different.

The two Moors, who had lately received some rolls of white cotton stuff to line their tents as reward for this trip, stoutly refused to take any further part in our antiquarian researches.

The negroes, who had also received presents, argued differently. "If the white women gave sugar and tea yesterday," they thought, "they will perhaps do the same again this evening, and as they treat us kindly, there is no reason for us not to follow and protect them today."

So with Dumbo and the children we spent the whole day

Magic Inscriptions and Ossuary at N'Dio

wandering in the rocky mazes of the mountain, roasting on the terraces, photographing, copying inscriptions, plunging into incredible labyrinths where human beings had marked their passage with magic drawings and heaps of broken pottery.

We were greatly impressed by the capacity of the ancient Gangaris for breaking pots! Everywhere, on the floor of the most inaccessible caves and at the bottom of the most uninhabitable rock-crevices, we found fragments of pottery ornamented with rude designs, like the modern *kanaris*. There were also fragments of balls of polished basalt. But we never found a single thing, whether of iron, wood or stone, that was unbroken.

Dumbo postponed as long as possible the moment for us to photograph the skulls. In climbing up to the ossuary I slipped on a loose stone, and only just managed to catch hold of the rock-face to save myself from falling. As I did so, a sharp pain darted through my right thumb. Immediately I remembered the thorn of Silliwol that I had many times attempted to remove, and then finally forgotten. I looked at it, and it seemed as though the thumb was swollen.... No doubt it was the heat, for my left hand, and my feet too, seemed somewhat swollen.

We went on with the photographs. Then a strange lassitude came over me and I felt rather sick and a little feverish. Marion got me to rest under a vault covered with rounds and crosses ... but to me it seemed draughty.

With the naive assurance of Europeans we took pleasure in thinking of the passes of the Assaba we were to visit, and Kiffa and the R'Kiss, Tidjikja and the Tagant, where there were Gangari ruins far more important than those we had been exploring. There we were, surrounded by our black courtiers, planning itineraries, fixing dates, and deciding to leave N'Dio first thing next morning to have time to see all we intended to before the storms of June.

Back in Khoukhou's hut my thumb was red and shiny, and Marion insisted on my bathing it for a long time in hot water. After a feverish and sleepless night it was swollen down to the wrist.

A fomentation was applied, while M'Hammed and Mokhtar-

Saloum looked at us with the contempt which people deserve when they have done everything possible to attract celestial vengeance on their caravan.

"Now you stop climbing mountains," said M'Hammed. "You take the good road to Kiffa by the Tak-Tak. No need to go to Goussas and tire the camels and break your head. Too difficult, Goussas. Mountain, it is always same everywhere; and it's no good, the mountain!"

"You leave us in peace. We have let them know at Kiffa and at Sélibaby that we were crossing by the Goussas pass. Everybody says it's the most beautiful."

"And you, if they tell you 'there are fine mountains in the Moon with *marabout* writings' you take your camel and run off to take photo?"

"We are going by the Goussas."

"*Inch' Allah!*"

And early next morning we rode off to the north.

***

At first everything went all right. Certainly I was not altogether comfortable, but when the guide is mounted on an ass the camels do not have to hurry.

The track kept close to the mountains which rose steeply on our right. We saw nothing of any animals except their tracks. About eleven o'clock we reached a large *marigot* where some Tadjakants were watering their herds. They sold us a sheep which they later helped us to eat.

By their miserable appearance one would hardly have thought that they were Himyarites and among the innumerable descendants of Solomon and the Queen of Sheba, nor that their ancestors had founded the sect of the Bekka'ias and the fortress of Tindouf before being driven southwards by later invaders.

While they drank tea with us they discoursed volubly, accompanying their words with easy sweeping gestures. They told us that we should certainly be well received that evening in their camp, and that next day they would take us to an isolated valley where we should be able to see a number of paintings in several colours representing men and animals. But alas! in spite of their desire to help us in every possible way, they could not provide the pack-camel that we had been looking for ever since Aleg. Robbers and diseases had only left them with a few inferior animals, and they needed all they had to go and pay their taxes at Kiffa before the end of the present moon. There was no time to be lost, for the storms would soon be playing havoc with the tracks. The *dioula* from Senegal had already been and had taken away half their flocks. He had said to their chief:

"Look here, you must have money for your taxes, and I who am your friend don't want you to be put in prison by the French. So I shall pay you five francs a head for your sheep, only, as I am a poor man myself, I will only pay half the money down, If you take your sheep to the market at Kayes you will have a long journey and the sheep will get thin on the way. Besides, the *administrateur* will be able to see your flocks and count them, and find out how many you concealed from him at the last assessment. And by the time you have paid your fine and the toll at the river and the dues of the market, you will return home poorer than when you set out."

One *ouguïa*! Five francs for a good fat sheep! The times were hard and the heart of Moulana (may his will be done!) was hardened against his people!

Moreover, though they did not know it, these wretched shepherds would never see more than the half of the agreed price. As for the *dioula*, he was beyond the reach of any control. He would take the sheep to Louga or one of the other Senegalese markets, where he would sell them at twenty-five francs a head.

Indeed, the times have changed in this country. It is now the black trader who despoils without scruple his former pillager. If they are caught by the French patrols, they are of course severely punished. But the scrub is vast and with many roundabout tracks, so it is not often that that happens. Thus, little by little, the flocks and herds dwindle, which are the only fortune of the nomads and provide almost their only food.

After our siesta, Marion and I decided to walk into the

mountains to take a photograph of a *guelta* near by.

At the same time we should be able to enjoy the luxury of a bathe and a drink of good clear water.

Mokhtar-Saloum had no objection to make, for it had been arranged for him to go straight on to the camp with Dumbo and our things and Boukhzeïma. The latter, having had no work to do lately, was now much better. But M'Hammed, who would have to accompany us to the tarn, assumed the airs of a martyr. For, from his point of view, *gueltas* were the most ill-famed places in all the mountains. Fortunately, a young Tadjakant slave was quite willing to come too to show us the way, and I took him on the croup of my camel.

Twenty minutes' ride brought us to the foot of the mountain in a prairie cut by ditches and riddled by rabbit holes dangerously hidden under the tall grass.

Marion was riding ahead in excellent spirits with a song on her lips. Suddenly, however, to my horror, I saw her camel go down. It had caught its leg in one of the rabbit holes. Marion was thrown from the saddle (a height of two metres) face downwards on to the sand, where she lay stunned. I dismounted as quickly as I could, and ran and picked her up. I found her half-conscious, with a lip cut and her face covered with blood. She quickly came round, however, and assured me she was all right, and even maintained that she had had a lucky fall. This was true in a sense, for a few paces further on she would have broken her skull on the stones.

M'Hammed, who was far from being astonished at any misfortune in this locality, took the opportunity to suggest our return. But Marion insisted on our going on, as we had already practically reached the *guelta*. A good bathe would make her feel quite herself again.

At the bottom of a canyon cut in the black earthy rock three tarns lay before us. At the edge of the first one we came to, M'Hammed pointed to some grooves in the ground which zig-zagged between the imprints of clawed feet.

"Track for crocodiles," he said. "The jinn make everything bad in the mountain."

As if the floods of the White Gorgol, swollen by the rains, were not enough to bring crocodiles to the lakes of the Assaba without the intervention of jinn!

"Crocodile is very bad!"

Then M'Hammed sat down by the camels, carefully filled his pipe, and watched us ironically.

Marion was set on bathing. There were so many footprints of gazelles and guinea-fowl and so many cat-fish making bubbles in the water that the crocodiles did not seem to be very hungry. Moreover, the negro boy was jumping like a young goat into the water of the furthest *guelta* to fill a waterbottle where the water was most clear.

We had seen crocodiles round this third tarn basking in the sun on the rocks, but as soon as they had seen us they had dived into the water. For a moment the surface was covered with ripples, disturbing the smooth reflection of the trees around, then a few minutes later it was a polished mirror once more.

At the water's edge the little slave was overjoyed at something he had found: two batches of crocodile's eggs, six dozen in all, which he collected carefully and wrapped up in his *boubou*. Then he plunged into the water again, bathing with obvious relish. After that he came out, picked up his eggs and made a sign that the place was free for us.

"The crocodiles certainly don't seem very aggressive," said Marion.

"Not to small negroes, anyhow," I answered. "They have a decided preference for literary people...."

"Bah! how should they know? They have never seen any before! Besides, if they suspect there will still be time for us to run away."

In a moment our tunics were off and we were immersed in the delicious tepid water in which all fever and muscular stiffness seemed instantly to dissolve. But we kept a weather eye on certain long grey objects crouching between the rocks at the furthest edge of the guelta. They gave, however, the comforting impression of being more frightened of us than we were of them.

An hour later we came suddenly upon another member of the local fauna, and at this meeting the roles were reversed. This time it was a magnificent lioness who thrust up her proud head over the tall grasses at a distance of no more than twenty paces.

The camels were terrified; their eyes looked wild with fear. They turned in panic and made off in great bounds that shook Marion's head painfully as well as my thumb.

As for the lioness, secure in her sense of power, she watched us calmly, though evidently she was ready to spring at the least menace.

This meeting could have been tragic enough, but luck was with us. By a miracle M'Hammed obeyed our urgent orders that he was not to shoot. A miracle indeed, for the skin was worth fifty francs to him! Whether he aimed well or badly at gazelles or bustards did not matter in the least. But with lions those who fumble are not let down lightly. One might even say that the real danger in such country as this is to carry a gun. Nothing makes one more nervous. . . . Not carrying firearms, we were left in peace—and the animals too.

The lioness watched us ride off and then returned to her personal affairs.

This was not to be our last emotion on this memorable day.

As soon as we got to the camp, Mokhtar-Saloum informed us of the death of our pretty little pet, Gatt', who had been trodden on by a camel.

It was a great loss, this savage little companion, so affectionate and so courageous. No bigger than one's fist, he could already keep dogs at bay. Each meal was accompanied by the fiercest growling against imaginary enemies. Then, suddenly replete, he would draw in his claws and jump on to Marion's shoulder, where he would be the gentlest and most innocent little kitten. He had been born in freedom, and had only been lent to us for a while, for at the first breeding season he would have been off to the wilds once more. Wild cats never permanently abandon their dignity and independence for the comforts of civilized life.

God be praised! We were given a quiet tent near the sheep-fold at some distance from the camp. Here we were free to think of ourselves and tend to our respective wounds. In the distance we could hear the tom-tom beating for a marriage feast, but we were neither of us feeling well enough to take part in any festivities.

We had a new item on our menu: crocodile eggs. These are much like duck's eggs, only a good deal bigger, and have been jestingly called 'drake's eggs.'

After we had eaten, Marion, who was really rather knocked up by her fall, went off to sleep in the tent. Outside, M'Hammed and Dumbo chattered in low tones. The others had gone off to the wedding.

I sat alone in front of a huge fire, bathing my swollen thumb in hot water. It was now obviously a whitlow. It had got quite stiff and had begun to be very painful. It was a keen, piercing pain, starting under the nail and drilling its way up my arm. It made me feel rather sick. I could hear the fever beating in my temples and my forehead was covered with sweat.

Rag-ends of thought darted through my brain: A whitlow . . . was a whitlow a serious complaint? . . . What troubled sleep Marion was having! . . . Suppose she has internal injuries, what could we do out here? ... At Kiffa there was only a medical assistant, a negro. . . . Nobody at all at Sélibaby. . . . An old male nurse at Kaédi and a French doctor who was always away shooting. . . . Kiffa—that's 250 kilometres. . . . And the mountains to cross, too. . . . How were we to manage? . . .

Once more I saw Marion falling from her camel, falling heavily on to the ground. Marion, my closest friend, the companion of my joys and trials—I had for a moment thought her dead. Suppose she had been! Uselessly I pictured the silent, sinister return, the gaunt silhouette of a riderless camel. . . .

The lioness, Gatt', the crocodiles, a monkey who had made faces at us while we were bathing—they all danced among the flames as I stared into the fire.

So much suffering for a miserable little thorn. . . . But you couldn't abandon a trip on account of a whitlow. . . . Francois, one of the fishermen from Treboul, had had one, but he had gone on fishing just the same. . . . Then he had sharpened his knife and cut off the end of his finger himself. . . . With one great chop, on the mess table. . . . He had shown us the stump, still bloody, at Villa-Cisneros. . . . But I should never have the courage. . . . Kaédi, 200 kilometres. . . . Kiffa, 250, five days' journey, perhaps six. . . . Two mountains. . . . "The jinn make everything bad in the mountain." . . . Two hundred and fifty. . . . Two hundred and fif. . .

The Sorceress

I must have fallen off to sleep, my hand remaining in the hot water. A sharp pain woke me up. I opened my eyes wide, and then wider, staring with horror at the strange creature I saw before me.

One might have taken it for a monstrous fetish made of wood and shrivelled leather, an embodied spirit of this baneful earth. The face was disfigured by a hideous grimace. The eyes were fixed upon me, and in them I could see the red reflection of the fire. . . . Perhaps it was a jinnee, *our* jinnee, the one that had been tracking our footsteps ever since we entered the Assaba!

I screamed for help, and at once M'Hammed was at my side, and with a threatening gesture driving off the evil thing. The gnome, thus exorcized, turned and limped off slowly, dragging its legs that were too short for the long body. The back was hunched. The knotty arms gripped a big stick.

"You got a fright for the sorceress?" asked M'Hammed. "Ach, it's no good: same thing as jackal."

Kneeling beside me, he whispered, for the sorceress was within earshot. She had stopped and was leaning against a tree muttering something. I could just see her white hair, her toothless mumbling mouth, her long flat breasts like tobacco-pouches, falling over the ragged loin-cloth. M'Hammed told me that, like all her kind, she was an old slave who had acquired a taste for human blood. During the night she sucked the blood of other slaves, or else she demanded it as the price for amulets, philtres or spells, whether of love or vengeance.

M'Hammed told me worse things still. These slaves, practised in witchcraft, could take the heart out of a sleeping man, who would then appear to be dead. By means of prayers, magic ceremonies and presents, the family got the vampire to return the stolen heart. At once the victim got up and resumed his normal existence just as if nothing whatever had happened to him.

All the same he was not quite the same as before. For instance, if he looked behind him over his shoulder, he could no longer go forward. And he could make another man swoon by staring in his eyes, because the power of witchcraft had remained in his heart.

A tumult of piteous bleating interrupted M'Hammed. The fence of the *zeriba* or sheep-fold made a crackling noise under the pressure of the crowd of frightened animals who were trying to escape. One cry rose above all the others. Shepherds rushed up with lighted brands in their hands, just in time to see a large speckled hyena carrying off a black ewe.

The sorceress had disappeared. By the position of the Southern Cross I knew midnight was past. At last this devilish day was over. Almost automatically, as on other nights, I told M'Hammed to have the camels ready early in the morning and, holding my aching hand against my breast, I lay down beside Marion and tried to sleep.

But when the morning came, neither the fresh air, nor the beauty of the grey mountains against a pearly sky, nor the sounds of the camels being brought in from the pasture, nor even the thought of the rock-paintings we were to have seen—no attraction was strong enough to get us up.

Besides a sprain in the neck, Marion was suffering from an attack of migraine. As for me, the infection had now reached my arm. There was really no question of our going, and we settled down to a day of rest.

In spite of a few bursts of hope, we were both thoroughly discouraged. Marion, who was a born fatalist, accepted our situation with a wise and silent resignation. I was just the opposite, and I must have made myself pretty well insupportable with my ragings against fate and my useless plans and decisions.

As a matter of fact I really had not much to grumble about. All things considered, the astonishing thing was that mischance had not descended upon us sooner, but had given us time to get from one end of Mauretania to the other.

We got together all our medical supplies and counted them up. The inventory was not impressive. We had been distributing drugs to the nomads as if we ourselves were proof against every illness. All we had left was a little aspirin and quinine which had got pulverized by being carried so long on the back of a camel. The box of dressings was almost empty. We had still some permanganate, but our solid iodine had disappeared and the bottle of alcohol been broken.

Our *tassoufra* of provisions revealed a similar state of depletion.

All we had left was some sugar and tea, a small bag of tobacco, a few handfuls of monkey-nuts, and some biscuits. And we had been warned that on the way to Kiffa we should find very few camps at this season on the other side of the Assaba.

The batteries for our electric torch had melted in the heat. So had our candles. M'Hammed and Mokhtar-Saloum had five cartridges left between them.

Having taken stock of our penury, there was nothing more for us to do but to wait for the empty and interminable hours to pass. My thumb prevented me writing and also made sleep impossible. Having nothing else to do I watched the little heat cyclones driving past. They were visible by a column of sand and dried leaves, which were sucked up in the vortex. At the first clump of bushes it would break up. It was not pleasant for any tent that happened to lie in the track of one. One caught ours, and the men had only just time to hurl themselves on its supports or it would have blown over on top of us.

When I bathed my thumb in the evening, M'Hammed offered to open it for me with his knife. With horror I refused.

Next morning we had to face the situation and come to some decision. My axillary glands were swollen, and I now had a carbuncle on the buttock. We came to the conclusion that it would be folly to stay where we were or to take any other route than that to Kiffa.

Mokhtar-Saloum was sent on ahead on the best camel with a letter to the District Commandant, asking him to send his lorry to meet us.

We had to say goodbye to the sweet-tempered Dumbo, whose good black face had always been lit up by a great white smile. His ass could not carry our things so far. After long negotiations, with many hitches, M'Hammed engaged a shepherd. He was almost an idiot, but he was the owner of an ox. He was to follow us with the baggage.

We were hoisted up painfully into our saddles and the conventional words of farewell were exchanged: "*Ouaddatek l'Moulana*, I confide you to God, your refuge is in Moulana." When addressed to us they seemed to be more than usually appropriate.

Certainly a whitlow does not prevent one's travelling, though it is capable of determining one's course. This one was to take me to the sick-quarters of Kayes, and further still into the operation theatre of the military hospital of Dakar in Senegal.

The first surgical operation took place only two hours after we had set out, under the shadow of a big tree. Near by, a spring trickled out of the mountain into the little basin it had cut in the rock and ran down into a long *marigot*. On the rocks around, monkeys and carrion birds watched the performance.

The pain in my thumb had got so intolerable that I had in the end accepted M'Hammed's offer. Whether it was from vanity or the natural cruelty of his race, to open my thumb seemed to give him exquisite pleasure. Or perhaps he had hopes of a present. In any case pity played no part in whatever emotions may have moved him. He got his little pointed knife out of his cartridge pouch, the knife with which I had seen him so many times cut a sheep's throat, and clean the feet of the camels. He sharpened it carefully, first on a stone and then on the steel of his lighter. After Marion had passed this improvised scalpel through a flame, he seized my hand and ruthlessly but deftly made a deep cut in my thumb. Blood and pus spurted out, and I fainted like any heroine of fiction.

After our siesta M'Hammed asked me for the beautiful calabash I had bought near Tak-Tak, one made of *dembaïe* wood, red with black grain, polished like marble. It was the price of my blood.

I protested as a matter of form:

"It is you, on the contrary, who ought to pay me a *dia* for having wounded me."

"No, no. If I make run your blood for bad, then I pay the *dia*. But if it's for good, then it's you who give present. It's same thing with my mother or sister. And at N'Dio I give my pipe to my *petit frère* who cut me a little here (and he pointed to a scar on his temple) because I had too much ache in my head. . . . Or else bad things happen."

We had had enough of 'bad things,' and M'Hammed got his calabash.

In the afternoon we crossed the Soufa pass. The ground was a mass of rock fragments, a sort of scree. The beauty of the pass was not equivalent to the trouble we had to get over it.

Marion was suffering a lot. She could feel every jerk of Boulilima in her neck. As for me, I was quite incapable of guiding Boudaïl. I had tied my stick and the bridle to the pommel and left the animal to look after itself and me too. Boudaïl was a good beast. I admired the prudent way in which he picked out the best track and tested the firmness of stones before trusting his weight to them. This instinct seemed to me the more marvellous by the fact that Boudaïl had been born and bred in the sands and had never seen mountains before. The soles of his feet were as soft as the palms of one's hands.

M'Hammed rode well ahead of us, leading the still unladen Boukhzeïma by the bridle. He was only worried by one care: not to damage the feet of the camel he was riding. It was his own property. Our guide brought up the rear with his ridiculous but sure-footed little brown ox. The sound of its steps seemed to frighten our camels and make them jump. This we did not like at all, as a fall on the sharp stones might easily have been fatal.

We found a shelter on a high, smooth ledge of rock, and the men made huge fires of brushwood. The flames threw distorted shadows of the camels on to the perpendicular wall of rock behind us. On the other side was a steep gorge in which two hyenas were fighting.

It was a fine setting for the *Rouaut Sba ous Gaboun*, the fable of the Lion and the Hyena, with which M'Hammed tried to entertain my sleepless hours, sitting by the fire smoking his little pipe.

The lion was old and ill, and as he did not like to live all alone he made friends with a female hyena. The lion hunted for their food while the hyena carried the water.

One morning the hyena looked at the sleeping lion. He looked so thin and aged that she thought it would be foolish for her to fetch water for one who would soon be of no help to her. So she lay down again and went to sleep.

The sun was already high when the lion woke up. Now lions,

The Eastern Slopes of the Assaba

like men, like to drink when they wake in the mornings—at all events M'Hammed assured me that they did. The lion looked for water, but found the waterbottle empty and his companion asleep. He immediately guessed the reason, and went off to hunt without saying anything; for he was still strong and far from stupid. He killed a large hyena, laid the carcass beside his companion and sat down patiently to wait.

It was a decidedly unpleasant surprise for the hyena on waking to find lying beside her the body of one of her sisters—and one much bigger and stronger than she was. Instantly she recovered her respect for the old lion, or at any rate her prudence.

"*Ouallahi! Ouallahi!*" she cried, jumping to her feet. "Where is the goatskin waterbottle, that I may run to fetch water? Fool that I am to sleep when the sun is burning hot and my poor old lion has not had anything to drink!"

Whoso wishes to be master of his tent must only show his weakness to God. . . .

In Moorish fables it is always the strongest or shrewdest that come off best. In this they reflect the cruel law of the desert, the law without justice, according to which the weak always go to the wall unless they are cunning enough to have the last laugh.

Those four days and a half from our departure from the camp of the Tadjakants on Wednesday, April 11th, to our arrival at Kiffa on the following Sunday, have remained in my memory as one vast nightmare. During the day it was the blinding, scorching scrub through which I must ride on and on, cost what it might. At night it was my sleepless watching of the Southern Cross as it turned slowly in the night sky while my companions slept. Day and night I had never a moment's relief from the atrocious pain which ran right through my hand and arm. Then there was the fearful heat, partly sun, partly fever, and a general feeling of weakness which obliged me to stop frequently for fear I should fall fainting from Boudaïl's back.

Sometimes we rode beside rivers of dry sand, bordered with reeds and flanked by cultivated fields, which in June would be

Kiffa, the Military Post

covered with rushing water. Here and there, but at rare intervals, there were pits in the river-bed, *oglats*, in which there was still a little dark stagnant water. To get some water M'Hammed would have to call a slave from the fields near by. For he had never wanted us to carry a *delou*, the leather bag mounted on a wooden hoop with which the water is drawn—probably for fear he would be called upon to undertake the degrading work himself.

We stopped under the palm trees beside almost dried-up marigots—El Hadj, Sani, Moïla—and drank with avidity their thick stagnant water.

One day some herdsmen who were watering a herd of zebus, stole a woollen vest that I had stuffed into my saddle to make a cushion under the carbuncle I had developed.

Should I on that account maintain, as so many Europeans have done, that the Moors are thieves? For four months we had been wandering from Port Étienne to Kiffa, and during that time had had many travelling companions of many different tribes. We had slept under many tents, rich and poor. We had had many different servants in the French posts. One of our escort—Cheikh, Armeddou or M'Hammed— had always had the key of our bags which lay scattered about on the sand. Our cartridge pouches containing our money lay on the ground near us as we slept. And every night, except when we were near lions or mountain bandits, our camels were left to roam about. No, we had long ago laid aside the burden of suspicion. Always the things that had been lost, scissors, sandals, a bracelet or a knife, were found sooner or later. And every morning all our camels were brought in. Our confidence had not cost us much: in all, two items, a little silver ring pinched by the son of the *mallem* who had sold it to us, and this woollen vest, stolen at El Hadj. No, from our experience I really could not say that the Moors were thieves.

On the other hand, the history of this people contains little else than marauding.... But that is a paradox I cannot attempt to explain.

The whole of this journey we never came upon a tent. What camps there were were hidden in the country well off our route. We did not dare wander from the track for fear of missing the lorry that was to come to meet us.

One evening at Sani a glare of light lit up the horizon to the north-east and brought us to our feet with beating hearts. Headlamps! ... It must be the lorry! ... It seemed to come nearer; but it was only the illusion of hope which made it seem to, for it was nothing more than a fire that had been lit by some nomads.

And this night passed like the others. Marion was now very much better. The chief symptom of her fall which now remained was an inordinate capacity and need for sleep. The two men, indifferent, slept too. I sat a little to one side and kept a small fire going to boil up my old dressings.

Attracted by the smell of our camels, hyenas howled around us. It was a melancholy sound, though there was no danger. When I went off to collect some brushwood I could hear them scampering away.

On the Saturday morning, near an *oglat*, we met Mokhtar-Saloum, who had come back from Kiffa with a parcel of medicaments and a letter from the adjutant to say that the lorry was under repair. The Commandant was at the moment away holding an inquiry some fifteen kilometres to the north of Kiffa in the camp of the Cherattit, who were engaged in a bitter religious dispute. The subject of the dispute was whether a row of beads, and the prayers to correspond to them, should be 99 in number or 100. There had been several broken heads as a result of the quarrel which the medical assistant was trying to mend.

Mokhtar-Saloum added casually that the latter, whom he described as a 'black European,' would be waiting for us at the palm trees of Kouroudjel. In the joy of hearing that succour was only two hours' ride further on, I sympathized with the fatigue which the *'petit frère'* complained of, congratulated him on his rapidity and paid for a fine *aouli* he had bought himself at Kiffa.

When the medical assistant arrived the first thing he told us was that Mokhtar-Saloum was a good-for-nothing, and that he had spent twenty-four hours amusing himself with the *griots* instead of bringing us the medicines. The fact was that the medical assistant had been sent for at the Cherattit's camp, and had had time to go to Kiffa for his things and then get to Kouroudjel three hours before our messenger.

However, I was no longer to be surprised by such conduct: we had seen too much of it since Boutilimit.

At last we could eat. A piece of bread, sweet potatoes and sardines provide the most delectable of feasts when one has starved for four days.

While we had been starving on this interminable track, a man had been looking for us on the Goussas pass. At M'Bout the District Commandant had taken in with a single glance of his experienced eye the poverty of our equipment and the inferiority of our escort, and he had had the thoughtfulness to send out a reliable man with supplies.

Our medical adviser was altogether reassuring about Marion's condition. Then when I was sufficiently restored by my meal he proceeded to perform my second operation. M'Hammed had cut across the thumb, but he cut longwise, getting right down to the bone. His scalpel was sharp though the point was broken. After this he washed the wound with water that had been carefully sterilized, to which had been added some more that had been taken straight from a neighbouring pool in which zebus were drinking. At Dakar he had been instructed, 'like the Whites,' always to boil any water used for surgery. But he had never understood why. For my part I was in no mood to protest.

Somehow or other I at last got a few hours' sleep. And I was now sustained by the certitude that tomorrow I should be at Kiffa—and in a bed!

Kiffa! Bed! These two words formed the sole content of mind during those last thirty kilometres. Beyond that my mind was a blank.

With my left hand and with my heels I pressed Boudaïl forward. He had been limping ever since we had crossed the pass, with a gash in one of his feet. Morning and evening M'Hammed tended it. Bending over the squatting camel he would say with absolute simplicity:

"You look away. I piss on foot of camel." A service that would no doubt have been willingly reciprocated if M'Hammed had had a bad foot.

To get to Kiffa! I rode on with the idea ringing through my head. I hardly saw the immense stretch of dry hay around us. I had no prudence descending slopes, no pity for my limping mount, no care for the saddle that rubbed my carbuncle, nor even much thought for the whitlow on my thumb. The concentration of my mind combined with my state of exhaustion to produce a condition bordering on anaesthesia.

To get to bed! I did not even want to stop to put on clean clothes, as did the Moors, when from the top of a hill the crenelated walls of the military post came finally into sight.

Thirty kilometres without a stop. We had started before dawn. It was nearly midday when we entered into the courtyard of the post. Men dressed in white gathered round us looking in silence at the two rescued Frenchwomen. Someone got my camel to kneel down. I was pulled from the saddle. The white-clothed men took me into a room, a half-darkened room, almost cool. In the middle was a great white rectangle. A bed at last! A bed in which I plunged into a sleep such as I had never known, a sleep that was heavy and long, and as profound as death.

Chapter IX

A Haven of Refuge

IF I had to be ill I could certainly not have chosen a better place to be laid up. I do not speak of ordinary hospitality, colonial or other. The devoted attentions which surrounded me, the friendliness which consoled and encouraged me, and helped me to stand up against adversity, were far in excess of what is usually implied by the word.

When Marion and I were sufficiently restored to look around us, our gaze was met by smiling faces, black and white, and we sensed a family atmosphere, the informality and cordiality of which were comforting beyond all words.

This homely atmosphere, combined nevertheless with strict military discipline, was characteristic of Kiffa. Every day in the little mess, as bare and white as a monastery, we would sit down to our midday meal with the officers, or we would find them on the verandah where we would go to breathe the cool evening air after a stifling day. Besides the District Commandant of the Assaba, there were two captains. One of them had commanded a nomad corps in Mauretania; the other had just come from a similar command at Agadès. There was also a resident lieutenant who had come straight from the Military College of Saint Cyr and who was impatient to get into one of the camel corps. In the form of memories or hopes, the Sahara embraced the whole lives of these three men.

But the famous family atmosphere of Kiffa was due most of all to a charming '*madame-Capitaine,*' who by her mere presence ensured harmony, good manners, and gaiety in the mess.

She was indeed the animating spirit of this humble building of dried earth, white-washed and decorated with native stuffs, furs, and painted leather. The garden, adjoining a *marigot*, provided an abundance of fruit and verdure. No home could have suited her better; for this one she had created herself from almost nothing, employing her own small hands getting browner every day, and making it a labour of love. It was a complete contrast to some of the other posts we had seen in which a bachelor commandant lived alone with his boredom.

Enough has not been said of the courage of colonial women—I mean the real ones—who, hiding their troubles and anxieties, make the task so much easier for the men who struggle in these distant and often desolate spots. They teach their brown or black sisters to respect the wisdom of the white woman. And they know how to look around them with an appreciative eye, seeing the beauty of alien people and exotic things, and the beauty of the immense horizon of this open country.

I have known some who, on horse or camel, would accompany their husbands on their tours of inspection, making a tour of inspection themselves in their own way, giving friendly words and good advice in the brown tents or the thatched huts. Others there are who have made different uses of their opportunities, taking to writing, painting or ethnography. Others have filled official posts or run commercial enterprises. Some, on the other hand, have been fully occupied looking after their families, protecting them from the many dangers which threaten white children in the tropics.

I cannot claim that I have an innate sense of discipline. On the other hand, I can certainly appreciate its benefits when applied to others! It was reassuring to see the Moors patiently squatting on the sand beyond the open gate, which they had not the right to pass except on business. When we went out they saluted, which was flattering.

It was very agreeable to be able to undress in one's room without being surprised by the *mallem*, or by some loafer in quest of Europeans to escort. We were thus at last able to get rid, at any rate, for the time being, of our lice.

Our own two men were transformed. Fear of punishment developed in them a politeness and attentiveness one would never have expected. M'Hammed had previously served one of the officers, and he had sung his praises all the way from M'Bout to Kiffa.

"That captain, it is my friend. Him good and strong altogether, Ach!" Which meant of course that the captain in question did not waste any words, meted out punishment when it was deserved, and did not confuse people's minds with indulgence, pardon, or gratitude, which are conceptions not readily assimilated by the Beïdane. With him the just price was paid for every delinquency. To obey is less onerous when the commander's will is inflexible.

Mokhtar-Saloum's insolence now completely disappeared. He would salute even in passing the lieutenant's empty room, and he lit the fire before dawn for my dressings and for our tea. To demonstrate his newly-found zeal he would even wash our clothes before they were dirty. And this was the man who in the scrub had many a time made us pay for a slave to wash his tunic.

It was a lesson to us, and one that we gave good heed to.

In spite of the peace and repose of this existence we were obsessed by a longing for the open country. To start out again as soon as possible was the idea always uppermost in our minds. Sometimes Marion sent for her camel and rode out towards the mountains, up to the furthest dunes, from which could be seen the route leading to Tidjikja.

The District Commandant would not hear of our going. He spoke of the imminent storms which would shortly be ravaging the country, and which every year take their toll of victims, and the absurdity of going off with my thumb not yet cured. He advanced many reasons for my taking the next lorry to Kayes, where proper medical attention was to be had. Normally a lorry came every fortnight with supplies, but it did not run during the rainy season, and one could not be sure whether the next journey might not be the last.

My hand was now purple and swollen right up to the wrist. In the middle of my thumb was the open suppurating sore. I hated the thought of going to Kayes, for that meant the end of our trip. In desperation I decided to have a third incision; but that only brought temporary relief. The Commandant hesitated to order me to Kayes, and the lorry came and went. It was promised, however, that it would make one more journey before the rains. In the meantime, I would have a chance to get well . . . but my thumb suppurated more vigorously than ever. . . . And then the infection spread and more whitlows appeared.

The lorry had brought mails. Belatedly we heard the news of the French successes in that part of Africa which in Mauretania is called the *Grand Nord*. The French had entered Tindouf and had linked up Morocco and Mauretania. . . . The champagne passed in honour of the occasion.

The days went by, sometimes bringing hope, sometimes discouragement. They were largely occupied with putting endless fomentations on my thumb. Besides that we went walks along the valley, where the Commandant was carefully rearing some young banana trees, whose fruit his successor would one day be able to eat, and three thousand date palms which might in fifteen or twenty years be the wealth of Kiffa.

We were delighted when the two captains asked us if we would like to come with them to Tamchakett where they had to make an inspection. "If the 'Press' would like to accompany us . . ." they said, and we did not have to be asked twice, for we wanted a little distraction.

Tamchakett was a little military post, more remote even than Kiffa, between the Affolla and the R'Kiss. The lorry we had asked for had by this time been got going again. We were to start off the following night, the idea being to get over the dunes during the hours of coolness when the ground was firmer, and to arrive at Tamchakett before the sun was high next morning.

That afternoon I went out on to the terrace. I looked out into the courtyard of the post and saw something which made me gasp with astonishment. Escorted by a guard, there was the awful sorceress who had so terrified me in the mountains. She was hobbling across the courtyard leaning heavily on her long stick. She looked wilder, more evil and more sordid than ever.

I asked what she was doing there, and her guard began a long story in his strange Franco-Bambara jargon, which I found very difficult to understand. I gathered, however, that she had arrived a few days before with the Tadjakants of Soufa. The interpreter's wife, *madame-femme-Interprete*, had had a dream of a sheep with a man's head, which was an evil omen. She had then sent for the sorceress, and had forbidden her to come and eat her heart during the night. Nevertheless she dreamt of the same sheep again, and there was a great to-do among the women of the place. In the end the Commandant, tired of listening to arguments and complaints, had thought it best to lock the old hag up, as much to protect her from an angry crowd as to keep her out of mischief.

What will seem in one place to be a coincidence will seem in another to be fraught with significance. All depends on the climate in which you are living. In France I am not particularly superstitious, but in Africa I was not quite the same person. And meeting this dreadful woman, reminding me as she did of one of the worst days of my life, I could not help feeling depressed. It wore off, however, as I busied myself getting ready for our departure and thought with pleasure of the new country we were to see.

At midnight the lorry, crammed with people and baggage, drove slowly through the gateway of the post, and bravely sallied forth into the country. The cold night air and the bright moonlight put everyone in good spirits. We shivered but we were happy.

At a quarter-past twelve one of the men who were accompanying us called out: "The spring, it has fallen down." But no one took him seriously, and he was called a fool.

Five minutes later, however, somebody expressed the opinion that one of the wheels was rubbing. A discussion ensued between the two captains, one of whom was driving, as to whether we should turn back or go ahead and trust to luck. This discussion lasted exactly five minutes when the question was decided, not by either of the captains, but by the car itself. Something happened inside the gear-box which brought us to a standstill.

There was now nothing for it but to get out and walk home, leaving the lorry where it was for the night. Luckily we had done no great distance, six or seven kilometres at the most. Once more the country of camel-riders and pedestrians had defended itself against mechanization!

The next day there were undeniable signs of another whitlow coming on my left thumb. This was now my sixth. I now felt there was no other course than to resign myself to my fate and take the next lorry to Kayes, which would be going on May 5th.

When it came we got the news of another air disaster in Rio de Oro. On April 26th one of the aeroplanes of Air France had crashed near Cape Bojador, on that desolate coast where four months earlier we had got our first welcome from the Moors —with bullets. In this crash two were injured, Gorée the pilot, and Bougrat, who was in command of the Dakar region. Reig, the mechanic, had been killed. Another aeroplane was sent to the rescue and brought in the injured, then returning for the body and the mails. When they got once more to the scene of the disaster, they found Reig's body mutilated and the mails ransacked. Four Ouled-Delims, Mohammed-ould-Khattat and his three sons, had committed these acts in revenge for a *dia* that had not been paid by some Trarzas belonging to French territory.

We had seen the wrecked plane, the Smara, while we were at Port Étienne. A fine craft it was. And Gorée too; he had looked silent and absorbed. We had exchanged good wishes. A little later the aeroplane had vanished into the night sky.

Before leaving for Kayes we wanted to see our camels once more, and we went out to see them being watered by M'Hammed and Mokhtar-Saloum.

The District Commandant was with us, and as soon as he saw Boukhzeïma he said:

"That's the best one. Left to graze for two months, he would be superb."

This opinion was offered quite spontaneously, the Commandant knowing nothing of the intrigue of which Boukhzeïma had been the object. However, all that was over; our journey was at an end, and it was no use crying over spilt milk. The only important thing was to prevent any further intrigues concerning the camels that we were to return to Abdallahi and Ould-Deïd. From various remarks that our two men had let fall, we had our suspicions that something was on foot. To put a spoke in their wheel we had decided to hand over the two camels to the care of the *Cadi* of Kiffa, who would send them off by the next caravan going to the Trarza.

It was Sunday and our last day at Kiffa. The flag hung motionless above the crenelated walls. The pet gazelle belonging to the non-commissioned officers was sleeping in the middle of the courtyard.

The shrill notes of a *tidinit* sounded like the song of a cicada in the breathless air. Through the gateway we could see the sharpshooters dancing, sometimes leaping like acrobats, sometimes miming with cleverly indecent gestures. Then a gramophone broke out hoarsely playing a worn-out record of a song once popular in Paris.

On the terrace of the Residence one of the captains, who had recently come from the East, was talking of his long marches through the desert with the veiled Touaregs.

The District Commandant, who was going next day to Dakar where formerly he had been stationed, was talking of the Trab-el-Beïdane. But it was a Trab-el-Beïdane that we did not yet know: the vast solitudes of the Inchiri, the Ouaran, and the Makteïr, in which one could go for days without seeing a single human being, nor a sheep, nor a well, nor a tree. He spoke with some nostalgia of the other parts of Mauretania that formerly he had known so well. He spoke too of tracks being lost . . . and of *razzias*. . . .

Suddenly a bugle sounded, and the conversation stopped abruptly, as also did the *tidinit* and the gramophone. The sharpshooters stood to attention just where they were. The officers stood up very straight in their starched 'whites' on which the anchors glittered. Their faces went grave. All eyes were turned on the flag which was slowly hauled down while the sunset call was sounded.

It was a moment of solemnity. We were in a little isolated spot lost in the scrub. But we knew that at that moment in seventeen other Mauretanian posts exactly the same ceremony was being gone through, and that knowledge gave us a feeling of closeness and solidarity with our own kind.

My thoughts turned to the flag we were watching. For some it had meant the greatness of a country, for others a life of adventure in these wilds of Africa. It was that flag that had called a halt to the raids of the warrior tribesmen and allowed their weaker brothers to show their faces in the open. Because of it the negroes could go out to collect gum or dates or quietly till their fields of *sorgho*. The former masters of this country had no hatred for this flag, but regarded it with fear and resignation. They had struggled bravely to the last. But *Inch' Allah*, it was useless to revolt against the will of Moulana, the All-Just and the All-Wise. The things of this world are small, and Paradise is at once immense and eternal. Believers and fatalists, they wisely bowed beneath the yoke, waiting patiently for the day that would put an end to all earthly tribulations.

Still watching that flag, my thoughts came closer home. It was because of it that we, two women, had been able to wander over the face of the Trab-el-Beïdane armed with no other weapon than our confidence, mixing with its people, learning their miseries and joys, and even, in brown woollen tents or thatched huts, enjoying the illusion that we were finding friends.

Or perhaps it was more than an illusion....

THE END

Glossary

*Adabaïe** - African village with round huts

Adress – aromatic wood (*Commiphora africana*) used for toothpicks and musical instruments

Aman [Ar. *aman*]– pardon

Aouli, haouli – turban, often of indigo-dyed cloth

Ardin - musical instrument of the harp-type

Azouzel [Hassaniya Ar. *ezuzaûl*] camel gelding

Banco – clay used for bricks

Basin moiré [French] – watered twilled cotton (bombazine)

Beïdan (sing. *Beïdani*) [Ar. *baydān*] – literally "whites" the name used for themselves by the Mauritanians of Arab or Berber, as opposed to African, origin.

Cadi [Ar. *qādī*]– judge

Chandorah indigo-dyed cloth especially used for head coverings and veils, the colour of the dye rubbing off the skin was much prized – perhaps from Chandor, Goa

Courbine – [Fr. *courbine*; *maigre*] giant seabass

Cro-cro - tropical sore, Leishmaniasis

Dami [Berber]- Zenaga term for gazelle

Delou [Ar. *dalw*]- large sheepskin bag for lifting water

Dhar [Berber]- chain of mountains

Dia [Ar. *diya'*]– blood price

Dioula - itinerant trader, from the W. African language much used for trade

Draa - tunic usually of indigo cotton

Fagkou – type of song, war-chant

Fal - camel stallion

Faro – lamb or sheepskin coverlet

Fatreh - *Aïd-el-Seghir* [Ar. 'īd al-fitr; 'īd al-saghīr], North African name for the feast at the end of Ramadan

Filaria medinensis - Guinea-worm

Gabelle [French, derived from Ar.]- French salt tax

Goumiers [French, derived from Ar.] - tribal irregulars and also Moroccan soldiers serving in auxiliary units

Gri-gri [pan-Sahara]– leather Koran case

Griot [pan-Sahara]– musician, singer

Guelta [Berber]– lake, reservoir

Guerba [Berber]- goatskins for carrying water

Guinée - indigo-dyed cloth originally exported from Pondicherry to Senegal and used as a monetary unit

Haouli [Berber; see Aouli]– turban generally made of *guinée*

Haratine (sing. *hartani*) [Berber]– freed slave, generally of African or mixed descent

Iguinin [Berber]- desert bush or small tree (*Capparis aphylla*)

Jihad [Ar. *jihād*] – holy war

Jinn [Ar. *jinn*] – genie, supernatural creature

Kora [Ar. *al-kura*] - ball game

Lanche [pan-Mediterranean]- one masted lateen-rigged ship

Lebda – leather mat
Litham [Ar. *lithām*]– veil, especially typical of Berber men
Malahfa [Ar. *milhafa*] - draped clothing
Mahssar [Ar. *misr*]- camp
Mallem (pl.*mallemin*) [Ar. *muʻallim*, pl. *maʻāllima*]– from *maʼallema*, master, or teacher of a craft, in Mauretania specifically a blacksmith
Marabouts [Ar. *murābit*] – Muslim holy men, especially in North Africa
Margouillats [French]- chameleons
Mechbour - raiding band
Méchoui [Ar. *mashwī*] - grilled meat
Médersa [Ar. *madrasa*] – school, especially used for Muslim religious institutions
Méhari (pl. *Méhara*) [Ar. *mahārī*] – riding camels
Mesk [Ar. *misk*]- musk, scent
Messouak [Ar. *miswāk*]- toothpick
Mocouaressa – a kind of lichen used for smoking
N'koubel [cf. *gabelle*]-salt tax
N'sri - sour milk and water
Oglat [Berber]- well pit in a riverbed
Ouarga [Ar. *warqa*]– wet tea leaves with sugar
Ouguïa [Ar. *ūqiya*] - Mauretanian currency, then 5 to the French Franc now c.436 to the GBP
Pistards [French] - desert patrol
Rahla [Ar. *rahla*]– (lit. the traveller) camel saddle
Razzia [Ar. *ghazwa*]– raid, often to capture animals and women
Roumis [Ar. *rūmī*]–(lit. Romans i.e. Byzantines) Christians
Sebkha [Ar. *sabkha*]- salt flats
Siroual [Ar. *sirwāl*]- baggy trousers
Talha [Ar. *talha*] - an aromatic plant (*Acacia tortilis*)
Tariqa [Ar. *tarīqa*]– Muslim religious orders of extreme importance, religious, social and political, expecially in North and Saharan Africa. They are Sufi and generally named after their founder
Tebbou [Berber]- camel stick
Techgal [Berber]- bed frame
Télamid [Ar. *tilmīdh*, pl. *talāmīdh*]- pupils, disciples
Tidinit [Berber]– a small long-necked lute of *adress* wood played by men
Tilimit [Berber]– long grass
Tisoufren (pl. of *tassoufra*) [Berber]- sheepskin traveling bags
Titarek [Hassaniya Ar. *titarik*]- a kind of broom plant used for making nets (*Leptadenia pyrotechnica*)
Zawiya [Ar. *zāwiya*]– buildings associated with a Sufi religious order or *tariqa*, sometimes housing the grave of the founder. In Mauretania the term is also used to designate scholarly – as opposed to warrior tribes or fractions.

* *Unattributed words are either from one of the African languages current in the region e.g. Peulh (Wolof), Pular (Fulani), etc. or from one of the Berber dialects.*

A

Adabaïe, (African village with round huts) 150
Adrar xi, xvi, xix, 6, 16, 27, 66-7, 71, 73, 75, 84, 86, 102, 150, 184
Adress (aromatic wood used for toothpicks) 57, 61, 95, 101
Aéropostale, pilots of xi
Aftout (salt flats) 122, 130
Ahel-Gazel (tribe) 40
Ahel-Grâa (tribe) 13
Ahmed-ben-Daman (tribe) 49
Air France 7, 10, 30; plane crash 220-1
Ait-Lhassen (tribe) 16
Akjoujt 32, 33, 45, 46
Aleg, French Fort 136, 146, 147, 148, 150, 151, 152, 153, 154, 157, 160, 161, 198
Aman (pardon) 86, 87
Amrouche, Jean xv
Amrouche, Marguerite Taos xv
Aouli (turban)15, 16, 17, 42, 90, 94, 99, 131, 141, 175, 213
Arabization xix
Archaeological site 191
Ardin or *ardine* (musical instrument) 58, 59
Arguin island xi, 20, 21
Arts et Coutumes des Maures xv, xvii, xxiii
Assaba vii, xxviii, 6, 153, 176-7, 180-7, 191, 196, 199, 204, 206, 209, 216
Atlantic xi, 6, 7, 33, 121
Azouzel (camel gelding) 28, 88, 95, 111, 120, 126, 137, 138, 140

B

Baboons 183
Banco (clay used for bricks) 63, 66, 75, 80, 135
Bandits 38, 41, 87, 92, 152, 185, 192
Barekallah (tribe) 13, 56
Basin moiré (watered twilled cotton - bombazine) 79
Bay of Biscay 1
Bay of Lévrier 17
Bay of Pelicans 17, 20
Beïdan - sing. *Beïdani* (literally "whites" the name used for themselves by the Mauritanians of Arab or Berber, as opposed to African, origin)
- *passim*, including 6, 19, 29, 33, 40, 45, 49, 62-72, 79-80, 83, 86, 90, 101-102, 108, 112, 116, 119, 140, 141, 145, 150, 158, 159, 164, 167, 171, 179-83, 193, 218, 222-3
Be'idania women unveiled 22
Belle-Hirondelle, the ship described 1, 5, 6, 7, 8, 10
Beni Hassan (tribe) xviii, xix
Beni Hilal (tribe) xviii
Beni Sulaym (tribe) xviii
Birds 8, 18, 20, 21, 146-147, 161, 179, 185, 207
Blacksmith 67
Blue dye 59
'Blue Sultan' 31, 87
Boghé 151, 152, 153
Books xii, xiii, xxii, 4, 23, 70, 74, 75, 132; abandoned in the sand 23, 75
Boutilimit – *passim*, including 30, 49, 50, 60-4, 68, 71-2, 76, 78, 86-90, 93, 95-6, 111-16, 119, 135, 137, 140, 150, 158, 167, 168, 214
Bracelets 22, 59, 68, 74
Bretons x, xi, xii, xxvii, 2, 121

Breton fishing boats x, xi, 2
Breton islands x
Brittany ix, x, xiv, 2, 4, 157
Bustard 96

C
Cadi (judge) 72, 80-4, 121, 124, 131, 147, 181, 221
Canary Islands 5
Canines extracted 110
Cap Blanc xi
Caravans xiii, 18, 23, 27, 34, 123, 125, 157
Casablanca
Chandorah (indigo-dyed cloth especially used for head coverings and veils) 94, 99, 124, 140, 179
Cheikh-Sidia 70, 71, 72, 74, 76, 83, 86, 117
Chemama 151, 161, 164
Cherchell (Caesaria) xviii
Chinguetti (center of learning) 75
Colonial Exhibition, Paris 1931 - 28, 76, 90, 142, 188
Colonial women 217
Compagnie du Sénégal 21
Coppolani, Xavier xix, xx, xxiv, 10, 71, 72, 117, 163, 164
Courbine (giant seabass) 27
Cowries 151
Crafts xiii, 68
Cray-fish 1, 8
Cro-cro (tropical sore, Leishmaniasis) 175
Crocodiles xxviii, 184, 199, 200, 202
Cross-dressing xi-xii

D
Dakar v, vii, 4, 12, 16, 72, 172, 207, 214, 221, 222

Dami (Zenaga term for gazelle) 142
Dancing 13, 47, 54, 59, 118, 128, 134, 158, 176, 222
Darfur xviii
Dates xxi, 53, 66, 70, 73, 77, 92, 196, 222
Delou (large sheepskin bag for lifting water) 66, 212
Dhar (chain of mountains) 33
Dia (blood price) 82, 83, 207, 221
Dioula (itinerant merchant, from the W. African language much used for trade) 12, 47, 66, 67, 198
Divorce 55, 81, 90
Douarnenez 1, 2
Dowry ix, 15, 104
Draa (tunic usually of indigo cotton) 15, 19, 72, 76, 79, 90, 175
Drums 3, 47, 88, 181
Durand-Ruel, Paul ix

E
El Bourak 155
El Khansa, the poetess 59
Elephants 136, 185
Enforced labour 98
Er Rashid xiv
Eve, magazine x, 9
'Events' of 1989
Evil spirits 33, 74, 106, 134, 186

F
Fable of the Lion and the Hyena 208-210
Fal (camel stallion) 28
Fantasia described 100-101
Faro (lamb or sheepskin coverlet) 50, 101, 109, 135
Fatreh - Aïd-el-Seghir (North African name for the feast at the end of Ramadan) 45, 47, 48

Filaria medinensis (Guinea-worm) 178
Flamingos 21, 23
Forced feeding 101, 108-111
Fournier, Mme "Twinka" ix, x

G
Gabelle, French salt tax 123
Gangari, ruins
Gazelle 96, 110, 141, 142, 144; suckled by a woman 160
General Gouraud xxvii, 16, 17, 29, 152
Ghana xviii
Gold xviii, 6, 28, 57, 68, 151, 188
Gouchneh island 22, 23
Goumiers (tribal irregulars and also Moroccan soldiers serving in auxiliary units) 32
Gri-gri (leather Koran case) 67, 70, 72
Griot (musician, singer) 102, 111, 180
Guelta (lake, reservoir) xxviii, 184, 199, 200
Guerba, (goatskins for carrying water) 36, 42
Guimi, 153-4, 158-9
Guinée (indigo-dyed cloth originally exported from Pondicherry to Senegal and used as a monetary unit) 12, 27, 29, 59, 66, 82, 90
Gum 6, 53, 61, 70, 76-7, 94, 98, 117-8, 123-4, 143-4, 162, 174, 222

H
Hair styles, among the Peulh 172
Haratine - sing. *Hartani* (freed slave, generally of African or mixed descent) 14, 44, 49-50, 55, 57, 60-1, 73, 88, 92, 94, 96, 99, 104, 107, 115, 125, 131, 137, 162, 169
Hassaniya dialect xii, xix
Henna 57, 66, 100, 108, 148
Holy war (see also *jihad*) 71
Hunting 96, 138, 140-141, 142, 181
Hunting clothes 140-142

I
Iboulkham (well)
Iguinin (desert bush) 61
Imraguen (slave-fishermen) 14, 19, 22 ; their way of life 23-28; unjust taxes and tribute paid by them 27; rape of their women by the warrior caste 27; 36, 37
Independence, Mauritania xv, xvi, xx
Inierk (wells)
Initi (prickly desert plant) 61, 93, 142

J
Jews 67
Jihad xviii, xix, xx
Jinn 18, 136, 190, 192, 193, 194, 199, 200, 202
Juba I of Numidia xvii, xviii

K
Karet – Odette du Puigaudeau's boat 1908-1956 x
Kayes 172, 194, 198, 207, 218, 220, 221
Kervaudu - Odette du Puigaudeau's childhood home ix
Keur-Massen 123
Kiffa vii, 54, 136, 140, 168, 184, 196-8, 202, 206, 210, 211-21
Kora (ball game) 47
Kreutzberger, Marcelle Borne – Marion Sénones x

La Grande Foire aux dattes xiii, xxi
La Pacification de la Mauritanie 152
La Piste Maroc – Sénégal xv
Lake Aleg
Lamtuna Berbers xviii
Lanche (one masted lateen-rigged ship) 12, 17, 18, 22
Lanvin, Jeanne ix
Law Court 79 - 85
Le Sel du desert xxiii
League of the Rights of Man 180, 181, 182
Lebda (leather mat) 56
Légion d'honneur 87
Libraries 75
Lice 95, 166, 217
Lions xxvii, 136, 174, 185, 186, 193, 201, 208, 212
Litham (veil, especially typical of Berber men) 6, 70

M

M'Bout 136, 169, 170, 176-7, 181, 214, 217
Ma al-'Aynayn xix, xx
Ma-el-Aïnin (tribe) 70, 71, 129
Mac-Mahon, Lieutenant 19, 40
Mahssar (camp) 60, 87, 89, 93, 94, 95, 97, 99, 100, 101, 119, 131, 137
Mal Lake 159, 161, 165
Malahfa (draped clothing) 16, 57, 81, 104, 129, 144, 148
Mallem - pl.*mallemin* (blacksmith) 67, 110, 212, 217
Manuscripts 75
Marabouts xix, 13, 22,-24, 53, 62-3, 70-4, 76, 80-1, 86, 98, 107, 116, 118, 121, 126, 132, 134, 155, 156-9, 161-5, 192-3, 197
Marauding tribes 62

Margouillats (chameleons) 150
Mechbour (raiding band) 156
Méchoui (grilled meat) 21, 38, 45, 55, 57, 93, 99, 132, 158, 160, 176
Mederdra 78, 87, 107, 115, 117-9, 121, 124, 131, 134, 137
Médersa (school) 63, 64, 77
Medical care 78-9
Medicine, traditional 144
Méhara, (riding camels) 27
Memrhar 12, 19, 20, 23, 24, 27,
Mesk (musk, scent) 95
Messouak, (toothpick) 157
Milk, and meat eaten together taboo 177
Mime 24, 126
Mocouaressa (lichen used for smoking) 162
Moors – *passim*, including xi, xii, xix, xxviii, 3, 9-15, 17-8, 30-3, 61-3, 75-8, 119-23, 132, 135-7, 142-3, 164-8,175-6, 193, 194, 212-7, 221
Mousouden (wells)
Murder trial 82-85
Musée d'Ethnographie xi
Musée de l'homme xv, xvi
Musée des Colonies xi
Muséum national d'histoire naturelle ix, x, xiii

N

N'Dio, place vii, 189, 190, 194-6, 207
N'Dio people, hunted by Arabs 187;hairstyle and costume 187-188; weaving cotton 188-189
N'koubel (salt tax) 123
N'sri, (sour milk and water) 98
N'Térert *(sebka)*121, 122, 124, 125, 126, 131

Naga Saleh 156
Nazism xiv
Nets 2-5, 7-10, 23, 27, 88
North African workers in France xv
Nouakschott x
Nouazibou (Port Étienne) 11
NSV (National Sozialistische Volkswohlfahrt) xiv
Nuclear testing xvi

O
Oglat (well pit in a river bed) 213
Omar-ben-Khalssum 59
Ophthalmia 27, 64, 78, 144
Ouaghadou 191
Ouarga (wet tea leaves with sugar) 93
Ouguïa (Mauritanian currency) 15, 67, 198
Ould Daddah xv, xvi, xx, xxiv
Ould-Deïd - *passim*, including 44, 49, 60, his history - 86-9, 92-6, 99, 101, 102, 104-5, 109-13, 124, 131, 137-40, 150, 159, 221
Ouled-Biri (tribe) 70, 73, 89
Ouled-Daman (tribe) 89, 96, 140, 142, 145, 146, 153
Ouled-Delim (tribe) 13, 14, 15, 17, 19, 30, 31, 87
Ouled-en-Nour (tribe) 71
Ouled-Normache (tribe) 153, 159
Ouled-Noun 16
Ouolom-Nére, sacred mountain 164-5

P
Pacification 152
Paris ix, x, xi, xiv, xxiii, xxiv, xxvii, 19, 28, 41, 90, 119, 142, 222
Peulhs vii, 170-4, marriage - 181
Pistards (desert patrol) xv

Plant names 60-1
Polisario Front xx
Port Étienne (Nouazibou) vii, 2, 7, 10, 11, 13, 15-9, 22, 23, 26-7, 30-1, 41, 64, 116, 212, 221
Prayer beads 213
Prostitutes 46, 66, 92, 135

Q
Qadiriya order xix

R
Rahla (camel saddle) 34
Razzias (raids) 10, 15, 87, 88, 92, 222
Reggane xvi
Reguïba (R'Guïebat) 24; permission to raid them requested – 112-3
Reporters, reputation of xxvii, xxviii
Rio de Oro xi, 4, 6, 9, 11, 13, 15, 22, 28, 30, 41, 112, 184, 220
Rites 93
Rites after childbirth 134
Rock inscriptions 184, 195-196
Rock paintings xiii, xiv, 192-193, 195-196, 197-198
Rosso 122, 126, 158
Roumis (Christians) 16

S
Saint-Louis du Sénégal xx
Sainte-Marie-de-Bathurst 4
Salt extraction 121-125
Salt ix, xiii, 33, 42, 88, 106, 115, 121, 122, 123, 124, 137, 166, 181
Sanhaja Berbers xviii
Sarakollés 170, 171, 179, 181, 187
Schools 63, 78, 147
Sebkha (salt flats) 121
Sel du desert xxiii

231

Sélibaby 178, 180, 181, 182, 183, 185, 186, 197, 202
Senegal, country and river xi, xvi, xviii, xix, xx, 6, 11, 14, 21, 23, 33, 62, 67, 71, 73, 104, 113, 117, 123, 151, 166, 170, 171, 179, 187, 198, 207
Sénones, Marion – *passim*, including ii, vii, x, xiii, xv, xvii, xxiii, xxvii, 2, 5, 17, 29, 88
S.F.F. (Service féminin français) xiv
Sheba, Queen of 50, 197
Ship-wrecks 20
Sijilmassa xviii
Singing 39, 58, 59, 98, 102, 126, 128; on the telephone 148-9, 193
Siroual (baggy trousers) 38, 75, 95, 99, 119, 142
Skulls 23, 192, 196
Slave-fishermen (see also *Imraguen*) xix
Slavery xii, xix
Slaves – passim, including xviii, xix, xx, 6, 14, 21, 24, 27, 30, 43, 45, 47, 49, 53-7, 60, 70-3, 77, 80, 83, 87-8, 93, 98, 100-1, 104, 117, 118, 121-6, 129-35, 145, 153, 158, 162-3, 182, 185, 204
Small children left naked, 18
Smara, capital of Ma al-'Aynayn xix, 87, 112, 221
Société de Geographie xxvii
Songs, religious – 118; 126, 129, 150
Soninke xviii
Sorcerers 180
Sorceress 204-205, 219
SOS Slaves xx
Stars, 5, 29; legends of - 155-156; 186
Sufi orders xix
Syphilis 78

T

Tagant xiii, xix, xxiii, xxiv, 6, 75, 84, 86, 159, 163, 184, 191, 196
Tak-Tak Pass 183, 184, 197, 207
Takrur xviii
Talha (aromatic plant) 66
Tamchakett, military post 219
Tariqas (Sufi brotherhoods) xix
Tassoufra - pl. *tisoufren* (sheepskin travelling bag) 36, 41, 67, 68, 105, 120, 137, 139, 155, 205
Taxation 76, 77; French, unjust 79
Tebbou (camel stick) 36, 162, 165
Techgal (bed frame) 158
Télamid (pupils, disciples) 73
Tenaloul 18, 22, 23
Tent – *passim*; described -131-132
Tiab (warrior tribe) 98
Tibesti xiv
Tichitt, center of learning 75
Tidra 23
Tigbarren 99
Tilimit (long grass) 72
Tin-Deila 49, 50
Tin-Djemaran, sebkha 122
Tindouf 197, 219
Tisoufren (pl. of *tassoufra*), sheepskin traveling bags 36, 49
Titarek (a kind of broom plant used for making nets) 27, 121
Tombs 6, 21
Toucouleur 151, 152, 164, 166,
Touidermi 121, 122, 124, 126, 131
Trab-el-Beïdane 6, 33, 49, 68, 70, 85, 90, 108, 116, 159, 164, 179, 222-3
Trade goods 66
Traders v, 1, 2, 123, 124, 190
Treaty of Algeciras xx
Tribute 13, 15, 17, 24, 27, 44,

74, 87, 96, 112, 175; paid by
  Imraguen - 24, 28
Tuberculosis 64, 78

U
Une Bretonne au desert xxi, xxiii

V
Vaccination 119
Villa-Cisneros vii, 7, 8, 10, 25, 202
Volubilis xviii

W
Weights and measures 67
Wells drying up 121
Western Sahara xx, xxi, xxix
Wild-cat 132, 135, 144
Wooden crosses 23

Z
Zawiya (religious center) xix
Zebus 43, 147, 165, 171-2, 212, 214
Zénega language 70, 163
Zeriba (sheep-fold) 204

www.ingramcontent.com/pod-product-compliance
Lightning Source LLC
Chambersburg PA
CBHW020750160426
43192CB00006B/293